A Guide to the Nuclear Arms Control Treaties

by

David B. Thomson

A Guide to the Nuclear Arms Control Treaties

by

David B. Thomson

LOS ALAMOS HISTORICAL SOCIETY
PUBLICATIONS
P.O. BOX 43, LOS ALAMOS, NEW MEXICO 87544

Los Alamos Historical Society
P.O. Box 43
Los Alamos, New Mexico 87544

LIBRARY OF CONGRESS CATALOGING-IN-PUBLICATON DATA

Thomson, David B. (David Browning), 1927–
A Guide to the Nuclear Arms Control Treaties/ David B. Thomson.
p. cm.
Includes bibliographical references.
"LA-UR-99-31-73."
ISBN 0-941232-26-3 (alk. paper)

1. Nuclear Weapons (International law)
2. Nuclear Arms Control—United States. I. Title.

KZ5665.T48 2001
341.7'34'026—dc21 00-068982

Cover photo: The author participated in this nuclear test at the Nevada Test Site, May 1953.

Foreword

The advent of nuclear weapons and their use to end World War II was followed by their role as a deterrent during the Cold War. The recognition by the United States and other world leaders of the horrendous death and destruction that a nuclear war could inflict on humanity subsequently led to negotiation of a succession of nuclear arms control treaties and related agreements aimed at reducing the threats of nuclear war. Implementing these treaties included negotiation and application of a variety of international verification mechanisms by the parties.

Principal treaties that led us to where we are today include the Limited Test Ban Treaty (LTBT), nuclear Nonproliferation Treaty (NPT), Threshold Test Ban Treaty (TTBT), Intermediate-Range Nuclear Forces (INF) Treaty, and Strategic Arms Reduction Treaties (START I and II). Along the way, the ABM treaty and the SALT II treaty (not ratified but replaced and greatly improved on by START I), as well as other related treaties and agreements, contributed to the process. Today, supporters of the arms control process await entry-into-force of START II, entry into force of the Comprehensive Test Ban Treaty (CTBT), negotiation of further reductions in strategic nuclear delivery vehicles, negotiation of major reductions and verification of all nuclear warheads, and verification and control of all nuclear weapons materials such as plutonium. Some want to reduce allowed nuclear warheads to very low levels, say, less than 300.

In this book the author provides an overview of the Cold-War nuclear-arms buildup, an overview of the principal negotiated nuclear arms control treaties, and a chapter devoted to the nuclear test ban treaties. A chapter is devoted to the NPT, its related International Atomic Energy Agency (IAEA) safeguards procedures, application of the NPT and other nonproliferation agreements to specific threats (such as Iraq), and the indefinite extension of the NPT. Separate chapters each are devoted to the INF treaty, the START I treaty, and the START II treaty. A chapter is devoted to vital new agreements being discussed with Russia (START III and plutonium controls, for example). In the last chapter some new multilateral treaties or initiatives, proposed by a variety of arms control groups, are reviewed.

This book was first written to provide Los Alamos National Laboratory staff and other interested parties with descriptive texts and summaries of the present principal nuclear arms control treaties and with brief summaries of some major new agreements that have been proposed. A major purpose has been to describe and summarize the verification procedures and mechanisms used for each of the treaties discussed. We hope that these summaries will be useful to those doing verification research and development, to those considering future arms control policy, and to interested citizens. Most of the text is descriptive.

Histories of negotiations are written briefly and as the author understands them. We have used charts extensively to summarize key detailed features of the principal treaties. Mostly in the last part of Chapter X does the author outline some of his own particular views as to directions for future initiatives.

There is a certain amount of overlap among some of the chapters resulting from an effort to give each chapter a degree of completeness within that topic.

This book was first written and distributed as Los Alamos National Laboratory Report #LA-UR-99-3173, July 1999. Since that time, two significant events have occurred that we mention here.

First, the Comprehensive Test Ban Treaty (CTBT), described in Chapter III, was abruptly brought to the Senate floor with only a few days of last minute consideration by the Senate Foreign Relations Committee, and only a few more days of debate on the Senate floor. In an action, resulting from a miscalculation by treaty proponents, diehard opposition by opponents, and intense partisanship by both sides, the Senate rejected the treaty 51-48 on October 13, 1999. It has been noted however that it may be brought up again for consideration by the Senate in the future. Meanwhile, as noted in Chapter III, the work of the PrepCom may continue.

Second, after President Vladimir Putin's election victory, the Russian Duma finally voted to ratify the START II treaty on April 14, 2000. The Duma's principal conditions were adoption of the amendments to the START II treaty agreed by the parties in September, 1997 (Chapter VIII); and the amendments to the ABM treaty negotiated in September, 1997 (Chapter IX). These amendments now require action by the US Senate if START II is to enter-into-force.

Because of the strong support in the US Senate for a national missile defense system (NMD), a strategy for achieving the necessary Senate actions will have to be worked out by the new US administration which takes office in January 2001 if START II is to be finally implemented. The author believes that prompt and strong initiatives should be taken by the new administration to achieve the goals of the START II treaty, to move toward START III, and to move the arms control agenda forward along the lines discussed in Chapters IX and X, if the potential threats of clandestine uses of nuclear weapons are to be substantially alleviated.

All interpretations, views, and opinions expressed herein are those of the author and do not necessarily reflect those of the Los Alamos National Laboratory, the University of California, the United States Government, or the Los Alamos Historical Society.

David B. Thomson
December 2000

Acknowledgments

The support and assistance of many persons contributed to the preparation and writing of this book. The author expresses deep appreciation to Steven Maaranen for support, most helpful discussions and suggestions during the preparation of this text as well as throughout the writing of the CNSS and CISA reports which preceded it. Steve's knowledge of US strategic policies and of the arms control process have been invaluable to the author for many years, as have his contributions to this writing, particularly with respect to the START treaties.
The author acknowledges valuable discussions and collaborations on many arms control issues with William Chambers over the years, and thanks him for his helpful suggestions after a careful reading of this book. Early support, a review of the text, and helpful suggestions by John Hopkins, are fully appreciated.

Donald Westervelt's broad experience and knowledge of the nuclear test ban treaties have been invaluable. Paul Mutschlecner made valuable suggestions with respect to test ban verification. Discussions with Delmar Bergen regarding the INF Treaty have been most useful and helpful. John Puckett supplied much valuable information concerning the NPT, IAEA, and related issues, and made several important suggestions. Gene Bosler provided a most helpful review of sections on the IAEA, NPT, and plutonium. Randall Erickson provided essential information and valuable suggestions with respect to the US/Russian plutonium agreements and verification. Maurice Bryson very helpfully reviewed sections on verification agencies, recent START III discussions, and the rest of the text. Discussions with William Beyer on needed future agreements have been most helpful, as has timely information from Pete Lyons and Pat Garrity. Discussions on selected topics with Joseph Pilat, Ronald Augustson, Thurman Talley, Donald Eilers, Nathan Busch, and Diane McCallum are most appreciated.

The author gratefully appreciates the support and encouragement of John Shaner, former CISA Director, and also of Paul White, NIS-RNP Director.

The author very much appreciates the efforts of Cynthia Phillips and Kathy Valdez of the Laboratory's Communication Arts and Services Group for their diligent and patient work in editing and formatting this book and guiding its final publication. Valuable library research was provided by Mona Mosier, Marie Harper, and Donna Berg. Helpful secretarial support has been provided by Anna Trujillo and Suzanne Montoya of CISA.

Finally, the author wishes to express appreciation to Matt Murphy, Bob Waters, and members of the Public Affairs Group of the US Arms Control and Disarmament Agency (ACDA) for supplying many of the basic reference documents. Conversations over the years with Edward Lacey, Stan Riveles, Lynn Rusten, Gerry Mally, Karin Look, and other members of ACDA have been most helpful. We note here that ACDA has recently been folded into the State Department by Congressional Legislation. Discussions over the years on START with Ambassador Linton Brooks, and also with Rodney Jones, are recalled with pleasure.

The views, opinions, and interpretations presented in this book are strictly the responsibility of the author and do not necessarily reflect those of the Los Alamos National Laboratory, the University of California, the United States government, or the individuals acknowledged above.

The author greatly appreciates the initiative of the Los Alamos Historical Society in making this book available to the general public.

Russian Nonproliferation Programs Office

The Russian Nonproliferation Programs (RNP) Office was established by Los Alamos National Laboratory in June 1999. The Office is a part of the Nonproliferation and International Security Division, and is a successor organization to the Center for International Security Affairs established in 1995. Its purpose is to provide leadership and oversight for key nonproliferation initiatives with the Russian Federation. These include the Material Protection, Control, and Accounting Program; the Initiative for Proliferation Prevention; and the Nuclear Cities Initiative. In addition, the Office serves as a focal point for coordination of other Laboratory interactions with the Former Soviet Union (FSU) and the Peoples Republic of China (PRC). The RNP Office also helps to ensure that all Laboratory interactions with the FSU and the PRC are consistent with US policy objectives.

A Guide to the Nuclear Arms Control Treaties

Contents

Charts

Figures

Tables

Appendices

Glossary

ABACC	Argentine-Brazilian Agency for Accounting and Control of Nuclear Materials
ABM	antiballistic missile
ACA	Arms Control Association
ACDA	(US) Arms Control and Disarmament Agency
ACIS	Arms Control Intelligence Staff
AEC	Atomic Energy Commission
ALCM	air-launched cruise missile
ASEAN	Association of Southeast Asia Nations
BCC	Bilateral Consultative Commission
BIC	Bilateral Implementation Commission (START II)
BM	ballistic missile
CD	Conference on Disarmament (UN)
C/E	conversion/elimination
CFE	Conventional Forces in Europe
CG	Coordinating Group
CIA	Central Intelligence Agency
CIS	Commonwealth of Independent States
CISA	Center for International Security Affairs (at Los Alamos National Laboratory, 1995–1999)
CISAC	Committee on International Security and Arms Control
CMC	Carnegie Moscow Center
CNSS	Center for National Security Studies (at Los Alamos National Laboratory, 1986–1994)
CRS	Congressional Research Service
CSCE	Conference on Security and Cooperation in Europe
CTBT	Comprehensive Test Ban Treaty
CTBTO	Comprehensive Test Ban Treaty Organization
CORRTEX	continuous reflectometry for radius vs time experiments
CTR	Cooperative Threat Reduction
CWC	Chemical Weapons Convention
DG	director general (CTBTO)
DoD	Department of Defense
DOE	Department of Energy
DSNW	destruction of strategic nuclear warheads

DSWA	Defense Special Weapons Agency
DTRA	Defense Threat Reduction Agency
ECOSOC	Economic and Social Council
EIF	entry into force
ENDC	(UN) Eighteen-Nation Disarmament Commission
FRG	Federal Republic of Germany
FSU	former Soviet Union
GAO	Government Accounting Office (US)
GLBM	ground-launched ballistic missile
GLCM	ground-launched cruise missile
GPO	Government Printing Office (US)
HB	heavy bomber
HEU	highly enriched uranium
HTGR	high-temperature gas-cooled reactor
IAEA	International Atomic Energy Agency
ICBM	intercontinental ballistic missile
IDC	International Data Center
IMS	International Monitoring System
INF	intermediate-range nuclear forces
INFT	Intermediate-Range Nuclear Forces Treaty
IRBM	intermediate-range ballistic missile
IVA	International Verification Agency (proposed)
JCIC	Joint Compliance and Inspection Commission (START I)
JCS	Joint Chiefs of Staff
JICC	Joint Implementation and Compliance Commission
JVE	joint verification experiment
kT	kiloton
LANL	Los Alamos National Laboratory (after 1980)
LASL	Los Alamos Scientific Laboratory (before 1980)
LEU	low enriched uranium
LLNL	Lawrence Livermore National Laboratory
LTBT	Limited Test Ban Treaty
MINATOM	Ministry of Atomic Energy (Russian)
MIRV	multiple independently targetable re-entry vehicles
MIRVed	missiles with multiple independently targetable re-entry vehicles
MLF	multilateral nuclear force (Europe, 1961)

MOA	Memorandum of Understanding on Warhead Attribution and Heavy Bomber Data (START II Treaty)
MOU	Memorandum of Understanding (START I Treaty)
MOX	mixed oxide
MPC&A	material protection, control and accounting (nuclear)
MTCR	missile technology control regime
NAS	National Academy of Sciences
NATO	North Atlantic Treaty Organization
NFZ	nuclear-free zone
NNW	nonnuclear weapon
NNWS	nonnuclear weapon state(s)
NPT	Treaty on the Nonproliferation of Nuclear Weapons
NRC	National Research Council
NRC	Nuclear Regulatory Commission
NRRC	Nuclear Risk Reduction Center
NSC	National Security Council
NST	Nuclear and Space Talks
NTM	national technical means
NTS	Nevada Test Site
NW	nuclear weapon
NWS	nuclear weapon state(s)
OSCC	Open Skies Consultative Commission
OSCE	Organization for Security and Cooperation in Europe
OSI	on-site inspection
OSIA	On-Site Inspection Agency
PNE	peaceful nuclear explosions
PNET	Peaceful Nuclear Explosions Treaty
POE	point of entry
PPCM	portal perimeter continuous monitoring
PRBSW	prevention of rapid buildup of strategic warheads
PRC	Peoples Republic of China
Pu	plutonium
R&D	research and development
RV	reentry vehicle
SAC	Strategic Air Command
SALT	Strategic Arms Limitation Talks

SALT II	Strategic Arms Limitation Talks II (SALT II Treaty)
SAR	synthetic aperture radar
SASC	Senate Armed Services Committee
SBSS	Science-Based Stockpile Stewardship
SCC	Standing Consultative Commission (ABM Treaty)
SDI	Strategic Defense Initiative
SFRC	Senate Foreign Relations Committee
SLBM	submarine-launched ballistic missile
SLCM	sea-launched cruise missile
SNDV	strategic nuclear delivery vehicle
SNWI	strategic nuclear warhead inventories
SQ	significant quantity
SRAM	short-range attack missile
SSCI	Senate Select Committee on Intelligence
SSR	satellite system receiver
START I	Strategic Arms Reduction Treaty (signed July 31, 1991)
START II	"Treaty between the United States of America and the Russian Federation on the further reduction and limitation of strategic offensive arms" (signed January 3, 1993)
START III	proposed treaty to follow the START I and START II treaties
SVC	Special Verification Commission (INF Treaty)
TLI	treaty-limited item
TMD	Theater Missile Defense
TS	technical secretariat (CTBTO)
TTBT	Threshold Test Ban Treaty
UK	United Kingdom
UN	United Nations
UNAEC	United Nations Atomic Energy Commission
UNSCOM	United Nations Special Commission on Iraq
US	United States
USEC	US Enrichment Corporation
USSR	Union of Soviet Socialist Republics
WH	warhead (nuclear)
WMD	weapons of mass destruction

Chapter I

The Nuclear Arms Race

The end of World War II brought relief and celebration to the peoples of the United States, Russia, England, and the other victorious allies. The heavy loss of life among both combatants and civilians had been tragic for both sides, and the damage to cities and infrastructure within most of Europe and Russia had been devastating. Even in victory however, the democratic allies, United States and England, and their communist ally, the Soviet Union, were wary of each other. Stalin had killed[1] millions of his own people and carried out other brutalities in the late thirties while consolidating his internal power. As the United States and Russia waged World War II as allies, Americans hoped that relations between the two countries would be much improved after the defeat of Hitler.

During World War II, the United States developed a new form of energy from nuclear fission under a top secret program, the Manhattan Project. This program resulted in the creation of the first atomic bomb, developed at a top secret facility in Los Alamos, New Mexico. The United States used these nuclear weapons at Hiroshima and Nagasaki in August 1945 (with deadly results) to end World War II in time[2] to save hundreds of thousands of American lives, and even more Japanese lives, that would have been lost if the invasion[3] of Japan had gone forward. Euphoria in the United States over the sudden end of the war was sobered by the fact that this new energy from nuclear fission was both a savior and a curse. Using nuclear energy from reactors to provide electricity gave promise to great benefits for mankind. The secrets of making nuclear weapons gave Americans confidence in their security. But the scientists, led by Robert Oppenheimer and Vannevar Bush, were aware[4] that the physics and technologies used during the Manhattan Project were based on laws of nature that could be discovered by others. Worse yet, secrets could be stolen. Within a few years,[5] other nations could have nuclear weapons. In October 1945, President Truman[6] called for "international arrangements" to prevent the use of atomic weapons and allow peaceful uses of atomic energy.

The Cold War Begins

Even before the final surrender of Germany in May 1945, secrecy behind the Russian lines caused Churchill to express concern to Truman, using the term "iron curtain" for the first time.[7] At the Potsdam Conference in July 1945, Truman was frustrated[8] by not being able to gain Stalin's support for free elections in Poland, Eastern Europe, and the Balkans, all areas then occupied by the Russian armies.

In February of 1946, Stalin[9] declared that Communism and capitalism were incompatible and that another war was inevitable. He kept the Russian Army in northern Iran despite an earlier promise to withdraw. In March, Iran protested to the United Nations (UN), and Russia returned the northern province to Iran in June, but Communist agitation continued. At the same time, sensational news first came from Ottawa of a Russian spy ring[10] that was trying to steal secrets of the atom bomb. In March 1946, Winston Churchill delivered his famous speech[11] at Fulton, Missouri, that declared "From Stettin in the Baltic, to Trieste in the Adriatic, an iron curtain had descended across the continent. Behind that line all the capitals of Central and Eastern Europe . . . Warsaw, Berlin, Prague, Vienna, Budapest, Belgrade, Bucharest, and Sofia, and the populations around them lie . . . under an increasing measure of control from Moscow." Churchill's speech was criticized by some in the press but supported by Harriman, Forrestal, Kennan, and Atchison. Truman pleaded "no comment" and sent a conciliatory letter to Stalin.

Truman appointed Bernard Baruch to head the American delegation to the UN Atomic Energy Commission. Baruch presented the plan[12] that would create a UN authority to control all uranium and plutonium worldwide and eventually ban individual national nuclear programs (ch. II). The Soviets, rejecting the on-site verification provisions of the plan, vetoed it in December 1946.[13] The plan died and so did progress in nuclear arms control for many years. The failure of the Baruch plan, the success of the Russian spy ring in obtaining early US nuclear weapons secrets, and the continued Soviet domination of Eastern Europe combined to intensify the dangers of the Cold War.

In late 1946, Clark Clifford and George Elsey completed a detailed analysis[14] of Soviet-American relations. Their work emphasized that the

Soviets had continually delayed post-war peace settlements, and this enabled them to keep excessively large Red Army occupation forces in Eastern Europe, including parts of Finland, Poland, Czechoslovakia, Hungary, Romania, and Bulgaria. Only US and UK forces prevented a takeover in Austria, and "Communist parties were growing in France and Italy." More ominously, they warned that Stalin was "supporting forces stronger than any potential combination of foreign powers," and was developing atomic weapons and strategic forces of great range. On March 12, 1947, following serious political disintegration in Greece, the president presented[15] the "Truman Doctrine" to a joint session of Congress, asking for $400 million in economic aid for Greece and Turkey to help free them from communist coercion.

In mid-1947, the Marshall Plan was developed[16] to provide economic aid to Europe to prevent economic collapse. The initial plan was discussed at a conference in Paris of European nations that included Russia and Eastern Europe. Conditions for US aid included Soviet help to rebuild parts of Western and Central Europe and open accounting of how US funds were spent. The Soviets would not accept this, withdrew, and pressured Czechoslovakia, Hungary, Poland, and the other Eastern European satellites not to take part. Eventually 17 nations did take part, and the Soviet withdrawal helped ensure US congressional support. Truman and Marshall, aided by Republican Senator Arthur Vandenberg, achieved congressional approval of the massive $17 billion aid plan in 1948. The Marshall Plan is credited[17] with saving Western Europe from economic collapse and likely communist domination.

In June 1948, the Russians clamped a blockade on all rail and highway traffic in and out of Berlin. Stalin hoped to force the Western allies to withdraw. Truman rejected use of an armored convoy to break the blockade, fearing a major war. Instead, he initiated a full-scale airlift, shipping supplies in large American and British cargo planes. The Berlin airlift,[18] with hundreds of flights a day, went on for several months. The Soviets eventually backed down rather than continue to risk nuclear war, making the airlift a big success. But the Berlin blockade episode had emphasized the hair trigger nature of the Cold War.

NATO

In response to the ever increasing Soviet danger, the United States, Canada, and ten European allies signed, on April 4, 1949, the North Atlantic Treaty from which evolved[19] the North Atlantic Treaty Organization (NATO). This treaty was preceded[20] by the Brussels Treaty (1948) and the Vandenberg Resolution (1948). In December 1950, the North Atlantic Council approved the French plan for creating a European Defense Force and authorized the creation[20] of a Supreme Headquarters. President Truman appointed General Dwight D. Eisenhower as supreme commander and announced that the number of US forces in Europe would be increased to four divisions.

NATO evolved[20] over the next several decades and has remained the core of the "transatlantic bargain," preserving the freedom and stability of Western Europe.

France developed an independent security policy and in 1966, under Charles de Gaulle, withdrew from NATO's integrated military command but not from NATO itself. This withdrawal was balanced by the development of military contributions of the Federal Republic of Germany and later by the addition of Spain. The United Kingdom eventually accepted a role in continental Europe's economic future by joining the European Community (EC). US strategic forces and nuclear umbrella remained at the core of NATO's defense.

Korea

The Cold War reached a crisis point when North Korea suddenly invaded South Korea in June 1950.[21] North Korea was controlled by Communist surrogates supported by Moscow. The United States and the UN responded with a hastily drawn up military defense.

The American-led defense of South Korea managed to drive the invaders from South Korea, but the US effort to liberate North Korea evolved into a stalemate when Chinese Communist forces[22] came across the Chinese North Korean border in massive numbers in late 1950. The active entry of Communist China on the side of Soviet aggression had broadened the dangers of the Cold War.

The Cold War and Los Alamos

Immediately after World War II, the United States demobilized rapidly.[17] At Los Alamos, many scientists, including Oppenheimer, returned to academic pursuits. The dismantling of wartime infrastructure cast doubt on the future of the laboratory at Los Alamos.[23] Dr. Norris Bradbury was asked to keep the laboratory running.[24] Bradbury persuaded key people, including Darol Froman, Raemer Schreiber, Al Graves, Marshall Holloway, and many others to stay on.[25] The management of nuclear energy and weapons was in a state of uncertainty and evolution,[22] and the United States had only a few nuclear weapons. Three nuclear weapons tests were conducted at Bikini Atoll in the summer of 1946.[26] In late 1946 Congress created the Atomic Energy Commission (AEC).[27] By 1949, the Los Alamos Laboratory had achieved the infrastructure and scientific base it needed to improve weapons designs. Weapons were now being produced at other AEC facilities, and Los Alamos could concentrate on new designs, nuclear testing, and related science. The urgency and value of Bradbury's initiatives in building the laboratory after the war became crystal clear when the Russians exploded a copy of the Trinity device in 1949.

The Nuclear Weapons Buildup

By 1950, the United States had about 800 nuclear warheads and the Russians were starting to build theirs. In response to vastly larger Soviet ground forces in Europe, the United States built a superior long-range bomber force[28] and created the Strategic Air Command (SAC), which provided the carriers for US strategic nuclear weapons. The US AEC created nuclear test facilities in the Pacific and at the Nevada Test Site (NTS) and conducted atmospheric tests every year from 1951 to 1958. Russian tests were conducted in greater secrecy but were observable from radioactive fallout. The first US test of a hydrogen bomb at Eniwetok, in November of 1952, was followed by the first Russian thermonuclear test in August 1953.[29] With these high-yield nuclear weapons, the potential dangers, should the Cold War become a "hot war," had reached catastrophic proportions.

President Eisenhower (1953 to 1960) was determined to maintain security but worked hard to end the threat of nuclear weapons. Under Eisenhower, the US nuclear deterrent was greatly strengthened, and tactical nuclear weapons were developed for defending Europe and Japan. However, Eisenhower's many initiatives for arms control were thwarted by the Soviets, who rejected effective verification in a variety of arms control proposals[30] (see ch. II). During the late 1950s, the potential dangers of the nuclear arms race increased with the development of intercontinental ballistic missiles (ICBMs) and submarine-launched missiles as nuclear weapon carriers. Suppression[30] of freedom in Hungary by Soviet forces in 1956 intensified the Cold War.

Grave Danger, Then a Beginning for Arms Control

A high point in the Cold War threat of nuclear catastrophe was reached in the early 1960s as a new president, John F. Kennedy, faced new threats by Soviet leader, Nikita Khrushchev, who appeared buoyed by Russia's new missile capabilities. The Soviets suddenly built the Berlin wall[31] in August 1961 to prevent East Germans from seeking freedom in the West. In late 1961, the Soviets abruptly broke the nuclear test moratorium (initiated by Eisenhower and Khrushchev in 1958) by conducting a series of powerful new atmospheric nuclear tests.[32] Khrushchev boasted of new high-yield weapons. Given his powerful missile forces, his threats were taken seriously. The United States resumed nuclear testing in the atmosphere, both at NTS and in the Pacific Ocean. Finally, later in 1962, the United States discovered that the Russians were building missile-launching sites in Cuba sufficient to pose a dangerous new nuclear threat to the United States. Kennedy eventually responded to the threat,[33] and Khrushchev withdrew his missiles.

As if they had sobered, the Russians became more reasonable in 1963, agreeing to the first Moscow–Washington hot line and then agreeing to a verifiable Limited Test Ban Treaty (LTBT),[34] signed by the United States and Russia in August. The LTBT paved the way for the signing of the Nonproliferation Treaty (NPT) by 60 nations in 1968 (see ch. II, ch. IV).

New Dangers as the Arms Race Continues

Despite the gains and hopes for arms control engendered by the LTBT and the NPT, the Cold War continued. In 1968, the Soviets again put down a bid for freedom in Eastern Europe, this time in Czechoslovakia.[35] The LTBT allowed nuclear testing underground, the technology of ballistic missiles was improving greatly, and the nuclear arms race between the United States and the USSR continued[36] in the late 1960s, through the 1970s, and into the early 1980s. In the late 1960s, the United States had substantial strategic nuclear forces, but by 1971, the Soviets had caught up with numbers of ICBM deployed carriers, as well as with heavier payloads. Despite the Strategic Arms Limitation Treaty (SALT) I agreements (1972),[37] which included the antiballistic missile (ABM) treaty and the negotiation of the SALT II treaty (1979),[38] the numbers of deployed strategic warheads continued to increase (see ch. II). The SALT treaties were limited by the continued refusal of the Soviets to accept on-site inspections. Verification was limited to national technical means (NTM), which could not directly verify numbers of deployed MIRVed warheads (missiles with multiple independently targetable re-entry vehicles or warheads). Thus the SALT agreements limited total deployed delivery vehicles (ICBMs, SLBMs, and bombers) but not warhead totals, and both parties deployed more MIRVed missiles. By the early 1980s, the Soviets had deployed approximately 300 SS-18 heavy ICBMs within SALT II limits. With 10 warheads each, the SS-18 force alone constituted about 3000 warheads, which provided a formidable strategic first-strike threat[39] to the entire US ICBM force.

In the late 1970s, the Soviets also deployed[40] a large force of intermediate-range ballistic missiles that grew to be capable of delivering a total of about 3000 warheads. This force was not limited by SALT II and represented a very serious first-strike threat to NATO. All capitals of Western Europe were at risk (warning time was about 18 minutes). The United States countered with intermediate-range nuclear forces (INF), Pershing ballistic missiles, and ground-launched cruise missiles (GLCMs) for a total of about 1000 warheads by 1986.

The nuclear arms race had reached a very high point in its potential for catastrophe.[41] These Cold War dangers were exacerbated by continued Soviet subversion[42] of vulnerable nations worldwide.

Should a nuclear war actually start, many scenarios were possible, most of them horrendous. Nuclear weapons exploded over even just a few cities of each of the adversaries would mean death and destruction of untold magnitude. Military planners and political leaders could never afford to assume scenarios involving nuclear strikes only at each side's missile or bomber bases. The examples of Hiroshima and Nagasaki have served as constant reminders of how horrible even limited nuclear war could be.

Mikhail Gorbachev

Every American president since the end of World War II had attempted to achieve effective nuclear arms control agreements with the Soviet Union and, while negotiating from a position of nuclear strength, had considered the use of nuclear weapons only as a last resort. President Reagan, first elected in 1980, rebuilt US conventional military forces and sought a treaty (which became the Strategic Arms Reduction Treaty, or START) that would achieve meaningful and verifiable reductions in deployed strategic weapons. Russian leaders Khrushchev and Brezhnev, while occasionally assuming threatening postures as they continued Communist Cold War initiatives, restrained themselves in their plans to use nuclear weapons, thus preventing the Cold War from becoming hot.

Not until Mikhail Gorbachev came to full power in the USSR in early 1985 did the Cold War begin to recede. Gorbachev introduced new ideas[43] that he termed "Perestroika." Immediate indicators of this new thinking were in arms control negotiations. Gorbachev and President Reagan made important progress on strategic arms control (START) at the Geneva (1985) and Reykjavik (1986) summits, and the first breakthrough occurred with the signing of the INF treaty in Washington, DC, December 1987. In the INF treaty,[44] Gorbachev agreed to a practical system of notifications and on-site inspections as part of a comprehensive verification package. This was the first time the Soviets had ever agreed to such on-site inspections of their nuclear deployments. The

INF treaty provided for the complete elimination of all deployed US and Soviet missile systems with a range of 300 to 3400 miles, and banned the production, storage, and deployment of such systems thereafter (ch. V). The treaty entered into force on June 1, 1988. The elimination of missiles, along with the on-site inspections (twenty per year for each side), proceeded for the three-year elimination period. By 1991, all the treaty-prohibited forces, including missiles carrying about 3000 Soviet nuclear warheads and the INF missiles carrying about 1000 US warheads, had been eliminated or accounted for.[45] The success of the INF treaty was a first major accomplishment signaling the end of the Cold War. This was followed by the reunification of Germany, the removal of the Berlin wall, and the liberation of the other Eastern European peoples.[46] Gorbachev's agreement to on-site inspections paved the way for the implementation of the Threshold Test Ban Treaty (TTBT) and the Conventional Forces in Europe (CFE) agreement, which also helped codify the end of the Cold War.

In 1986, Presidents Reagan and Gorbachev quickly agreed on the major limits (1600 strategic delivery vehicles and 6000 accountable warheads) and the principle of on-site verification for the proposed START I treaty, but the details were difficult. The two sides had differing force structures and disagreed on inspections and downloading; Presidents Bush and Gorbachev finally signed the START I treaty on July 1, 1991. The comprehensive treaty[47] reduces strategic delivery vehicles and deployed strategic warheads by nearly half. The treaty's notification, verification, and on-site inspection procedures are comprehensive and fully demonstrated Gorbachev's commitment to a "new openness" (ch. VII).

The Breakup of the Soviet Union

In December 1991, the USSR broke up into fifteen independent republics. Four of these, Russia, Ukraine, Belarus, and Kazakhstan, contained all the START-limited weapons and equipment. The critical legal question on the status of the treaty was resolved in May 1992 at Lisbon, Portugal, when these four nations and the United States signed the "Lisbon Protocol,"[48] an addition to the START I treaty that bound the five nations to all the conditions of the original treaty (ch. VII).

Russia assumed the obligations of the former USSR, and Ukraine, Belarus, and Kazakhstan pledged to become non-nuclear-weapon members of the NPT. The US Senate and the Russian parliament ratified the new treaty in the fall of 1992. Not until November 1994 did the other three parties ratify the START treaty and accede to the NPT (Ukraine last, after much internal political turbulence). The first data exchanges and baseline inspections were completed by July 1995.[49] START I provided a measure of stability during the early hectic days of the breakup of the USSR.

Further Reductions

To further reduce the dangers of excessive nuclear weapons, Presidents Bush and Yeltsin held a summit in June 1992 and agreed on an outline for START II that would decrease strategic deployments; after hard negotiations, the two presidents signed START II[50] on January 3, 1993, just before Bush left office. START II will reduce deployed strategic warheads to no more than 3500 for each side (down from 6000 in START I) and will eliminate all MIRVed ICBMs, including the heavy Soviet SS-18s (ch. VIII).

As of mid-1999, START II still had not entered into force. The first major delay was obtaining ratification of START I and the NPT by Ukraine (ch. VII). Next, US Senate ratification[51] was delayed until January 1996 (ch. VIII). The principal delay, however, has been in Russia, where a new Duma (elected in December 1995) resisted approval of the treaty. Throughout 1996, 1997, and 1998, political opposition[52] to START II within Russia remained strong (ch. VIII). Communists, other hard-liners, and Yeltsin's opponents in the Duma have resisted action on the treaty. Some Russians voiced objections about the US developments in antimissile defense. Some Russian military analysts have been concerned that eliminating all MIRVed ICBMs places a burden on Russian resources, especially if they are to replace SS-18 and SS-24 missiles with new single-warhead missiles in an effort to maintain parity with the United States under START II. Politically, many Russians have expressed concern about NATO expansion.[53] Many of these concerns, as expressed within Russia, have merit but may be exaggerated by carry-over thinking from the Cold War years. The Russians are a proud and patriotic people who have suffered much throughout history, both at the hands of invaders (Hitler in World War II) and their own dictatorial leaders (Stalin and Brezhnev, for example). They have not yet realized the full benefits of increased political freedom and/or a free economy, and with a greatly reduced conventional military capability, some cling to their nuclear weapons as a bargaining chip. Years of cold-war thinking, coupled with the previous lack of a free press and individual freedom over many decades, have made it difficult for the Russian people to achieve the full benefits promised by the end of the Cold War.

At Helsinki in March 1997, Presidents Clinton and Yeltsin reached agreements[54] (see ch. VIII and IX) on START II implementation and another proposed treaty, START III, that would further limit and verify nuclear deployments. Subsequently, the Russian-NATO Founding Act[55] was signed in an effort to alleviate Russian concerns over NATO and to enhance future NATO-Russian cooperation. To further accommodate some of the Russian concerns, the United States and Russia signed (September 1997) amendments to the START II treaty to extend the date for the strategic force reductions from 2003 to 2007. Concurrently, they signed an amendment to the ABM treaty to limit theater missile-defense systems to capabilities below those believed needed for ABM systems. Whether these agreements (ch. IX) will enable the necessary support for START II within the Duma remains to be seen.

While the nuclear arms race has been arrested with the advent of the INF and START treaties, and nuclear proliferation was substantially limited by the extension of the NPT in 1995 (see ch. II and IV), the superpower arms race has left the world with thousands of nuclear weapons, deployed and nondeployed, in the hands of several nations (including China, the United Kingdom, and France) that are not yet under the control of nuclear-weapon-limitation treaties. In addition, the threat of proliferation of nuclear weapons by other parties, such as Iraq, Iran, North Korea, and Libya, has grown in recent years. A major result of the United States-led-coalition actions against Iraq in the Gulf War (1991) has been the continuing effort to find and destroy the nuclear weapons program in Iraq. Another nuclear arms race threatens to erupt between India and Pakistan, with neither side yet committed to either the NPT or the Comprehensive Test Ban Treaty (CTBT). In addition, with the large numbers of nondeployed nuclear warheads and quantities of nuclear weapons materials (weapons-grade uranium and plutonium, much of it in the FSU) that exist outside any credible international control authority, the possibility of nuclear weapons use by terrorists (or others) is believed to be greater than ever.

The threat of the superpower nuclear arms race has been greatly reduced, but much critical and urgent work remains to be done to achieve full and credible control of nuclear weapons worldwide. Some of these needs were discussed by Allison, Carter, and coauthors[56] in 1993. The following chapters address these issues.

References and Notes

1. *World Almanac Book of Facts*, 1994, Robert Famighetti, ed. (Funk and Wagnallis Corp., Mahuah, New Jersey) p. 517. Millions of people perished in the Soviet Union from 1929 to 1938 as a result of Stalin's political purges and suppression of ethnic groups. See also *World War II Almanac 1931–1945*, Robert Goralski, ed. (Bonanza Books, New York, 1981), p. 115. In the Katyn Massacre, 4,000 Polish officers were shot in the head by the NKVD after being removed from a body of 180,000 Polish prisoners of war taken by the Soviets at the end of the September 1939 German invasion of Poland. An additional 6000 Polish officers were never accounted for. This is but one of many examples of Stalin's brutality before and during World War II.
2. David McCullough, *Truman* (Simon & Schuster, New York, 1992).
3. McGeorge Bundy, *Danger and Survival* (Random House, New York, 1988) pp. 58–93.
4. Bundy, *Danger and Survival*, p. 132.
5. Bundy, *Danger and Survival*, pp. 141–142.
6. Bundy, *Danger and Survival*, pp. 142–148.
7. McCullough, *Truman*, p. 383.
8. McCullough, *Truman*, p. 449.
9. McCullough, *Truman*, p. 486.
10. Richard Rhodes, *Dark Sun–The Making of the Hydrogen Bomb* (Simon & Schuster, New York, 1995), ch. 13.
11. McCullough, *Truman*, pp. 486–490.
12. Bundy, *Danger and Survival*, pp. 158–169. The plan was first developed by Acheson, Lilienthal, and Oppenheimer.
13. Bundy, *Danger and Survival*, pp. 166–176.
14. McCullough, *Truman*, pp. 543–544.
15. McCullough, *Truman*, pp. 546–549.
16. McCullough, *Truman*, pp. 561–565.
17. Dwight D. Eisenhower, *Mandate for Change* (Doubleday and Co., Garden City, New York, 1963), pp. 80–81. Also see McCullough, Truman, p. 583.
18. McCullough, *Truman*, pp. 630–631, 647–648, 699, 734–735.
19. Stanley R. Sloan, NATO's *Future-Towards A New Transatlantic Bargain*, National Defense University Press (US GPO, Washington, DC, 1985).
20. Sloan, ch. 1 (origins); ch. 3 (evolution of NATO).
21. McCullough, *Truman*, pp. 775–783.
22. McCullough, *Truman*, pp. 814–820.

23. *The First 20 Years at Los Alamos*, Los Alamos Scientific Laboratory News (January 1, 1963) pp. 31–32.
24. *The Atom* **7**, No. 8, Los Alamos Scientific Laboratory News (September 1970). In October 1945, Robert Oppenheimer, with General Leslie Groves, asked Dr. Norris Bradbury to direct the Los Alamos Laboratory. He did so for 25 years.
25. *The Atom*, Los Alamos Scientific Laboratory News (January 1, 1963). Others who stayed at the Laboratory included Carson Mark, Bill Ogle, Max Roy, Ralph Carlisle Smith, and many others.
26. *The Atom*, Los Alamos Scientific Laboratory News (January 1, 1963). The Bikini Atol tests studied naval effects and provided needed nuclear data.
27. *The Atom*, Los Alamos Scientific Laboratory News (January 1, 1963). The McMahon Act of 1946 created the AEC, which took over the atomic energy program on January 1, 1947. This put Los Alamos Laboratory on a firm base. The Congress created a Joint (House-Senate) Committee on Atomic Energy (JCAE) which played a key role for several decades.
28. Bundy, *Danger and Survival*, pp. 319–325.
29. Rhodes, *Dark Sun*, ch. 25.
30. Dwight D. Eisenhower, *Mandate for Change*, pp. 445–458, and *Waging Peace* (Doubleday and Co., Garden City, New York, 1965). Also see Bundy, *Danger and Survival*, pp. 236–305. The brutal suppression of Hungary in 1956 illustrated Soviet domination of Eastern Europe (see *Waging Peace*, ch. III).
31. Bundy, *Danger and Survival*, pp. 358–371.
32. Charles R. Morris, *Iron Destinies, Lost Opportunities* (Harper & Row Publishers, New York) p. 173. The Soviet tests were extensive, forty in all, the largest being about 50 megatons. Some were conducted at high altitude and many produced large amounts of radioactive fallout worldwide.
33. Morris, pp. 173–174. The world stood "at the brink of war" before Khrushchev withdrew his missiles and ended the crisis.
34. *Arms Control Agreements: Texts and Histories of Negotiations*, 1982 ed. US Arms Control and Disarmament Agency, Washington, DC, 1982.
35. Famighetti, *World Almanac Book of Facts 1994*, p. 520.
36. *Arms Control Agreements: Texts and Histories of Negotiations*, 1982 ed. Also see Henry Kissinger, White House Years (Little, Brown and Co., Boston, Massachusetts, 1979) pp. 196–198, 1216–1222, and 1229–1246.
37. *Arms Control Agreements: Texts and Histories of Negotiations*, 1982 ed. (see SALT I, Strategic Arms Limitation Talks).

38. *Arms Control Agreements: Texts and Histories of Negotiations*, 1982 ed. (SALT II), and "The SALT II Treaty," SFRC exec. report 96-14, November 1979.
39. The elimination of the dangerous Soviet MIRVed heavy ICBMS (SS-18s) is a decades-old, high-priority US arms control objective. See "The START Treaty," SFRC exec. report 102-53, September 1992. Also see Linton F. Brooks, "Strategic Nuclear Arms Control: Status and Prospects," Los Alamos National Laboratory report LA-UR-94-952, CNSS seminar at Los Alamos National Laboratory February 25, 1994.
40. US SFRC, *The INF Treaty*, April 1988, exec. report 100-15. See INF (intermediate-range nuclear force) deployments.
41. Caspar Weinberger, *Soviet Military Power*, US DoD report, March 1986.
42. See, for example, *Soviet Active Measures*, Hearings before the Subcommittee on European Affairs," SFRC, Sept. 12 and 13, 1985, Sen. Hrg. 99-44, Part 2 of 5.
43. Mikhail Gorbachev, *Perestroika-New Thinking for Our Country and the World* (Harper & Row Publishers, New York, 1987).
44. "The INF Treaty," SFRC exec. report 100-15, April 14,1988.
45. Arms Control and Disarmament Agency (ACDA), Annual Report for 1991 (July 1992).
46. James A. Baker, *The Politics of Diplomacy* (G. P. Putnam's Sons, New York, 1995).
47. "Treaty with the Union of Soviet Socialists Republics on the Reduction and Limitation of Strategic Offensive Arms (the START treaty)," Message to the US Senate by the president of the United States, Treaty Doc. 102-20, 102nd Congress, November 25, 1991, US GPO, Washington, DC. Document includes complete treaty text, protocols on eliminations, inspections, notifications, throw-weight, telemetry, JCIC, signed statements, and the Memorandum of Understanding (MOU). The MOU gives the detailed list of deployments for each party as of 1991. The president's message includes an article-by-article analysis. The START treaties (START I and START II) and their implementation are described and summarized in detail in the Los Alamos National Laboratory Report, LA-UR-97-2045, "The START Treaties: Implementation and Status," David B. Thomson, May 1997.
48. "Message from the President of the United States to the US Senate Transmitting the Protocol to the START Treaty, signed at Lisbon, Portugal, on May 23, 1992," treaty document 102-32, June 23, 1992.

49. The difficult process of obtaining full ratification of the START I treaty is described in the Los Alamos National Report, LA-UR-97-2045 (listed in ref. 47, above). This report also summarizes treaty implementation activities as of early 1997, including the very significant reductions in strategic nuclear deployments by the parties.
50. "Message from the President Transmitting the START II Treaty to the US Senate (Including its Protocols and Memorandum of Attribution, MOA)," treaty document 103-1, Jan. 20, 1993. Includes article-by-article analysis. The START II treaty is also summarized in detail in LA-UR-97-2045 (listed in ref. 47 above).
51. The process of START II ratification by the US Senate is described in some detail in LA-UR-97-2045 (listed in ref. 47).
52. Recent Russian political opposition to the START II treaty is discussed in LA-UR-97-2045.
53. NATO expansion issues are discussed by Hans Binnendijk, "NATO Enlargement: Sailing between Scylla and Charybdis," in Strategic Forum, Institute for National Strategic Studies (INSS), No. 55, November 1995 (NDU Press, 202-475-1913). Opposition to NATO expansion within the US arms control community is well expressed by Jack Mendelsohn, "NATO Expansion: A Decision to Regret," *Arms Control Today*, The Arms Control Association, Washington, DC, Vol. 27, No. 4, June/July 1997, p. 2.
54. Agreements reached at the March 1997 Helsinki Summit by Presidents Clinton and Yeltsin in an effort to facilitate Russian ratification of START II are discussed in LA-UR-97-2045.
55. "Founding Act on Mutual Relations, Cooperation and Security Between NATO and the Russian Federation," signed in Paris, May 27, 1997, *Arms Control Today*, The Arms Control Association, Washington, DC, Vol. 27, No. 3, May 1997, pp. 21–24, and pp. 19–20. Also see "Cold War Rivalry Buried by NATO-Russian Deal," *Jane's Defence Weekly*, 4 June 1997, p. 3.
56. Graham Allison, Ashton Carter, Steven Miller, and Philip Zelikow, eds., "Cooperative Denuclearization: From Pledges to Deeds," Center for Science and International Affairs, Harvard University, Cambridge, MA (1993).

Chapter II

Historical Overview of Nuclear Arms Control Negotiations

Euphoria and relief prevailed in the United States over the successful use of nuclear weapons at Hiroshima and Nagasaki to end World War II in August 1945. This elation was heavily dampened by the tremendous death and devastation caused in these cities by the use of a single weapon. Possessing the secrets of making nuclear weapons gave the American people confidence in their security, but it also made them critically concerned for the future of mankind and hopeful that these weapons would never have to be used again.

The Baruch Plan

In November 1945, Vannevar Bush and President Truman agreed that a United Nations (UN) commission might become a means[1] for controlling nuclear weapons. Committees headed by Dean Acheson and David Lilienthal, and guided by J. Robert Oppenheimer, produced the Acheson-Lilienthal Report (March 1946). The plan[2] called for a UN Atomic Development Authority that would (1) control all uranium and plutonium worldwide, (2) ban individual national nuclear programs, (3) conduct research on the peaceful use of atomic energy, and (4) make violations easier to detect with all allowable work done under the UN. The United States and others would negotiate to gradually turn their know-how and nuclear materials over to the UN.

In March 1946, Truman named Bernard Baruch as chief US negotiator for the plan. Baruch added that there would be (1) swift and sure penalties for violations and (2) no big-power "veto" on enforcement or inspections.[3] Baruch presented the plan to the UN Atomic Energy Commission (UNAEC) in New York on June 17, 1946.[4] The Russians insisted on having the veto in all cases, including verification. The plan was debated[5] in the UNAEC and the final vote taken in December. The USSR vetoed the plan. The Baruch Plan as conceived by Oppenheimer and others required openness and cooperation that Joseph Stalin would never consider. The plan died.[5]

The Eisenhower Years

In 1953, new president Dwight D. Eisenhower was determined to achieve peace and security.[6] The USSR had deployed quantities of tanks and artillery forces in Europe that could overwhelm the North Atlantic Treaty Organization (NATO) and US forces. Eisenhower believed the economic way to deter Russian aggression was to strengthen US strategic forces and deploy tactical nuclear weapons in Europe.
Los Alamos was asked to develop a variety of new weapons, both low- and high-yield. "Ike" also supported peaceful uses of nuclear energy and called for the creation of an International Atomic Energy Agency (IAEA).[7]

While building up US nuclear forces, Eisenhower sought to limit[8] the nuclear arms race through negotiations. Ike proposed[8] an "open skies" agreement to allow aerial observations over the territories of each of the parties as a way of guarding against surprise attack. He also proposed[8] on-site inspections to restrict future nuclear material production to peaceful uses. The Soviets rejected both proposals. From the mid-fifties on, Ike worked for a verifiable nuclear test ban.[9] The Soviets claimed to want such a ban, but in negotiations, always opposed on-site verification. In late 1958, Eisenhower declared a unilateral moratorium on US nuclear testing in an effort to help negotiations and alleviate fallout concerns.[10] The Soviets followed with a similar unilateral moratorium. In 1960, Ike proposed a threshold test ban banning tests greater than five kilotons (kT), but the Soviets rejected the related inspections.[11]
To enhance verification, Project Vela was started in FY60 and funding was increased for FY61.

When Ike left office in January 1961, the Soviets had rejected all his proposals for verifiable control of nuclear arms or testing.[12] Eisenhower had provided, however, for strong US strategic forces.[13] Overwhelming US nuclear retaliatory power combined with experienced leadership had successfully minimized the chances of Soviet attack.

The Limited Nuclear Test Ban Treaty of 1963

After the Cuban missile crisis in 1962, the Soviets sobered and relations improved in 1963. In June the United States and Russia created the "hot line" between Moscow and Washington, enabling the leaders to quickly talk to each other,[14] and they worked on the test ban.[15] World public opinion was vocal against the flagrant renewal of high-yield nuclear tests by the Soviets in 1961 and the resulting US response. Nuclear fallout from high-yield tests in the atmosphere was a great concern.

After eight years of test ban negotiations, the issues had been explored. Agreement was stymied by Soviet refusal to allow the inspections necessary for verification. Atmospheric tests can be detected by a variety of means from outside the territory of any nation (by national technical means, NTM), but underground tests generally require on-site monitoring for verification. The solution, to ban atmospheric tests and allow underground tests, was proposed by Eisenhower in 1958 and encouraged by Senator Hubert Humphrey. As late as 1962,[15] the Soviets were insisting that underground tests be prohibited by the treaty (without inspections). In June 1963, Khrushchev agreed, surprisingly, to a treaty banning all tests in the atmosphere and space, but allowing underground tests. Clandestine atmospheric testing could be observed from stations outside the testing country (ground stations, aircraft, and Vela satellites) and did not require on-site inspections for verification, as discussed in ch. III. The treaty was negotiated and signed on August 5, 1963.

The test ban treaty was supported by public opinion and most of the US scientific community. However, Senate ratification required a two-thirds majority, and some key senators opposed it or had doubts. The Senate Foreign Relations Committee (SFRC) held 11 hearings on the Test Ban Treaty during August.[16] Dr. Norris Bradbury, director of Los Alamos Scientific Laboratory, testified persuasively in support of the treaty, as discussed in ch. III. With strong bipartisan support, and after three weeks of floor debate in September, the Senate ratified the test ban treaty by a vote of 80 to 19.

When the treaty entered into force in October 1963, over 60 nations had signed it. Today over 120 nations have joined, helping reduce proliferation. The Limited Test Ban Treaty (LTBT) was a great success. The LTBT accomplished the following: (1) showed for the first time that the superpowers could reach nuclear weapons agreement, (2) eliminated the worldwide fallout from nuclear tests, and (3) set the stage for the Nonproliferation Treaty of 1968. Also, under the treaty, the laboratories were able to provide the needed weapons designs. We note that the US Arms Control and Disarmament Agency (ACDA) was created[17] just before the LTBT was signed, and played a role in explaining it to the public.

The Nonproliferation Treaty (NPT)

By 1964, three nations had joined the United States and Russia as nuclear powers: the United Kingdom in 1952, France in 1960, and China in 1964. In 1966, five countries had nuclear reactors, but about 300[18] power reactors were projected to be built worldwide. Some of these could be modified to produce weapons-grade plutonium. If many nations possessed nuclear weapons, the risks of nuclear war could greatly increase as a result of accident, unauthorized use, or escalation of conflicts. On June 12, 1968, after specific negotiations beginning in 1965, the General Assembly approved the "Treaty on the Nonproliferation of Nuclear Weapons" (NPT). The United States, the USSR, the United Kingdom, and 59 other countries signed the treaty in July 1, 1968, and it entered into force on March 5, 1970.[18]

The NPT recognizes states that exploded nuclear weapons before January 1967 as nuclear weapons states, namely the United States, the United Kingdom, Russia, France, and China. All other member states are recognized as non-nuclear-weapons states. NPT provisions[18] include the following: (1) nuclear-weapons states may not transfer nuclear weapons to non-nuclear-weapons states or assist a non-nuclear-weapons state in acquiring nuclear weapons; and (2) non-nuclear-weapons states may not manufacture or acquire nuclear weapons and must accept IAEA safeguards[18] to prevent diversion of fissionable materials to weapons uses. Now 178 nations are members, with France and China joining in 1992.

Since the 1970s, nations have negotiated safeguard agreements with the IAEA, and safeguards inspections have been carried out routinely at many declared nonweapon sites. The NPT has been decisive in preventing proliferation by many nations. Iraq, North Korea, and possibly Iran are considered to be possible violators.

The treaty called for a review conference every five years and for a special review and extension conference 25 years after its entry into force, to either amend it, extend it, or let it lapse. By 1995, many members were unhappy that the nuclear powers had not achieved the disarmament goals of the preamble. Others were concerned about their security and/or the supply of allowed nuclear materials. The conference ended in New York in May 1995, with the parties extending the treaty indefinitely in a parliamentary maneuver that did not require a formal vote, as discussed in ch. IV. Many nonnuclear members are still concerned about their security, however.

India, Pakistan, and Israel have not joined the NPT, and India and Pakistan recently concluded a series of underground nuclear tests (ch. III and IV), provocative actions that threaten the whole nonproliferation regime in central Asia.[19]

The SALT Treaties

In spite of the LTBT and the NPT, the nuclear arms race between the United States and USSR continued in the late 1960s. The United States had substantial strategic forces[20] then: 1054 ICBMs, 650 SLBMs, and about 400 B-52 long-range heavy bombers. These amounts became ceilings that Congress did not want to exceed. Russia, starting with lower numbers of delivery vehicles and warheads, caught up in 1971[20] with heavier intercontinental ballistic missile (ICBM) payloads. In November 1969, the United States and the Soviets began the Strategic Arms Limitation Talks (SALT). Presidents Nixon and Brezhnev signed SALT I, which included the antiballistic missile (ABM) treaty and an Interim Agreement on Strategic Offensive Arms, in May 1972.[20]

The SALT agreements were limited by the continued refusal of the Soviets to accept on-site verification, which they considered too intrusive. SALT verification was therefore limited to NTM,[21] which includes photographic observation by earth-orbiting satellites. NTM also includes radar observations of the range and velocities of individual rocket tests (ICBMs, for example) obtained from stations outside the nation being observed. The NTM evidence enables the observing nation to determine numbers of deployed missile sites, missiles, bombers, and submarines capable of launching missiles. NTM cannot by itself verify the numbers or characteristics of the nuclear warheads carried on board any given delivery vehicle.

The ABM treaty[20,22] limited each side to two ABM sites, one centered at the nation's capital and one centered at an ICBM launching site. (The parties were limited to 100 ABM launchers at each ABM site.) The SALT I Interim Agreement on Offensive Strategic Deployments required both parties to pledge not to construct any new fixed land-based ICBM launchers. The sides agreed not to convert existing ICBM launchers into heavy ICBM launchers and not to increase their SLBMs or submarines for SLBMs. This agreement lasted five years and was planned to be superseded by the SALT II treaty.

The ABM treaty, ratified in August 1972, limited strategic deployments for the first time. By limiting[22] defensive deployments of one party, the ABM treaty was supposed to limit the incentive for the other party to build more offensive delivery systems designed to overwhelm the adversary. However, fifteen years would pass before another treaty designed to limit missile deployments was both signed and ratified.

In November 1974 at Vladivostok, President Ford with Secretary of State Kissinger and General Secretary Brezhnev agreed that a SALT II treaty[23] should be negotiated that included a limit of 2400 strategic nuclear delivery vehicles (SNDVs are ICBMs, SLBMs, and heavy bombers) for each side. President Carter (with Secretary of State Cyrus Vance) assumed office in 1977 and continued the SALT II negotiations. SALT II was finally signed by Carter and Brezhnev in June 1979.[23] SALT II provided parity only in numbers of delivery vehicles and included a number of sublimits and other restrictions. The principal SALT II limits were as follows:

Strategic Nuclear Delivery Vehicle	Number of Vehicles Allowed
Total SNDVs	2400 (to be reduced to 2250 by 1981)
MIRVed ICBMs and bombers with air-launched cruise missiles (ALCMs)	1320
MIRVed ICBMs and SLBMs	1200
ICBM launchers	820

Restrictions were also placed on new heavy ICBMs, other new missile types, rapid reload, missiles tests, and so forth, but these were very hard to verify by NTM alone.

Vigorous Senate hearings and debate[23] on the SALT II treaty were held in the summer and fall of 1979. Many amendments to the resolution of ratification passed or failed by only one or two votes. The SFRC finally recommended ratification but only by a vote of nine to six, with numerous reservations. Because of the Soviet invasion of Afghanistan and other international and domestic political considerations, SALT II was never brought to the Senate floor for a vote. For several years, both parties stated they would abide by its limits, however, and it was eventually replaced by the START treaty. The Soviet buildup of heavy SS-18s and other threatening MIRVed missiles (ch. I) occurred while SALT II was being observed in a strictly legal sense-but there were no limits on deployed warheads and no on-site inspections to help verify such deployed warheads. In addition, the Soviets were deploying mobile missiles (such as the SS-24 and SS-25), which were harder to verify by NTM alone.

The Intermediate-Range Nuclear Forces (INF) Treaty

Following the rapid Soviet buildup of intermediate-range nuclear missiles threatening NATO in the late 1970s, discussed in ch. I, the United States initiated plans to deploy Pershing II missiles and ground-launched cruise missiles (GLCMs) to counter the threat. In 1982, the United States and Russia started negotiations on a treaty to limit such forces. As in previous arms control negotiations, the Soviet refusal to allow adequate verification prevented a practical treaty.

As noted in ch. I, Mikhail Gorbachev's rise to full power in the USSR in early 1985 reversed the Cold War as Gorbachev introduced "Perestroika." Immediate indicators of this "new thinking" were in arms control negotiations. Gorbachev and President Reagan made important progress on strategic arms control (START) at the Geneva (1985) and Reykjavik (1986) summits, and the first breakthrough occurred with the signing of the INF treaty in Washington, DC, December 1987. In the INF treaty,[24] Gorbachev agreed to a practical system of notifications and on-site inspections as part of a comprehensive verification package.

This was the first time ever that the Soviets had agreed to such on-site inspections of their nuclear deployments. The INF treaty provided for the complete elimination of all deployed US and Soviet missile systems with a range of 300 to 3400 miles, and banned the production, storage, and deployment of such systems thereafter. After ratification, the treaty entered into force on June 1, 1988. On-site inspections (20 per year for each side) and the elimination of missiles proceeded for the three-year elimination period. By 1991, all the treaty-prohibited forces, including missiles carrying 3000 Soviet nuclear warheads and the INF missiles carrying about 1000 US warheads, had been eliminated or accounted for.

The INF treaty and its implementation is described in detail in ch. V. The success of the INF treaty was a first major accomplishment signaling the end of the Cold War. Gorbachev's agreement to on-site inspections also paved the way for the implementation of the Threshold Test Ban Treaty (TTBT) discussed in ch. III and the Treaty on Conventional Forces in Europe (CFE).[25]

The START I Treaty

In 1982, President Reagan first proposed a strategic arms reduction treaty (START) with major reductions in nuclear deployments and with adequate on-site verification. Under Brezhnev, the Soviets were not about to agree to the inspections. After Gorbachev came to power, the presidents quickly agreed (in 1986) on the major limits (1600 strategic delivery vehicles and 6000 accountable warheads) and on the principle of on-site verification for the proposed START I treaty. The details were harder. The two sides' differing force-structures created sublimit issues. Difficulties with inspections and the issue of downloading MIRVed ICBMs persisted until the final signing. George Bush became president and pushed for a treaty. Finally in Moscow, July 1, 1991, Presidents Bush and Gorbachev signed the START I treaty. The voluminous treaty[26] reduces strategic delivery vehicles from about 2500 to 1600 for each side. Deployed strategic warheads are reduced from about 10,200 each to 6000. The treaty's notification, verification, and on-site inspection procedures are the most comprehensive ever negotiated for a nuclear treaty. But much more effort was needed.

In December 1991, the USSR broke up into 15 independent republics. Four of these, Russia, Ukraine, Belarus, and Kazakhstan, contained all the START-limited weapons and equipment. The critical legal question on the status of the treaty was resolved by Secretary of State James Baker in May 1992 at Lisbon, Portugal, when these four nations and the United States signed the "Lisbon Protocol," [27] an addition to the START I treaty that bound the five nations to all the conditions of the original treaty. Russia assumed the obligations of the former USSR, and Ukraine, Belarus, and Kazakhstan pledged to become non-nuclear-weapon members of the NPT. The US Senate and the Russian parliament ratified the new treaty in the fall of 1992. Not until November 1994 had the other three parties all ratified the START treaty and acceded to the NPT (Ukraine last, after much negotiating and internal political turbulence). The first data exchanges and extensive baseline inspections (visits to about 50 sites by US inspectors) were completed by July 1995, and the strategic deployments of the former Soviet Union were now under the detailed scrutiny of the On-Site Inspection Agency (OSIA). Also, START I had provided a measure of stability during the early hectic days of the breakup of the USSR. START I and its implementation are described in detail in ch. VII.

START II and the Cold War Legacy

To further reduce the dangers of excessive nuclear weapons, Presidents Bush and Yeltsin held a summit in June 1992 and agreed on an outline for the START II treaty to further reduce strategic deployments. US and Russian negotiators worked hard to put the summit statement into agreed-upon treaty language, and the two presidents signed the START II treaty[28] on January 3, 1993, just before Bush left office. START II is a bilateral treaty that will reduce deployed strategic warheads to no more than 3500 for each side (down from 6000 in START I) and will eliminate all MIRVed ICBMs, including the heavy Soviet SS-18s. START II uses the comprehensive START I verification procedures and depends on the implementation of START I. START II is described in detail in ch. VIII.

As of early 1999, START II had not entered into force. The first major delay was obtaining ratification of START I by Ukraine. Next, US Senate ratification[29] was delayed until January 1996. The principal delay, however, has been in Russia, where a new Duma (elected in December 1995) resisted approval of the treaty. Throughout 1996, 1997, 1998, and well into 1999, political opposition to START II within Russia was strong. Yeltsin's opponents in the Duma, Communists and other hard-liners, have resisted action on the treaty. Some Russians have been concerned about American developments in antimissile defense. Some Russian military analysts have stated a concern that eliminating all MIRVed ICBMs places a burden on Russian resources, especially if they are to replace SS-18 and SS-24 missiles with new single-warhead missiles in an effort to maintain parity with the United States under START II. Politically, many Russians have expressed concern about NATO expansion.

In March 1997, Presidents Clinton and Yeltsin reached agreements[30] on START II implementation and a proposed START III treaty that would further limit and verify nuclear deployments. Subsequently, the Russian-NATO Founding Act[31] was signed in an effort to alleviate Russian concerns over NATO and to enhance future NATO-Russian cooperation. To further accommodate some of the Russian concerns, the United States and Russia signed (September 1997) amendments to START II to extend the date for the strategic force reductions from the year 2003 to 2007. Concurrently, they signed an amendment to the ABM treaty to limit theater missile-defense systems to capabilities below those believed needed for ABM systems. Whether these agreements will garner the necessary support for START II within the Duma remains to be seen. START II is described, and ratification and implementation issues are detailed, in ch. VIII.

The Future of Nuclear Arms Control

The ratification of the START II treaty by the Russian Duma may be a critical milestone. Firstly, the continued step-by-step mutual reductions in the nuclear weapon stockpiles of the United States and Russia depend on achieving START II or some new treaty in its place. Secondly, in 1995, the NPT was extended indefinitely by the 25-year review conference (ch. IV), but that extension was based on many factors, including the promised continued reduction of nuclear deployments by the nuclear superpowers. Failure to achieve START II could have serious repercussions in the continued observance and enhancement of the NPT worldwide. The response of the international community to the recent provocative testing of nuclear weapons by India and Pakistan will be even more critical to the future of the NPT. These issues are discussed in ch. IV.

Many arms control advocates believe that nuclear weapons must be reduced to very low levels (say, about 300) if the nations of the world are to be free of the threat of nuclear devastation that existed during the Cold War years. The author suggests, however, that many steps are needed to achieve such a goal. Some of these steps are discussed in ch. X, as are other issues concerning the future of nuclear arms control.

References and Notes

1. McGeorge Bundy, *Danger and Survival* (Random House, New York, 1988) pp. 142–148.
2. Bundy, *Danger and Survival*, pp. 158–161.
3. Charles R. Morris, *Iron Destinies, Lost Opportunities* (Harper & Row Publishers, New York, 1988) pp. 30–31.
4. Bundy, *Danger and Survival*, pp. 161–169.
5. Bundy, *Danger and Survival*, pp. 166–176. In December 1946, the Baruch Plan was voted on in the UN, and passed 10-0-2. The Russian veto killed it. Baruch resigned in January 1947. Discussion continued in the UN in 1947 and 1948, but with the same result.
6. Bundy, *Danger and Survival*, pp. 236–305. Also see Dwight D. Eisenhower, *Mandate for Change* (Doubleday and Co., Garden City, New York, 1963), pp. 445–458; and *Waging Peace* (Doubleday and Co., Garden City, New York, 1965), pp. 466–484. Ike's goals included a strong national defense within reasonable budgets, worldwide peace and security, an end to dangers of nuclear war, and exploiting atomic energy for peace.
7. Dwight D. Eisenhower, *Waging Peace*, pp. 468–469. Ike called for international cooperation in atomic energy in a major UN speech in 1953 and encouraged creation of the International Atomic Energy Authority (IAEA), which occurred by 1957. International scientific conferences in 1955 and 1958 distributed information worldwide on the peaceful uses of nuclear energy. The IAEA became technically capable and promoted peaceful nuclear activities worldwide.
8. Dwight D. Eisenhower, *Mandate for Change*, pp. 519–521; and *Waging Peace*, pp. 469–471. In 1955, Ike made the first "open skies" proposal to guard against surprise attack. The Soviets fully rejected the idea. See also *Waging Peace*, pp. 466–484. Eisenhower named Harold Stassen as the first ever presidential disarmament adviser. In 1957 he submitted proposals, complete with on-site inspections, for restricting future nuclear material production to peaceful purposes. The Soviets fully rejected the proposals.
9. Eisenhower, *Waging Peace*, pp. 477–484. In October 1958, Ike announced a two-year moratorium on nuclear testing, to facilitate negotiations. The moratorium was to last as long as the Soviets did not test. The Soviets refrained from testing also until they broke the moratorium in 1961.
10. Bundy, *Danger and Survival*, pp. 328–329.
11. Eisenhower, *Waging Peace*, p. 480–481. Project Vela funding: FY60 at $10 M; FY61 at $66 M.
12. Eisenhower, *Waging Peace*, pp. 467–484.

13. Eisenhower, *Waging Peace*, pp. 205–212. Eisenhower initiated the Atlas, Titan, and Minuteman ICBM programs, and the development of the Jupiter and Thor intermediate-range ballistic missiles. See p. 483: the first Polaris SLBM was fired from a nuclear-powered submarine in 1960.
14. "Arms Control and Disarmament Agreements," (ACDA, 1982 ed.) US ACDA, Washington, DC. See hot line agreement.
15. ACDA 1982 ed. Note that proposals for including a test ban with a ban or limit on production of nuclear materials, or for treating the testing issue separately, had been promoted by each side at one time or another. Also note that Senator Hubert Humphrey, chairman of the Senate Subcommittee on Disarmament, had worked hard for the test ban treaty.
16. "Nuclear Test Ban Treaty," hearings, SFRC, August 12–15, 19–23, 26, and 27, 1963. Note that an atmospheric test ban treaty had been proposed by Eisenhower in 1958. Also note that Los Alamos developed the Vela satellite detection system and a ground-based fluorescence detection system. These greatly enhanced LTBT verification. See Dr. Norris Bradbury's testimony.
17. The Limited Test Ban Treaty negotiations had involved many complex technical issues, as did the elusive goals of limitations on production of nuclear weapons materials and the elimination of proliferation of nuclear weapons to other nations. During the negotiations, the president needed experts from the DoD, AEC, State Department, and other agencies. Harold Stassen was the first disarmament adviser, but his staff was small. In 1961, Congress created the US Arms Control and Disarmament agency (ACDA), whose director reports directly to the president and, with the secretary of state, provides ambassadors for negotiations. ACDA has a staff of experts who conduct research and inform the public. Dr. William C. Foster was the first director.
18. ACDA, 1982 ed., pp. 82–98. Also see ch. IV, below.
19. Joseph Cirincione and Toby Dalton, "India Tests Three Nuclear Devices," Proliferation Brief Vol. 1, No. 3, May 8, 1998, Carnegie Endowment for International Peace, 1779 Mass. Ave., NW, Washington, DC, 20036.
20. ACDA 1982 ed. Also see Henry Kissinger, *White House Years*, (Little, Brown and Co., Boston, Massachusetts, 1979), pp. 196–198, pp. 1216–1222, and pp. 1229–1246. By the late 1960s, the United States had 1054 ICBMs, 650 SLBMs, and about 400 B-52 bombers. These became ceilings which Congress did not want to exceed. In the SALT I Interim Agreement (1972), the two sides agreed not to convert existing ICBM launchers into heavy ICBM launchers and not to increase their SLBMs or submarines for SLBMs. The interim agreement lasted for five years.

21. *Verification and Arms Control,* William C. Potter, Ed. (Lexington Books, Lexington, MA, 1985).
22. ACDA, 1982 ed., pp. 161–163. In 1974, a protocol was added to the ABM treaty that limited each side to one ABM site.
23. ACDA, 1982 ed., and "The SALT II Treaty," SFRC exec. report 96-14, November, 1979. SALT II sublimits were 1320 MIRVed ICBMs and bombers with ALCMs, 1200 MIRVed ICBMs and SLBMs, 820 ICBM launchers, and restrictions on new heavy ICBMs, other new types, rapid reload, missile tests, and so forth. After many committee resolutions passed or failed by one or two vote margins, the SFRC finally recommended ratification by a vote of 9 to 6, with numerous reservations, in November 1979. Because of the Soviet invasion of Afghanistan and other international and domestic political considerations, SALT II was never brought to the Senate floor for a vote.
24. "The INF Treaty," SFRC exec. report 100-15, April 14, 1988.
25. James A. Baker, *The Politics of Diplomacy* (G. P. Putnam's Sons, New York, 1995).
26. "Treaty with the Union of Soviet Socialists Republics on the Reduction and Limitation of Strategic Offensive Arms (the START treaty)," message to the US Senate by the president of the United States, Treaty Doc. 102-20, 102nd Congress, November 25, 1991, US GPO, Washington, DC.
27. "Message from the President of the United States to the US Senate Transmitting the Protocol to the START Treaty, Signed at Lisbon, Portugal, on May 23, 1992," Treaty Doc. 102-32, June 23, 1992.
28. "Message from the President Transmitting the START II Treaty to the US Senate (Including its Protocols and Memorandum of Attribution, MOA)," Treaty Doc. 103-1, January 20, 1993. Includes article-by-article analysis.
29. David B. Thomson, "The START Treaties: Implementation and Status," Los Alamos National Laboratory report LA-UR-97-2045 (May 1997).
30. Agreements reached at the March 1997 Helsinki Summit by Presidents Clinton and Yeltsin in an effort to facilitate Russian ratification of START II are discussed in LA-UR-97-2045.
31. "Founding Act on Mutual Relations, Cooperation and Security Between NATO and the Russian Federation," signed in Paris, May 27, 1997, *Arms Control Today*, the Arms Control Association, Washington, DC, Vol. 27, No. 3, May 1997, pp. 21–24 and pp. 19–20. Also see "Cold War Rivalry Buried by NATO-Russian Deal," *Jane's Defence Weekly*, 4 June 1997, p. 3.

Chapter III

The Nuclear Test Ban Treaties

Nuclear Testing

In the earlier days of the nuclear arms race, the rapid buildup of nuclear weapons stockpiles by the United States and the USSR in the 1950s was preceded and accompanied by numerous nuclear weapons tests.[1,2] From 1951 to 1962, the United States conducted most of its tests in the yield range of a few to about fifty kilotons at the Nevada Test Site (NTS). Higher yield tests in the atmosphere, up to about 15 megatons, were conducted at the Pacific test facilities at Eniwetok, Johnston Atoll, and the Bikini atoll. The Russians tested their nuclear weapons in Kazakhstan at Semipalatinsk and at other facilities. After 1963, the United States tested nuclear weapons underground at Nevada and Amchitka Island, and the Soviets tested underground at Semipalatinsk and Novaya Zemlya Island, each at yields of up to one or several megatons.

Los Alamos had been tasked with developing a variety of new weapons designs. This task included the goals of (1) using the expensive nuclear fuels plutonium (Pu) and highly enriched uranium (HEU) more efficiently; (2) satisfying a wide range of military missions including deployment of tactical nuclear weapons in Europe; (3) incorporating the new thermonuclear weapons[3] (H-bomb, first tested in the Pacific Ocean with the Mike shot in November 1952) into deliverable weapons systems; and (4) mating nuclear weapons with the ever changing means of delivery, such as long-range and shorter range bombers; intermediate-range ballistic missiles (IRBMs); intercontinental ballistic missiles (ICBMs); submarine-launched ballistic missiles (SLBMs), and tactical artillery. The United States considered its nuclear weapons as primarily a deterrent to massive attack by the Soviet Union, most likely by ground forces in Europe. US nuclear forces had to be deliverable under a variety of scenarios, and of sufficient numbers to provide a credible deterrent to any first strike by the Soviets. This required a vigorous program of nuclear weapons technology development at Los Alamos and at the Lawrence Livermore National Laboratory (LLNL). The ever more sophisticated nuclear weapons designs required nuclear tests to verify the accuracy of the physics designs and the deliverability of the weapons.[4] In addition, military and civilian defense programs made use of these tests to obtain vital information on the effects[5] of nuclear weapons on potential targets. The Soviets conducted a robust nuclear test program with similar technical purposes.[6]

Radioactive fallout from nuclear explosive tests was highlighted as a worldwide concern by the 1954 US Bravo test[7] in the Pacific Ocean, which gave a high yield (about 15 megatons), more than twice what had been predicted. Heavy fallout from this test landed on a Japanese fishing boat[7] that was downwind from the test and within the boundaries of the test range. Serious fallout also landed on some Micronesian Islanders. Radiation sickness suffered by several dozen of the Japanese fishermen, one of whom died, fueled international concern about nuclear testing. Subsequent discovery of radioactive strontium-90, in measurable quantities in locations far from American and Russian test sites, added to the worldwide concerns about fallout.[8] Serious detrimental fallout effects within the USSR, from Soviet tests, went largely unreported.

Eisenhower's Arms Control Proposals

During the mid-1950s, concern about nuclear testing had been generally related to nuclear disarmament. President Eisenhower appointed Harold Stassen as the first US presidential adviser on disarmament and initiated a number of arms control proposals[9] that involved verifiable controls on the production and use of nuclear weapons materials (Pu and HEU), aerial overflights (open skies) as a guard against surprise attack, and verifiable cessation of nuclear weapons testing. All of these proposals required on-site inspections on (or over) the territories of the parties, and the Soviets resolutely rejected them. The Soviets made several proposals that involved pledges, but not verification.

By 1958, worldwide concern for radioactive fallout had reached major proportions, including major demonstrations. Negotiations[10] were conducted in Geneva for a comprehensive test ban, but the Soviets rejected the on-site inspections needed to verify underground tests.

In 1959, Eisenhower proposed[10] a limited test ban treaty that would eliminate testing in the atmosphere but allow underground testing. Such a test ban was fully verifiable from stations and detectors outside the testing nation and would eliminate the dangers posed by the continued buildup of fallout all over the world. Khrushchev quickly rejected this proposal, asserting that the ban must include underground tests. However, Eisenhower and Khrushchev did agree in 1958 to cease testing for a year, during which time they would continue to negotiate a treaty. Near the end of his term, Eisenhower came to the conclusion[11] that the Soviets were not going to agree to a verifiable treaty and declared that the United States would resume testing if necessary. He decided to wait, however, and leave a decision to actually renew testing to the newly elected president, John Kennedy.

Crisis, Then Agreement

President Kennedy faced a series of tests from Premier Khrushchev. First the Soviets constructed a wall around Berlin in August 1961 (ch. I). Then they provocatively broke their own test moratorium with a series of atmospheric tests,[12] including several at multimegaton yields. The United States responded with tests of its own in late 1961 and in 1962. Next came the Soviet threat with nuclear armed missiles in Cuba[13] in the fall of 1962 (ch. I).

As if sobered by his own provocative actions, Khrushchev became more agreeable in 1963. In June, the United States and Soviets established the hot line,[14] a direct communications link between the White House and the Kremlin. The hot line was aimed at making it possible for the leaders of the two countries, through direct and readily available communications, to alleviate crises of the type that occurred during the Cuban missile crisis and to prevent an "accidental" war, caused by misreading the other side's intentions.

Then the Soviets agreed to negotiate[15] the Limited Test Ban Treaty, which banned nuclear tests in the atmosphere, oceans, and space, but allowed underground testing, essentially as proposed by Eisenhower in 1958. As recently as 1962, the Soviets had rejected this proposal, submitted this time by the Kennedy administration. The Soviets had been insisting that the test ban include underground tests for which they wouldn't agree to adequate verification.

The Limited Test Ban Treaty of 1963

On July 2, 1963, Khrushchev announced willingness to negotiate the atmospheric test ban, and negotiations began in Geneva among the United States, the United Kingdom, and the USSR. The details were quickly agreed to and the treaty [16,17] was signed in Moscow on August 5, 1963.

The treaty, known as the Limited Test Ban Treaty (LTBT), prohibits the parties from carrying out nuclear explosions in the atmosphere, in outer space, under water, or in any other medium for which " such explosion causes radioactive debris to be present outside the territorial limits of the State under whose jurisdiction such explosion is conducted." The parties are also prohibited from participating in any atmospheric nuclear explosion within any other nation's territory.

The treaty is open to any nation to sign and implement. Amendments to the treaty may be submitted at an amendment conference but must be approved by a majority of the treaty parties, including all of the original parties. With three months' notice, any party may withdraw from the treaty at any time, if extraordinary events related to the treaty "have jeopardized (its) supreme interests." The preamble to the treaty states that the principal aim of the parties is "the achievement of an agreement on general and complete disarmament under strict international control."

Verification

The LTBT does not provide for a verification regime but it was understood that each party would use national technical means (NTM) to obtain evidence of violations. Any nation, exercising NTM and possessing the appropriate equipment, may observe nuclear atmospheric tests from outside the borders of any other nation by a variety of means.[17–21] These include observations of the following:

- fireball optics and radio-frequency signals,
- acoustics,
- optical signals created by the absorption of soft x-rays from the nuclear explosion in the upper atmosphere, and

- the soft x-rays and neutrons emitted from the nuclear explosion and observed by detectors attached to space-based satellites orbiting the earth.

Observing the fission products and other components of the radioactive fallout gives the most detailed data about the characteristics of the nuclear bomb producing the fallout. These detection methods had been well developed by the United States at the time of the signing of the LTBT in 1963, were available to the Russians at the same time, and were generally available to other nations though not to the same degree of sophistication as to the United States.

Seismic detection of underground and ground-level atmospheric nuclear tests was generally available to the international community, particularly in view of the long-time international use of seismic detectors for observing earthquake phenomenon. In 1963, however, seismic detection alone was not sufficient to distinguish small underground nuclear explosions from non-nuclear seismic events (particularly if high-explosive shots were fired simultaneously to mask the nuclear test). By 1963, experience at NTS had shown that nuclear weapons could be tested underground (at yields of up to about 1 MT). If such tests were well contained, most observations (such as fallout, optical signals, neutrons, and x-rays) used to detect atmospheric and high-altitude tests could not be used to detect underground tests. One had to rely primarily on seismic signals. Thus, on-site inspections were needed to complement verification systems designed to monitor or enforce any agreement to ban underground testing.

Ratification and Implementation

The US Senate immediately took up the treaty and the Foreign Relations Committee (SFRC) held eleven days of hearings[17] in August 1963. Members of the Senate Armed Services Committee and the Joint Committee on Atomic Energy participated in the hearings. A good majority of the American people supported ratification of the treaty, as did most of the scientific community and major leaders of both political parties. The administration's case for the treaty was ably presented by Secretary of State Dean Rusk, Secretary of Defense Robert McNamara, and others. Dr. Harold Brown, director of defense research, development, and engineering in the Department of Defense (DoD), gave a very thorough presentation of the technical issues including verification. In the Senate however, there was strong opposition to the treaty, led by conservative Senator Barry Goldwater, who did not trust the Soviet Communist leaders. At the hearings, technical opposition[17] to the treaty was led by Dr. Edward Teller of the Lawrence Livermore National Laboratory (LLNL). Dr. John Foster, LLNL director, noting Teller's concerns, expressed concern himself "as to whether or not the weapons laboratories will be able to fulfill their responsibilities to the nation," under the treaty. He also expressed concern as to whether the treaty would allow us to solve future problems. In particular, both Teller and Foster believed the atmospheric test ban would limit the ability of the United States to develop an antiballistic missile defense.

Therefore, the testimony[18] of Dr. Norris Bradbury, Director of the Los Alamos Scientific Laboratory, was crucial. In 1963, Los Alamos had been responsible for designing more than 80% of the US nuclear weapons in the stockpile. Los Alamos had much of the experience with the techniques of verification of atmospheric shots including optical observations, radiochemistry analysis of fission products and fallout from the tests, and the design and testing of the satellite-detection system being developed under the Vela Hotel (verification research) program. Dr. Bradbury stated that every current delivery system for which the DoD required a nuclear weapon had one. He also believed that, under the treaty, every anticipated future delivery system would be supplied the necessary warhead. He stated that, from the data we had received to date with underground testing (in Nevada), we would be able to conduct tests with yields as high as one megaton, or higher, under the treaty. He stated we could provide weapons with very high yields (tens of megatons) if that were required, though he noted such requirements had not recently been emphasized. He believed that the United States had sufficient atmospheric and other test data, as well as sufficient "on the shelf" tested designs, to be able to meet future ABM system requirements. He confirmed that US verification would be effective. In short, Bradbury believed that American security would not be at a disadvantage, relative to the Soviets, with both parties ratifying the LTBT.

Dr. Bradbury's testimony, and the scientific evidence, were persuasive. The LTBT was ratified on the Senate floor on September 24, 1963, by a vote of 80 to 19. Sixteen more negative votes would have killed it. The three initial parties (US, UK, and USSR) deposited their instruments of ratification on October 10, 1963, and the treaty entered into force. Over 60 parties joined the treaty by the end of 1963, but by 1990, France and China (PRC) had not signed.

In supporting[17] the treaty, the DoD and the Joint Chiefs of Staff had called for a funded "readiness program"[22] to enable the DoD and the AEC to promptly resume testing in the atmosphere if the Soviets broke out of the treaty and tested in the atmosphere or other prohibited environments (as they had provocatively resumed testing in 1961). The readiness program was strongly supported[18] by Dr. Bradbury and Dr. Foster. Under the readiness program, the laboratories (Los Alamos, Livermore, and Sandia) kept personnel and equipment on hand and ready to conduct atmospheric tests on short notice should the need arise.

The DoD and AEC kept the Pacific nuclear test sites at Johnston Atoll "moth-balled" in case high-yield and/or high-altitude tests were necessary. The Air Force earmarked three KC-135 transport planes (airframes similar to Boeing 707s), one for each laboratory (Los Alamos, Livermore, and Sandia), each outfitted with diagnostic equipment suitable to assist in conducting atmospheric tests on short notice. With the three planes ready to go, a nuclear test could be carried out with a good complement of diagnostics.

The laboratories and the Air Force were able to use this equipment for other scientific experiments (such as solar eclipse expeditions) over the years, while maintaining the basic test capability. Funding for this readiness continued until about 1975. The capability was never needed for an American atmospheric nuclear test, but lent credibility and confidence to US security during the early years under the LTBT.

The LTBT was a major success.[23] By 1995, the number of members had grown to over 120 nations. There were no definitive violations by parties to the treaty. The United States, Russia, and United Kingdom have not tested in the atmosphere (or space or underwater) since it was signed, but each carried out a vigorous testing program underground until the early 1990s. Both the United States and Russia were able to develop very sophisticated underground test and diagnostic programs that enabled them to get the data needed for their warhead developments without resorting to atmospheric tests. The international fallout problems of the 1950s and early 1960s receded. Perhaps most importantly, the 1963 LTBT paved the way for the Nonproliferation Treaty of 1968 (see ch. IV). However, France began nuclear testing in 1960, as did China in 1964. Early on, both tested in the atmosphere and neither signed the LTBT.

The Threshold Test Ban Treaty (TTBT)

The signing of the SALT I agreements,[24] including the ABM treaty, by President Nixon and General Secretary Brezhnev in 1972 initiated an era of "detente" during which the parties explored the possibility of further limitations on nuclear weapons. A principal goal was to negotiate a treaty limiting strategic offensive deployments (ch. II). In early 1974, the two parties also agreed to consider a Threshold Test Ban Treaty (TTBT) that would, as it turned out, limit the allowed underground testing of nuclear weapons to tests of design yields no greater than 150 kilotons, and experts from the two sides began discussions.[25] Nixon and Brezhnev signed [24,25] the TTBT in July 1974, only a few weeks before Nixon resigned as president because of Watergate.

The threshold yield[26] was the result of much interagency debate. Kissinger and negotiators wanted lower values, while the JCS and the AEC wanted higher values. The value of 150 kilotons was large enough to fulfill most of the likely missions for an ICBM or SLBM warhead, and large enough to provide a significant signal for seismic detection from outside the testing party's territory. It was substantially smaller than one megaton, a typical maximum value normally tested at the American and Russian test sites. Thus the TTBT, if observed, could significantly limit the tested yield of new warheads that could be designed for future delivery systems such as MIRVed ballistic missiles and cruise missiles.

The TTBT included a protocol[27] that called for the tests to be conducted within specific agreed geographical locations, for which the geological characteristics were known or could be obtained by calibration shots. The coordinates of each test were to be supplied to the other party. The protocol called for additional exchanges of geographical and other data that would assist the parties in verifying, from seismic stations outside the testing party's territory, that the allowed tests did not exceed the 150-kiloton (design yield) limit.

Following the signing of the TTBT, the parties negotiated a treaty on peaceful nuclear explosions (PNET). The PNET defined the allowed nuclear explosions as being only those for peaceful purposes (such as big earth moving projects). The PNET[27] provided the following:

- an upper limit of a 150-kiloton yield for any single explosive device-group explosions that have an aggregate yield of up to 1.5 megatons may be carried out only if the individual explosive devices can be clearly measured as not exceeding 150 kilotons;
- such experiments must be conducted outside the boundaries of the weapons tests sites;
- explosions must be conducted in compliance with the LTBT; and
- nuclear explosions must be observed on site.

The PNET was signed on May 28, 1976, by US President Gerald Ford and USSR General Secretary L. Brezhnev. The TTBT and the PNET were then submitted to the US Senate in July 1976. No final Senate action was then taken on the treaties, however.

Because there were no provisions for on-site verification, members of the Senate and the American defense community were concerned that the TTBT did not provide sufficient accuracy in verifying[28] underground nuclear weapons tests. There was no assurance that tests declared to be within the 150-kiloton limit might not actually be as high as 200 to 300 kilotons and not so determined by the seismic stations outside the Soviet Union. In view of the rapid buildup of Soviet forces (MIRVed heavy SS-18s, SS-24s, and mobile SS-25s; see ch. I), verifying the 150-kiloton limit was important if the treaty was to be ratified. There was confidence, however, that consistent clandestine testing at several hundred kilotons, or higher, would be at least indicated by the NTM seismic detection stations. Therefore, the United States and Russia each declared that they would observe the 150-kiloton limit of the treaty, pending agreement of adequate verification, unless it was determined that one of the parties had significantly exceeded the limit.

As of the early 1980s, there was seismic evidence[28] that a number of Soviet tests had been significantly in excess of 150 kilotons, but not enough evidence to "clearly assert" that the Soviets had violated the 150-kiloton limit. The Reagan administration sought to engage the Soviets in discussions on improving verification of the TTBT, but the Soviets rejected this approach and stated that they were observing the threshold.

Verification and Ratification of the TTBT

As with the INF and START treaties, the rise to power of Mikhail Gorbachev in 1985 (see ch. I and II) led to a major improvement in the Russian approach to openness and treaty verification. They agreed that on-site inspections could be used with the TTBT. In 1987, the sides agreed to negotiate a Joint Verification Experiment (JVE). In May 1988, they signed the agreement,[29] which provided that each side would conduct a nuclear test at its site with the other side present. Each side would use its own verification instruments based on the hydrodynamics method to measure directly the yields of the tests. The parties also used data from the teleseismic method, for comparison. The JVEs were carried out as planned, with tests conducted on August 17, 1988, at NTS, and on September 14 at Semipalatinsk. The experiments demonstrated the effectiveness and accuracy of the hydrodynamic[30] measurement method (CORRTEX) for verifying, on site, the yields of tests under the TTBT and PNET.

In May 1990, the two sides agreed[31] on texts[32] of the new verification protocols, based on the successful JVE results, for the TTBT and the PNET. The protocols were signed by Presidents Bush and Gorbachev on June 1. The TTBT and the PNET, with these new verification protocols, were approved by the US Senate in September by a vote of 98 to 0. The two treaties were ratified by the Supreme Soviet in October by a vote of 347 to 0; they entered into force on December 11, 1990.[31]

The TTBT Verification Protocol (1990) provides for implementing the hydrodynamic measurement method, the teleseismic method, and on-site inspections of the nuclear test emplacement hole, which will enable the parties to observe each other's nuclear tests when appropriate (more than 50 kT, see Chart III-A) and measure the yields. Chart III-A summarizes the 11 sections of the protocol.[32]

After entry-into-force in December 1990, each party made plans for verifying tests planned by the other party in 1991 and 1992. Two Soviet tests planned for late 1991 were postponed indefinitely following the breakup of the USSR in December 1991. The Russians verified one US test in 1992. Subsequent unilateral test moratoriums by the United States and Russia have been in effect, partly in anticipation of the Comprehensive Test Ban Treaty.

Comprehensive Test Ban Treaty (CTBT) Negotiations

Since the mid-1950s, many arms control advocates have urged a comprehensive nuclear test ban treaty, which, as a means for limiting the arms race, would eliminate all nuclear weapons tests. As noted above, President Eisenhower had repeatedly urged the Soviets to agree to the on-site inspections necessary for verification of a CTBT. Also as noted, the signing of the LTBT in 1963 and the signing of the nonproliferation treaty (NPT) in 1968 (ch. IV) slowed down but did not stop the expansion of the arms race beyond the five nations that had tested nuclear weapons by 1968. The preamble to the LTBT stated that a goal of the parties was "to achieve the discontinuance of all test explosions of nuclear weapons for all time, determined to continue negotiations to this end . . . ." The preamble to the NPT reaffirmed this objective. Arresting the buildup of deliverable nuclear warheads by the superpowers (United States and USSR) took priority in arms control negotiations (ch. II) throughout the 1970s, 1980s, and into the 1990s. The LTBT eliminated possible health dangers of radioactive fallout, and the NPT provided the major treaty contribution to limiting proliferation of nuclear weapons. Much of the nonproliferation effort in the 1970s and 1980s was devoted to obtaining IAEA safeguards agreements (ch. IV) among the members of the NPT.

When first taking office in 1977, President Jimmy Carter declared his intention to "proceed quickly with a comprehensive test ban treaty." Trilateral (US, UK, and USSR) negotiations began in Geneva in July 1977, without benefit of a full (US) interagency study. The initial US goal was stated as a zero-yield CTB of indefinite duration. The USSR position included that continuation beyond a third or fifth year depended on adherence by France and China. Secretary of Energy, James Schlesinger, and the Joint Chiefs of Staff (JCS) supported the position that the reliability and safety of the US nuclear weapons stockpile would require a small amount of continued underground testing under a CTB of indefinite duration. [33] In December 1977, Secretary of Defense Harold Brown and National Security Adviser Zbigniew Brzezinski produced a memo which stressed the importance of less than 15-kT tests to maintain confidence in the stockpile. The International Security Affairs (ISA) branch of the DoD made a recommendation for experiments below 100 tons to preserve confidence in stockpile reliability under a CTBT. In 1978 the DOE, in testimony to the House Armed Services Committee, recommended a threshold value of 3–5 kT as the minimum needed to maintain stockpile confidence. As SALT II negotiations and other issues pressed to the forefront, the push for a CTBT receded during the later years of the Carter administration.[33] The issue of a needed low-yield threshold came to the forefront again in the early 1990s as the Clinton administration accelerated negotiations leading to the CTBT.

Before and during the 25-year Review Conference on Extension of the NPT (See ch. IV) held in 1995, many leaders called for the negotiation of a comprehensive test ban treaty that would be binding on the five recognized nuclear powers as well as all other nations.[34] The indefinite extension of the NPT that took place at the review conference in 1995 was believed to have been achieved (ch. IV) only after the direct or implicit promise by the nuclear powers to reduce existing nuclear deployments as well as to sign a comprehensive nuclear test ban.

In 1992, Congress mandated a moratorium on US nuclear tests. These had been conducted underground since 1963. In 1995, President Clinton announced an extension of the moratorium[35] through 1996, pending negotiation of a CTBT. At the UN, negotiations on a CTBT began at the Conference on Disarmament (CD) in January 1994, following the unanimous adoption of a resolution calling for a CTBT in the United Nations General Assembly in December 1993. We note here that France and China had finally joined the NPT as nuclear weapons states in 1992. The CTBT negotiations covered both contentious issues[36] and detailed verification issues.[37] Treaty language was finally agreed on by all the members of the CD except India. It was submitted to the UN by Australia in September 1996. By majority vote, the UN General assembly opened it for signature. The United States and other nations signed it on September 24, 1996.[38] After the treaty had been signed by more than 140 other states and thoroughly deliberated on in the executive branch, President Clinton submitted[38] the treaty to the US Senate for ratification in September 1997.

Summary of the CTBT

The treaty[38] preamble stresses the need for progressive efforts to reduce nuclear weapons globally with the "ultimate goal of eliminating those weapons and of general and complete disarmament under strict and effective international control."

Article I establishes that all state parties to the CTBT agree to refrain from conducting or participating in "any nuclear weapon test explosion or any other nuclear explosion," and to "prohibit and prevent any such nuclear explosion at any place under its jurisdiction or control." These terms are discussed in detail in the president's article-by-article analysis[39] included with the formal submission of the treaty to the Senate.

Article II establishes the CTBT Organization (CTBTO), which will ensure implementation and verification of the treaty and provide states-parties with a forum for consultation and cooperation. The treaty organization includes three principal bodies:

- The Conference of States Parties will be the overall governing body that will handle treaty-related policy issues and oversee the implementation of the treaty, including the activities of the Executive Council and the Technical Secretariat. The Conference will meet annually unless otherwise decided. It will consist of all the states parties.
- The Executive Council, consisting of 51 members, will meet regularly and act as the treaty's principal decision-making body. It will comprise ten states-parties from Africa, seven from Eastern Europe, nine from Latin America and the Caribbean, seven from the Middle East and South Asia, ten from North America and Western Europe, and eight from Southeast Asia, the Pacific and the

Far East. The states in each region are listed in Annex 1 of the treaty. The members of the Executive Council will be elected by the Conference so that at least one third of the seats allotted for each region are filled on the basis of the treaty-applicable nuclear capabilities of the parties. Such capabilities include the number of monitoring facilities contributed to the verification system. The remaining seats will be determined by rotation or elections so that each state-party eventually serve on the Council.

- The Technical Secretariat will be the primary body responsible for the verification procedures. It will supervise the international monitoring system (IMS) and process and analyze the system's data. It will also manage the International Data Center (IDC) and perform procedural tasks related to the on-site inspections. The Director-General, the head and chief executive officer of the Technical Secretariat, will be appointed by the Conference upon recommendation of the Executive Council.

Article III obligates each state-party to implement the treaty within its constitutional processes. Article IV and the verification protocol establish the treaty's verification regime, consisting of four basic elements:

- the International Monitoring System (IMS),
- consultation and clarification through the CTB treaty organization,
- on-site inspections, and
- confidence-building measures.

The IMS will detect and identify nuclear explosions prohibited in Article I. It is comprised of a network of 50 primary and 120 auxiliary seismological monitoring stations designed to detect seismic activity and distinguish between natural events (such as earthquakes) and nuclear explosions. The IMS will also incorporate 80 radionuclide stations and 16 radionuclide laboratories to seek to identify radioactive particles released during a nuclear explosion. The IMS will also include 60 infrasound (acoustic) and 11 hydroacoustic stations designed to pick up the sound of nuclear explosions in the atmosphere and under water. The locations of the stations are listed in Annex 1 of the protocol.

Information collected by the IMS will be transmitted to the International Data Center (IDC), an essential part of the Technical Secretariat responsible for data storage and processing. The IDC will make both raw data and processed data available to the states parties.

The consultation and clarification elements of the treaty organization give procedures for states parties to resolve differing interpretations of the data and determine possible instances of noncompliance requiring on-site inspections. Each state-party has the right to request an on-site inspection based on data from the IMS and/or NTM (national technical means). The Executive Council will make a decision for an on-site inspection within 96 hours of receiving a request from a state-party. An OSI requires approval of at least 30 of the council's 51 members.

An on-site inspection request must include the approximate geographical coordinates, the estimated depth of the ambiguous event, the proposed boundaries of the area to be inspected (less than 1000 square kilometers), the state-party (parties) to be inspected, the estimated time of the event, and all evidence upon which the request is based. If the Executive Council is presented with an on-site inspection request that is frivolous or abusive, it may impose punitive measures on the requesting party, such as financial compensation for expenses of the Technical Secretariat, and may suspend the party's right to request future inspections. To assist the Technical Secretariat in interpreting data, each party will voluntarily notify the others of any chemical explosion of more than 300 tons on its territory. Each party may assist in calibrating IMS stations.

Article V empowers the conference to employ punitive measures. Article VI describes the mechanisms for resolving disputes pertaining to treaty interpretation or application.

Article VII describes the treaty amendment process. An amendment requires approval by a simple majority at an amendment conference with "no state party casting a negative vote."

Article VIII provides for a review conference ten years after the treaty enters into force. At this conference, peaceful nuclear explosions (PNEs) may be put on the agenda but are most likely to remain prohibited because a change must be approved "without objection" at two successive conferences.

Article IX provides that the CTBT will be in effect for an unlimited time, but also allows each state-party the right to withdraw from the treaty because of "extraordinary events related to the treaty that have jeopardized its supreme interests." Article X states that the treaty's annexes, protocol, and annexes to the protocol are formal parts of the treaty. Article XI declares the treaty open to all states for signature before it enters into force. Article XII maintains that each party will ratify the treaty according to its own constitutional processes. Article XIII allows any state that was not a member before entry into force to accede at any time thereafter.

Under Article XIV, the treaty will not enter into force for 180 days after it has been signed and ratified by 44 states—including the five nuclear-weapon states (United States, Russia, Britain, France, and China) and the three "threshold states" (India, Israel, and Pakistan). The 44 states, listed in Treaty Annex 2, are all members of the recently expanded CD, and all possess nuclear power and research reactors as determined by the IAEA. If the treaty has not entered into force three years after the date of its opening for signature, then a conference shall be held by the ratifying states to decide (by consensus) what measures should be taken to accelerate ratification.

Article XV stipulates that the treaty is not subject to reservations. Article XVI establishes the UN secretary general as the depositary. Article XVII provides six languages for authenticity.

The provisions of the treaty are tabulated in Chart III-B. Verification procedures are summarized in Chart III-C.

CTBT Ratification and Issues

After the contentious negotiations in the UN CD, which developed the final text of the CTBT, unexpectedly strong international support for the treaty emerged when the UN General Assembly voted 158 to 3 to endorse the text in September 1996.[36] However, as of March 1999, the SFRC has not yet held hearings on the CTBT, and only 28 of the 152 signatory nations have ratified it.[41]

A strong case for supporting the treaty has been made [36,40,42] by members of the US "arms control community," but a number of problems have worked against its immediate ratification by the United

States. A principal argument for supporting the treaty is the often expressed belief by many of the nonnuclear-weapons states-parties to the NPT that the five nuclear-weapons states should work to achieve a CTBT as called for in the preamble to the LTBT. The expectation of a comprehensive test ban was a significant component of the negotiation of the extension of the NPT at the review conference in 1995 (see ch. IV). However, the perceived value[43] of nuclear deterrence and its success during the Cold War led some distinguished leaders in the US defense community to question[44] whether international conditions are right for the United States to ratify a "zero yield" CTBT, given the large number of nations that basically depend on the United States for their security.

James Schlesinger (secretary of energy under President Carter; secretary of defense under Presidents Nixon and Ford; and chair of the AEC and director of the CIA under President Nixon), along with Robert Barker (assistant to the secretary of defense for atomic energy under Presidents Bush and Reagan), questioned[44] the ability of the United States to maintain the reliability and safety of the nuclear stockpile over a period of decades (particularly if new warheads are needed for new delivery systems) under the terms of the CTBT as signed in 1996. Barker noted that no tests had been conducted for the five years (1992 to 1996) preceding the signing of the CTBT, even though some were needed, and no tests would be conducted thereafter under the CTBT.

However, at the same hearing,[44] Victor Reis, assistant secretary of energy for Defense Programs, expressed the strong belief that the stockpile stewardship program (which he had developed in consultation with the directors of the three nuclear weapons laboratories at Los Alamos, Sandia, and Livermore) would give the United States confidence in the safety and reliability of its nuclear stockpile under the CTBT. Concurrent to submitting the CTBT to the Senate for ratification, the administration had instigated, through the national nuclear weapons laboratories, the "science-based stockpile stewardship" (SBSS) program [38,40,45,46] to use detailed scientific measurements, enhanced computer modeling, and vigorous component-monitoring to ensure the safety and reliability of the nuclear weapons stockpiles within the constraints of the CTBT. Letters[45] to the Senate from former (1986 to 1997) Los Alamos Director Sig Hecker expressed confidence in the value of the stockpile stewardship program but also indicated previous needs for nuclear testing. At hearings[46] before the Subcommittee on Strategic Forces, Senate Armed Services Committee (SASC), held on March 19, 1998, the three weapons laboratory directors (John Browne from LANL, Paul Robinson from SNL, and Bruce Tartar from LLNL) explained and supported the stockpile stewardship program and urged strong and continued administration and congressional support for the program under a CTBT. Browne stated,[46] "I am confident that we can certify the safety and reliability of our nuclear stockpile without nuclear testing if the stockpile stewardship program continues to receive strong support from the Administration and Congress over the next decade."

The complexities faced by the Senate in deciding whether or not to ratify the CTBT are illustrated by the divergent answers given to the same questions by Spurgeon Keeny (ACDA deputy director from 1977 to 1981) for the CTBT, and by Kathleen Bailey (ACDA assistant director for nonproliferation from 1987 to 1991) against the CTBT.[47] The questions concerned the ability of the CTBT to prevent nuclear proliferation, as well as the ability to verify the CTBT. Their answers were given at hearings of the Subcommittee on International Security and Nonproliferation, Senate Governmental Affairs Committee, on March 18, 1998.

Perhaps a basic impediment to final entry-into-force of the CTBT has been the failure of the Russian Duma to ratify START II (see ch. VIII, START II). Implementing the START II treaty is an essential component of the superpowers' building down of their large nuclear arsenals, again an expectation that encouraged the extension of the NPT in 1995 (see ch. IV). Also, without a START II treaty and documented further reductions (such as START III), some may feel the United States will need further flexibility (including some tests) to maintain its deterrent posture with a greatly reduced nuclear stockpile.

An immediate uncertainty of the CTBT's future developed suddenly with the very recent provocative testing[48] of five nuclear devices by India in May 1998. This testing was followed a few days later by Pakistan with several nuclear tests.[48] India had refused[36] to sign the

CTBT at the time of the opening for signatures in September 1996, and according to Article XIV (noted above), the CTBT cannot enter into force without the accession of the threshold states of India, Pakistan, and Israel, as well as the nuclear-weapon states (United States, Russia, Britain, France, and China). The international reaction[49] to the Indian and Pakistani tests was general condemnation of the tests. Immediate action was the imposition of economic sanctions prescribed by US Congressional law. By early 1999, Deputy Secretary of State Strobe Talbott had solicited promises[50] from officials of both India and Pakistan to sign the CTBT.

Several uncertainties (START II implementation, impact of the Indian/Pakistani tests, US Senate action, and ratification by other states—44 states must ratify) make the path to CTBT entry-into-force very difficult. Meanwhile, the CTBT remains a pledge by its many signatories.

Progress is being made in implementing the CTBT verification mechanisms. The Preparatory Commission (Prepcom, Chart III-B) was established[38,51] in November 1996, at a meeting at the United Nations. The Prepcom met four times in 1997 and three times in 1998.[51] The provisional IDC, established in Washington, DC, has been operating. The provisional technical secretariat (PTS) has been established by the Prepcom and is operating in Vienna. National data centers are important parts of the IDC. The IDC receives data from the national data centers for analysis. The US national data center is operating in Florida. Establishing the International Monitoring System (IMS) for the CTBTO is an important task now engaging the Prepcom.

The signing of the CTBT and its implementation are important to the continued viability of the NPT, as noted in ch. IV.

[In October, 1999, the US Senate abruptly brought up the CTBT for a floor vote without adequate hearings by the Senate Foreign Relations Committee. The floor vote was taken in a partisan atmosphere without full consideration of conditions to the resolution of ratification that might have alleviated perceived deficiencies. The Treaty was rejected by a vote of 51–48. It has been noted that it may be considered again by the Senate at an appropriate time.]

References and Notes

1. Necia Grant Cooper, ed., "The Evolution of the Laboratory/ Los Alamos National Laboratory," *Los Alamos Science*, Vol. 4, No. 7, Winter/Spring, 1983, LA-UR-83-475 (40th Anniversary Issue).
2. Thomas B. Cochran, Oleg Bukharin, Robert S. Norris, *Making the Russian Bomb: From Stalin to Yeltsin*, Westview Press, Boulder, CO, 1995.
3. Richard Rhodes, *Dark Sun-The Making of the Hydrogen Bomb* (Simon & Schuster, New York, 1995).
4. Cooper, "The Evolution of the Laboratory . . . ;" see Bradbury years, pp. 26–53.
5. Samuel Glasstone and Philip J. Dolan, "The Effects of Nuclear Weapons," US DoD and ERDA, US GPO, Washington, DC, 1977.
6. Thomas B. Cochran, et al., "Soviet Nuclear Weapons," (Nuclear Weapons Data Book, V. 4), Harper & Row, NY, 1989.
7. Richard Rhodes, *Dark Sun–The Making of the Hydrogen Bomb* (Simon & Schuster, New York, 1995) pp. 541–542.
8. For discussion of Sr 90, see ref. 5, pp. 442–450.
9. Dwight D. Eisenhower, *Waging Peace*, Doubleday & Co., Garden City, NY, 1965, ch. XX.
10. Eisenhower, *Waging Peace*, pp. 476–479. Eisenhower initiated (with Khrushchev's agreement) a meeting of technical experts to develop a common understanding of the technicalities of nuclear testing (both underground and atmospheric) and its verification. The committee met in Geneva in July 1958 and comprised representatives of the US, UK, France, USSR, Poland, Czechoslovakia, and Rumania. The committee worked with a spirit of "cooperation and objectivity." Their report covered detection of nuclear explosions, recording of seismic signals, collection of radioactive debris, and related technology. They discussed detection of explosions up to 50 kilometers altitude. Their report defined a control system to guard against infraction of a test ban. This system included a worldwide network of 160 land-based posts and about 10 ships. The Soviet technicians agreed. Based on this technical report, political negotiations for a comprehensive test ban were initiated in October 1958. The US, USSR, and UK each announced unilateral (one year) test moratoriums. Soviet negotiators immediately insisted on a veto of any requested on-site inspections of seismic events, and made other proposals which, as Eisenhower says, "made it obvious that they had no intention of agreeing to a practical control system." In April 1959 Eisenhower proposed a

limited nuclear test ban, only prohibiting nuclear tests in the atmosphere (up to 50 kilometers height). Khrushchev immediately turned it down, ignoring worldwide concerns for fallout.

11. Eisenhower, *Waging Peace*, pp. 479–484.
12. Charles R. Morris, *Iron Destinies, Lost Opportunities*, Harper & Row Publishers, NY, p. 173. The Soviet tests were extensive, more than 40 major tests, the largest being about 50 megatons. Some were conducted at high altitude, and many produced large amounts of radioactive fallout worldwide.
13. Morris, *Iron Destinies, Lost Opportunities,* pp. 173–174. The world stood "at the brink of war" before Khrushchev ended the crisis.
14. US Arms Control and Disarmament Agency, "Arms Control and Disarmament Agreements," texts and histories of negotiations, ACDA, Washington, DC, (ACDA, 1982 ed.). See hot line agreement.
15. ACDA, 1982 ed. See Limited Test Ban Treaty.
16. ACDA, 1982 ed. pp. 41–43.
17. "Nuclear Test Ban Treaty," SFRC hearings, August 12, 13, 14, 15, 19, 20, 21, 22, 23, 26, and 27, 1963, US GPO, Washington, DC, 1963.
18. "Nuclear Test Ban Treaty," SFRC hearings, 1963, pp. 579–612. At that time, the Los Alamos Scientific Laboratory was responsible for more than 80% of the US nuclear stockpile.
19. Tsipis, Hafemeister, and Janeway, Editors, "Arms Control Verification," Pergamon-Brassey's Publishers, Washington, New York, Oxford (1986).
20. William C. Potter, ed., *Verification and Arms Control,* Lexington Books (DC Heath & Co.), Lexington, Massachusetts; Toronto, Canada (1985).
21. D. R. Westervelt and H. Hoerlin, "The Los Alamos Air Fluorescence Detection System," Proceedings of the IEEE, Vol. 53, No. 12, Dec. 1965, 2067–2072; and Sidney Singer, "The Vela Satellite Program for Detection of High-Altitude Nuclear Detonations," Proceedings of the IEEE, Vol. 53, No. 12, December 1965, pp. 1935–1948.
22. See letters to SASC from DoD and JCS, Aug. 23, 1963, pp. 977–983, ref. 17. The Congress subsequently authorized additional funding for the three weapons laboratories (Los Alamos, Livermore, and Sandia) to maintain equipment and trained personnel in a "state of readiness" to rapidly conduct any urgently needed atmospheric tests. This "readiness" included maintenance of the Johnston Island test site and included three KC-135

(Boeing 707 airframes) aircraft (one for each laboratory) equipped with cameras and other instruments needed to diagnose atmospheric nuclear weapon tests. The "readiness" program was part of a fourfold AEC and DoD "safeguards" initiative to be undertaken under the LTBT (pp. 977–983, ref. 17).

23. McGeorge Bundy, *Danger and Survival*, Random House, NY, 1988. Note pp. 460–461. France, under deGaulle, fired their first nuclear weapon (an atmospheric test) in 1960 and continued tests for several years (pp. 472–487). China conducted an atmospheric test in 1964 and in 1967 conducted a 3-MT thermonuclear test in the atmosphere (pp. 525–535).
24. Richard Nixon, *The Memoirs of Richard Nixon*, Vol. 2, Warner Books, Inc., New York, NY (1978). Summit I, SALT I, pp. 89–104; Summit III, TTBT and ABM protocol pp. 605–624.
25. US Arms Control and Disarmament Agency, "Arms Control and Disarmament Agreements," 1990 ed., (ACDA, 1990 ed.), Washington, DC. See pp. 184–210 for TTBT and PNET, texts, and background.
26. The 150-kT limit was related to reducing the dangers of a first strike by the other party. See ref. 25, pp. 184–186.
27. See ref. 25, pp. 189–190 for TTBT Protocol on exchange of data on coordinates of test sites, coordinates and time of conducted tests, data for calibration tests, and other information. See ref. 25, pp. 191–210 for text and discussion of PNET. During negotiations of the PNET, the US insisted that such explosions not have a yield any greater than the 150-kT limit of the TTBT, and that when PNEs were conducted in sequence to increase the excavation effectiveness, that the individual explosions be timed and spaced so that the yields of the individual explosions could be determined. This time extension decreased the excavation effectiveness. We note that the PNET did provide for on-site observations (by the other party), a first for such Soviet agreement. The Soviets never did conduct PNEs at >150 kT, though they had argued for greater excavation capability during the negotiations.
28. Potter, *Verification and Arms Control*, ch. IV.
29. US Arms Control and Disarmament Agency, "Annual Report to Congress for 1988," March 14, 1989, Washington, DC. See JVEs, pp. 33–34.
30. R. Duff, R. Bass, W. Storey, D. Eilers, T. McKown, and C. W. Olsen, "Close-in Shock Wave Diagnostics on MIDDLENOTE and MISSION CYBER," Proc. on 7th Symposium on Containment of Underground Nuclear Explosions, Vol. 1, 1993 (held September 13–17, 1993, Kent, WA).

31. US Arms Control and Disarmament Agency, "Annual Report to Congress for 1990," p. 17.
32. US Arms Control and Disarmament Agency, "Protocol to the Treaty Between the United States of America and the Union of Soviet Socialist Republics on the Limitation of Underground Nuclear Tests," June 1990.
33. D. R. Westervelt, "A History of the Permitted Experiments Issue in the Carter Administration," Los Alamos National Laboratory, 1993, informal paper,
34. Thomas Graham, Jr., "Preparing for the 1995 NPT Conference," Interview in *Arms Control Today*, July/August 1994, pp. 10–13. Also see Rebecca Johnson, "The Comprehensive Test Ban Treaty: Hanging in the Balance," *Arms Control Today*, July 1996, pp. 3–8.
35. US Arms Control and Disarmament Agency, "Annual Report to Congress for 1995," Washington, DC, July 26, 1996, pp. 10–11.
36. Spurgeon M. Keeny, Jr., Joseph Cirincione, Richard L. Garwin, Gregory E. van der Vink, and John Isaacs, "The Signing of the Comprehensive Test Ban Treaty," Arms Control Association Press Briefing, September 20, 1996, published in *Arms Control Today*, September, 1996 (The Arms Control Association, 1726 M Street, NW, Suite 20, Washington, DC, 20036).
37. Verification issues are discussed by John Isaacs, ref. 36.
38. Comprehensive Nuclear Test-Ban Treaty (1996), message to the US Senate by the president, treaty document 105-28, September 23, 1997. Treaty includes two annexes, a protocol, and two annexes to the protocol, and referred to SFRC with article-by-article analysis. Doc. 105-28 also includes establishment of Preparatory Commission, November 19, 1996.
39. Definitions of "any other nuclear explosives" are in president's article-by-article analysis, ref. 38. Also see ref. 40.
40. Richard L. Garwin, "The Future of Nuclear Weapons Without Nuclear Testing," *Arms Control Today*, November/December 1997.
41. "Comprehensive Test Ban Treaty Signatories/Ratifiers," Fact Sheet, Office of Public Affairs, US ACDA, Washington, DC, February 4, 1999.
42. Spurgeon M. Keeny, Jr., and Craig Cerniello, "The CTB Treaty: An Historic Opportunity to Strengthen the Nonproliferation Regime," *Arms Control Today*, August 1996.
43. John C. Hopkins and Steven Maaranen, "Nuclear Weapons in Post-Cold War Deterrence," in *Post-Cold War Conflict Deterrence*, Naval Studies Board, National Research Council study (National Academy Press, Washington, DC, 1997).

44. US Senate Committee on Governmental Affairs, Subcommittee on International Security and Nonproliferation, testimony by James Schlesinger (secretary of defense, 1973–1975; secretary of energy, 1978–1980; chair of Atomic Energy Commission, 1969–1971); Victor Reis (asst. secretary of energy for Defense Programs, 1993–1997); and Robert Barker (asst. to dir., LLNL; former asst. secretary of defense for nuclear affairs, 1986–1992; former nuclear weapons designer); October 27, 1997.
45. US Senate Committee on Governmental Affairs, Subcommittee on International Security and Nonproliferation, Siegfried Hecker (LANL Director, 1986–1997), letter to Senator Kyl (Sept. 24, 1977); and letter to secretaries Pena and Cohen (Sept. 9, 1997), included in Appendix of Senate Hearing, ref. 44.
46. US Senate Committee on Armed Services, Subcommittee on Strategic Forces, March 19, 1998. Testimonies of Dr. John C. Brown (director, Los Alamos National Laboratory, LANL); Dr. C. Paul Robinson (director, Sandia National Laboratory, SNL), and Dr. Bruce Tartar (director, Lawrence Livermore National Laboratory, LLNL).
47. US Senate Government Affairs Committee, Subcommittee on International Security and Proliferation, Testimony of Spurgeon Keeny (ACA President; former Deputy Dir., ACDA, 1977–1981) and Kathleen C. Bailey (Sr. Fellow at LLNL; former asst. dir. at ACDA for Nonproliferation, 1987–1991), March 18, 1998, in *Arms Control Today*, March 1998, pp. 7–11.
48. Spurgeon M. Keeny, Jr., "South Asia's Nuclear Wake-Up Call," *Arms Control Today*, Washington, DC, May 1998, p. 2; and Irwin Goodwin, "Nuclear Devices Tested by India and Pakistan Perplex Scientists and Shake Prospects of CTBT," *Physics Today*, July 1998, pp. 45–46.
49. Howard Diamond, "India Conducts Nuclear Tests, Pakistan Follows Suit," pp. 22–27; Craig Cerniello, "South Asian Nuclear Tests Cloud Prospects for CTBT Ratification," pp. 24–27; and George Bunn, "Nuclear Tests Violate International Norm," pp. 26–27, *Arms Control Today*, May 1998.
50. Kathy Gannon (AP), "US Deputy: Pakistan, India Stick to Nukes," *Albuquerque Journal*, February 3, 1999. Deputy Secretary of State Talbott is quoted as saying India and Pakistan have not agreed to give up nuclear weapons or join the NPT, but have promised to sign the CTBT by mid–1999.
51. "Annual Report to Congress for 1997," US ACDA, Washington, DC, July 1998. For Prepcom, see pp. 86–87.

CHART III-A.
Summary of Provisions of the TTBT Verification Protocol of 1990

Section	Key Provisions	
I. Definitions	Explosive canister	Container covering nuclear explosives
	Designated personnel	Appointed by the verifying party to carry out its verification procedures
	Hydrodynamic method	Yield measured by observing shock vs. time
	Seismic method	Yield derived from observing elastic ground motion
	On-site inspection	Verify conditions of emplacement hole
	Emplacement hole	Any drill hole/tunnel in which explosive canister and associated equipment is placed for a test
	Satellite hole	Any hole/shaft used for hydrodynamic yield
	(Section I contains a total of 32 definitions.)	
II. Test Sites	For the United States: the Nevada Test Site (NTS) For the USSR: Northern Test Site (Novaya Zemla) Semipalatinsk (Kazakhstan) Precise geographic descriptions must be exchanged. Provision is made for defining new test sites.	
III. Verification Measures	The Verifying party has right to carry out • hydrodynamic method (sect. V) for tests having planned yield of >50 KT • seismic method (sect. VI) for tests of yield >50 KT • OSI (Sect. VII) of emplacement hole for tests of yield >35 KT (only if party not using hydro method for >50 KT). • For each of first five years after EIF, verifying party has right to use hydro method for tests of 2 highest yields (if testing party does do at least 2 >50 KT tests).	

CHART III-A. (Cont.)
Summary of Provisions of the TTBT Verification Protocol of 1990

Section	Key Provisions
III. Verification Measures (Cont.)	• For 6th yr., and each year thereafter, verifying party has right to use hydro method for one test of highest yield (if testing party only does not do at least one >50 KT test). • Additional measures regarding case of two or more tests at once, large volume emplacement holes, rights of designated personnel, etc., are provided.
IV. Notifications	• Each party shall use the NRRC and notify the other about the number of planned tests each year that equal or exceed 35 KT and 50 KT. • Testing party shall notify verifier, >200 days prior to test, date and location of tests, yield range (>35 KT, >50 KT), geologic information for specified cases, etc. • Within 20 days of receipt of notice, verifying party shall notify testing party whether it intends to carry out verification methods and if so, which ones. • Notifications of procedures for reference test for case of non standard configurations • Notifications for cases of exact test time, delays, etc. • Other Notifications as specified in section IV.
V. Hydrodynamic Method	• For cases of tests of planned yields <50 KT, and for tests of planned yields >50 KT, defines hydrodynamic measurement zone in terms of specified emplacement hole, allowed satellite hole location and dimensions, stemming material, other characteristics. • Provides for testing party to drill satellite hole, which meets specified requirements, prior to arrival of designated personnel of verifying party. • Provides for verifying (designated) personnel to observe stemming of emplacement hole; to carry out surveys and geodetic measurements of emplacement and satellite holes and to install the needed equipment for the hydromeasurement in the satellite hole.

CHART III-A. (Cont.)
Summary of Provisions of the TTBT Verification Protocol of 1990

Section	Key Provisions
V. Hydrodynamic Method (Cont.)	• Provides for hydrodynamic recording facility for use of verifying party during dry runs and during the test, and provides for monitoring facility for use of testing party. • Provides for use of photographs of the installation of the hydromeasurement equipment, stemming of satellite holes, emplacement of explosive canisters, etc. • Provides for other details and options that may be used in carrying out the hydrodynamic measurement method for specified nuclear tests.
VI. Seismic Measurement Method	• Provides for the verifying party to carry out independent seismic measurement at three designated seismic stations located within territory of testing party • Specifies minimum signal/noise ratio to be available to each verifying party at the designated seismic stations • Designates the three designated seismic stations now located (and operating) in each of the two parties (United States and USSR) • Each party must provide specific information, upon EIF, concerning seismic, geologic, and other characteristics at each of its designated seismic stations • If requested, each testing party shall provide the verifying party specific capabilities at each designated seismic station, including a work area, a bore hole for seismic sensors, a surface vault for seismic sensors, and other equipment and capabilities as designated in section VI. • Rights and procedures of designated personnel of the verifying party are prescribed in detail for carrying out the seismic measurement method for nuclear tests.

CHART III-A. (Cont.)
Summary of Provisions of the TTBT Verification Protocol of 1990

Section	Key Provisions
VII. On-site Inspection	• Provides for designated personnel of the verifying party to carry out inspections of the emplacement hole and its environment to confirm the validity of the geological, geophysical, and geometrical information provided by the testing party under Sect. IV. • Using their own equipment, designated personnel of the verifying party may carryout specified physical measurements (em measurements, radar, acoustic sounding, logging, etc.) to determine depth and cross section of emplacement hole and other specified characteristics. Core samples of rock fragments may be extracted. • Designated personnel of the verifying party may observe the emplacement of each explosive canister and determine its exact location, may observe the stemming process, may obtain photographs, etc. • Procedures for the activities of the designated personnel are specified.
VIII. Equipment	Equipment needed by designated personnel of the verifying party is listed and provision for its use is specified in excruciating detail. Typical equipment specified includes sensing element and cables (hydromeasurement meas.), trigger conditioner, command and monitoring facility, measuring and calibration instruments, recording facilities, electrical power supplies and cables for specified purposes, directional and magnetic survey, specified seismic sensors, seismic recording equipment, data processing computers, etc. The equipment list includes that needed for activities specified in Sections IV, V, and VI. Satellite communications, office equipment, medical and health equipment and protective gears, closed circuit television for remote observations, etc. etc. are to be provided or brought in.

CHART III-A. (Cont.)
Summary of Provisions of the TTBT Verification Protocol of 1990

Section	Key Provisions
IX. Designated and Transport Personnel	• Within 10 days after EIF, each party provides the other party a list of proposed designated personnel (<300) who will carry out activities for the verifying party, and transport personnel (<200) who shall provide transportation for the designated personnel. Each party may accept or reject names on the lists within 20 days, and rejected persons are replaced. Violation of the protocol terms by an individual may be grounds for replacement. • Designated and transport personnel may enter the host country through the designated ports of entry, and will have the immunities of diplomatic agents as specified in this protocol and the Vienna Convention on Diplomatic Relations. • Living and working quarters are provided. These personnel shall not engage in any commercial activity. Procedures for cases of abuse are provided.
X. Personnel Logistics	• Procedures for entry, transport, food, lodging, and provision of services for designated and transport personnel are spelled out. • Team leaders, etc., are specified for verifying personnel.
XI. Consultation and Coordination	• The Bilateral Consultative Commission (BCC) is established as a forum for implementing the treaty (TTBT). The BCC may consider: any questions relating to implementation of the treaty and this protocol, suggestions for amendments, technical or administrative changes to the protocol, questions relating to compliance, new verification technologies, matters specified in the protocol as requiring agreement of the parties, and questions relating to costs of verification. The BCC shall establish and may amend its operating procedures.

CHART III-A. (Cont.)
Summary of Provisions of the TTBT Verification Protocol of 1990

Section	Key Provisions
XI. Consultation and Coordination (Cont.)	• For each nuclear test, the parties shall establish a Coordinating Group (CG) of the BCC responsible for coordinating the activities of the testing and verifying parties. The CG shall be made up from the lists of approved designated personnel. The first meeting of the CG shall be in the capital of the testing party <25 days after notification of verifying activities. Procedures for meetings and decisions of the CG are provided. • The verifying party designates a team leader for its designated personnel for each test. At completion of verification activities of each test, the team leader shall provide a written report as delineated in the protocol. • Public release of results of observations, etc., may take place only with mutual agreement of the parties.

Source: Reference 32.

CHART III-B.
Summary of Provisions of the CTBT

Function	Key Provisions
Obligation	State-parties will not carry out any nuclear weapons test explosion or any nuclear explosion on their territory or any other territory State-parties will not participate in any nuclear explosion by others.[a]
CTBT Organization (CTBTO)	Carries out implementation and verification of CTBT Comprises all state-parties who have signed and acceded to CTBT Consists of Conference of States Parties (Conference), Executive Council, Technical Secretariat (TS), International Data Center (IDC), and Director-General (chief executive of Technical Secretariat). Located in Vienna, Austria Costs are paid annually by States Parties as with U. N. assessments; a party in arrears more than two years has no vote until adjudicated.
The Conference	Composed of all state parties with one vote each, Shall meet within 30 days of EIF, and annually unless decides otherwise. Special sessions: called by conference, by Executive Council, or when requested by party supported by majority of conference. May convene as treaty amendment conference or review conference. Majority constitutes quorum. Decisions of substance made by consensus; or after two 24 hour deferments, by a two thirds majority. May add a state to the list of States in Annex 1 as decision of substance. Any other change to Annex 1 must be by consensus. The Conference shall be the principal organ of the organization, shall oversee implementation, and review compliance.
The Conference shall	Adopt the annual report, program, and budget. Decide on scale of financial contributions by parties. Elect the members of the Executive Council. Appoint the Director-General, head of the Technical Secretariat.

CHART III-B. (Cont.)
Summary of Provisions of the CTBT

Function	Key Provisions
The Conference shall (Cont.)	Approve rules of procedure of the Executive Council. Review technical developments, compliance issues, etc. relating to CTBT. Review/approve guidelines, manuals from Preparatory Commission. Establish subsidiary organs necessary to exercise its functions. Update Annex 1 as appropriate.
Executive Council	Consists of 51 members. Shall represent regions as follows (no. of states-parties): 10 Africa 9 Latin American & Caribbean 7 Eastern Europe 7 Middle East & South Asia 10 N. America & W. Europe 8 SE Asia, Pacific, & Far East (Annex 1 lists states-parties in each region) At least one-third of members to Exec. Council from each region shall be allocated on basis of security interests and nuclear capabilities relative to CTBT (Art. II.B.29) as well as contributions (facilities, financial) to CTBTO. Each member holds office for two years. One vote per member. Council elaborates its rules/procedures subject to Conference approval. Council shall: Elect chairman from its members. Meet regularly, and as otherwise needed. Council procedures require simple majority. Council decisions on substantive matters require two thirds majority. Promote implementation and compliance. Supervise Technical Secretariat. Recommend appointment of Director-General. Make necessary recommendations to Conference. Cooperate with National Authority of each State-party. May request special session of the Conference. Submit draft annual program and budget to the Conference.

CHART III-B. (Cont.)
Summary of Provisions of the CTBT

Function	Key Provisions
Executive Council (Cont.)	Submit draft report on implementation, draft report on Council activities, etc. Make arrangements for Conference sessions, including draft agenda. Examine change proposals on administrative and technical matters. Conclude Conference approved agreements with states-parties, other states and organizations, and supervise implementation. This includes agreements relating to verification activities. Approve operational manuals and changes proposed by Tech Secretariat. Facilitate information exchanges. Facilitate consultation and clarification among the parties. Consider and act on requests for on-site inspections (Art. IV) Consider any noncompliance concern by a state-party. If further action is necessary, notify all parties and make recommendations to the Conference (Art. V).
Technical Secretariat (TS)	Is headed and administered by Director-General (DG). Assists the states-parties in the implementation of the treaty. Assists the Conference and the Executive Council. Provides Administrative support. Includes the International Data Center (IDC). Carries out the verification and other functions delegated to it. Supervises the International Monitoring System (IMC). Operates the IDC. Processes and reports IMS data. Provides technical assistance for monitoring stations. Assists Executive Council in facilitating consultation among states-parties.

CHART III-B. (Cont.)
Summary of Provisions of the CTBT

Function	Key Provisions
Technical Secretariat (TS) (Cont.)	Facilitates requests for on-site inspections and Executive Council consideration thereof. Facilitates conduct of on-site inspections and reporting to Exec. Council. Negotiates agreements with states-parties & other entities relating to verification (subject to approval of Executive Council). Develops and maintains operations manuals to guide the verification regime (subject to approval of Executive Council). Executes administrative functions including preparing draft program, draft budget, and draft report on CTBT implementation, for submission to Executive Council. Processes communications on behalf of the CTBTO. Administers CTBTO responsibilities related to any agreement with other international organizations. Maintains clear accounting of all costs, including IMS facilities. Promptly informs Executive Council of any problems regarding its functions.
Director General (DG)	Head and chief administrative officer of Technical Secretariat Appointed by the Conference, with recommendation of Executive Council. Serves one four year term, renewable for one added four year term. Appoints all staff, scientific, technical, and other personnel of Secretariat. May establish temporary working groups of experts. Shall recruit staff of highest professional expertise and integrity. Serve as agent through which all requests and notifications are transmitted. With staff, serve as international officers responsible only to CTBTO. DG and staff shall not receive instructions from any government or other source external to CTBTO. DG recruits staff on wide geographical basis. DG shall keep total staff to minimum necessary to perform duties.

CHART III-B. (Cont.)
Summary of Provisions of the CTBT

Function	Key Provisions
Immunities	Delegates and advisers of states-parties, and all CTBTO staff shall on the territory of states-parties have legal capacity to exercise their functions. Such legal capacity shall be defined in agreements between the CTBTO and the appropriate state-parties.
Entry into force	CTBT will not enter into force until it has been signed and ratified by 44 states, including the five nuclear-weapons states (United States, Russia, United Kingdom, France, China), the three "threshold states" (India, Pakistan, Israel), etc., as listed in Annex 2. EIF will occur 180 days after all 44 states have deposited their ratification. The 44 states are all participating members of the CD, and all possess nuclear power and research reactors as determined by the IAEA.
Amendments	Any time after EIF, any state-party may propose amendments to this treaty, its protocol, or its Annexes (see Article VII for procedures). An Amendment Conference (composed of all states-parties) shall be held >60 days after notification. Amendment may be approved by a simple majority, with no negative votes.
Disputes	Disputes concerning interpretation of the CTBT shall be settled within provisions of Article VI, shall involve mutual consultations, be considered by the Conference and the Executive Council, and may if necessary be referred to the International Court of Justice.
Duration/ Withdrawal	The CTBT is of unlimited duration. Any states-party may withdraw (with six months notice) if events have "jeopardized its supreme interests."
Accession/ Depository	The Secretary General of the UN is the depository of the CTBT. Any nation, not a member at time of EIF, may accede any time later.

CHART III-B. (Cont.)
Summary of Provisions of the CTBT

Function	Key Provisions
PREPCOM	Preparatory Commission for the CTBT (adopted at meeting of all CTBT signatories, Nov. 19, 1996, see refs. 38, 51). Convened by UN Secretary General within 60 days after 50 states signed treaty. Composed of all states which have signed treaty (134 member states, 11/96). All decisions are attempted by consensus. If no consensus: <24 hrs. make: decisions of substance by 2/3rd majority; decisions of procedure by simple majority.
PREPCOM shall	Elect chairman and officers Establish procedures Appoint Executive secretary Establish a Provisional Technical Secretariat (PTS) Provide for necessary staff (by rules of Art. II, Par. 50.). Provisionally establish the International Monitoring System (IMS) networks. Operate the International Data Center (IDC), provisionally. Make arrangements for first session of Conference of States for the CTBT. Use funds provided by the signatory states. Prepare studies and reports as necessary. Prepare operational manuals needed for the IDC & IMS. Conduct other activities as called for in the Prepcom Agreement (refs. 38, 51).

[a] The President's message[38] stresses that activities that may involve the release of energy such as Inertial Confinement Fusion (ICF), hydrodynamic experiments with fissile materials (subcritical), fast burst reactors, and material studies with high explosives do <u>not</u> constitute a "nuclear explosion," and are allowed under the CTBT.

Source: Reference 38.

CHART III-C.
Summary of Verification Provisions of the CTBT Protocol on Monitoring, Data Collection, and On-site Inspections

Function	Provisions for Verification of Compliance with the CTBT
IMS	International Monitoring System.[a] Established in Article IV of CTB treaty. Consists of those facilities specified in Annex 1 of Protocol to CTBT. Shall be supervised and coordinated by the Technical Secretariat (TS) under guidelines established by the Conference and the Executive Council (see Chart III-B.)
IMS Components	Seismic Network Radionuclide Network Infrasound Network; Hydroacoustic System.
Seismic Network	Primary network consists of 50 seismological monitoring stations listed in Table1-A of Annex 1 of the Protocol. For each station, the state responsible, the location, the coordinates, and the type, are listed. Each station meets technical requirements of Manual for seismological monitoring. Uninterrupted data shall be transmitted on-line to the International Data Center (IDC). An Auxiliary network consists of 120 seismological monitoring stations listed in Table 1-B of Annex 1 of Protocol. For each station, the state responsible, the location, the coordinates, and the type, are listed. On request, must be able to transmit data directly (or through a national data center) to the IDC. East station meets same technical requirements as for primary network.
Radionuclide Network	Network of 80 stations to be established as specified in Table 2-A of Annex 1 of the Protocol. For each station, the state responsible, the location, and the coordinates are listed. All stations shall be capable of monitoring relevant particulate matter in the atmosphere (nuclear test fallout). Forty of the stations must be capable of observing relevant noble gases.

CHART III-C. (Cont.)
Summary of Verification Provisions of the CTBT
Protocol on Monitoring, Data Collection, and On-site Inspections

Function	Provisions for Verification of Compliance with the CTBT
Radionuclide Network (Cont.)	The radionuclide network shall be supported by radionuclide laboratories, certified by the Technical Secretariat (TS), capable of analysis of samples collected by the radionuclide stations. Table 2-B of Annex 1 lists 16 such laboratories, including the state responsible, the name, and the location of each laboratory. Results of analysis of collected samples shall be provided to the IDC in accordance with CTBTO procedures.
Hydroacoustic Network	Six hydrophone and five T-phase stations are specified in Table 3 of Annex 1. The state responsible, the location, and type of each station is specified. These stations shall provide data to the IDC as prescribed by the CTBTO.
Infrasound Network	INFRASOUND Network of 60 infrasound stations specified in Table 4 of Annex 1 of Protocol. The state responsible, the location, and the coordinates are listed for each station. Each station shall meet the technical requirements in the Infrasound Monitoring Manual (approved by the CTBTO).
IDC	The International Data Center (IDC) shall receive, collect, process, report, and archive data from IMS facilities, including results of analysis at certified laboratories. IDC procedures are approved by the Conference. IDC is operated by the Technical Secretariat (Chart III-B.).
IDC Products	The IDC shall apply automatic processing methods and interactive human analysis to raw IMS data to create IDC products for all states-parties. Include lists of all signals detected & event bulletins with standard event screening. Include executive summaries of data archived by IDC. At state-party's request, provide special studies, with expert analysis of IMS data.

CHART III-C. (Cont.)
Summary of Verification Provisions of the CTBT
Protocol on Monitoring, Data Collection, and On-site Inspections

Function	Provisions for Verification of Compliance with the CTBT
IDC Services	Provide states-parties access to all IMS data and IDC products. Provide technical assistance in receiving and processing IMS data to individual states-parties as required. Continuously monitor/report operational status of IMS.
NTM	National Technical Means (NTM). Technical observations and analysis by a single nation (or in collaboration with its allies) to determine the activities of other nations with respect to its national security. This includes compliance of an arms control treaty or agreement (or other agreement) by other nations. NTM generally involves use of equipment on satellites (cameras, radio-frequency receivers, nuclear detectors,), detection equipment at ground based stations outside the territory of a nation being observed, etc. Includes intelligence information. See reference 20 for thorough discussion of NTM. Many arms control agreements provide for cooperation by observed party with specific NTM measures as "confidence building" measures.
OSIs	ON-SITE INSPECTIONS (OSIs) are provided to determine if events observed by IMS (or NTM) appear to be nuclear explosion really are nuclear explosions. OSIs shall be carried out in area where event(s) occurred that triggered the inspection request. The area shall be <1000 sq. km., continuous, and have no linear distance >50 km. in any direction. Duration of inspection <60 days from date of CTBTO approval (Art. IV); may be extended <70 days (Art. IV).

CHART III-C. (Cont.)
Summary of Verification Provisions of the CTBT
Protocol on Monitoring, Data Collection, and On-site Inspections

Function	Provisions for Verification of Compliance with the CTBT
OSIs (Cont.)	If area specified in the request extends to territory of more than one state-party, OSI provisions apply to each state-party with territory in the area. If transit required through territory of state-party not being inspected, that party shall facilitate the transit, and the inspected party shall fulfill the obligations of an inspected party and provide the necessary support for the inspection. If designated area is on territory of a state not party to CTBT but controlled by a state-party member of the CTBT, then that party has all the obligations of an inspected party and take all measures to ensure access for the OSI.
Inspection Team	Director-General shall determine size of inspection team and select its members from list of CTBTO approved qualified inspectors & inspection assistants. No national of requesting state-party, or of inspected state-party may be on team. The team size shall be the minimum necessary to do the OSI. Team size <40 persons, except during the drilling. Inspected state-party shall provide for team's transportation, communications, interpreters, working space, lodging, meals, medical care and required amenities. Inspected state-party shall be reimbursed by CTBTO. CTBTO shall provide detailed operations manual for OSIs.

CHART III-C. (Cont.)
Summary of Verification Provisions of the CTBT
Protocol on Monitoring, Data Collection, and On-site Inspections

Function	Provisions for Verification of Compliance with the CTBT
Inspectors and Assistants	Inspectors are qualified especially for this function. Inspection assistants are designated, such as technical & administrative personnel, air crew, interpreters, etc. Inspectors & assistants are nominated by states-parties (and for TS staff by the DG) on basis of expertise and experience. Within 60 days after EIF, TS will transmit initial list (names, nationalities, date of birth, sex, rank as inspectors or assistants) to all states-parties. Each submitted name is regarded as accepted unless a state-party (within thirty days of receipt of list) declares its in writing its non-acceptance of any name. May include reason for objection. TS shall immediately confirm receipt of objection and that person may not participate in inspections on the territory of the state-party that declared the objection. Replacement inspectors and assistants are designated in the same manner. A state-party may object to approved inspector assistant at later date. Such objection comes into effect within 30 days of objection.
Inspectors and Assistants (Procedures)	• The TS shall keep the list of approved inspectors and assistants up to date and notify all states-parties of additions or changes. • If state-party has been notified of inspection, it shall not seek removal of approved inspector or assistant named in the inspection mandate. • If DG feels non-acceptance of sufficient number of inspectors or assistants by a state-party impedes the designation of sufficient inspectors and/or assistants to carry out the inspection, DG shall refer issue to Executive Council. • Each approved inspector and assistant shall receive relevant training provided by the TS pursuant to CTBTO's Operations Manual for OSIs.

CHART III-C. (Cont.)
Summary of Verification Provisions of the CTBT
Protocol on Monitoring, Data Collection, and On-site Inspections

Function	Provisions for Verification of Compliance with the CTBT
OSI Observers	State-party requesting the inspection may request an inspector or assistant from the approved list to serve as its observer for the inspection (as per Art IV, P. 61). Observer may be national of requesting party. Inspected party has right of refusal of the proposed observer; but is noted in report. If two or more state-parties request the inspection, may have two or more observers not to exceed aggregate of three observers.
Immunities	Following acceptance of list of inspectors and inspection assistants, and upon application by an inspector assistant, each state-party shall provide necessary entry/exit/transit visas or documents for that person to carry out the duties/ functions for the OSI. Members of the inspection team shall have the following privileges & immunities: inviolability and immunities accorded diplomatic agents as set forth in Vienna Convention on Diplomatic Relations (April 18, 1961, Art. 29 & Art. 31); inviolate living quarters and offices (Vienna Convention, Art. 30); inviolability of papers and correspondence (Vienna Convention, Art. 30); right to use communications with the TS; inviolability of approved equipment and material samples; exemption from dues and taxes (Vienna Convention, Art. 34); exemption from custom duties of items for strictly personnel use; and same currency and exchange facilities diplomats on temporary official missions. Inspection team members transiting territory of state-parties other than the inspected party are to be accorded the same privileges and immunities as diplomatic agents (Vienna Convention, Art. 40

CHART III-C. (Cont.)
Summary of Verification Provisions of the CTBT
Protocol on Monitoring, Data Collection, and On-site Inspections

Function	Provisions for Verification of Compliance with the CTBT
Immunities (Cont.)	Inspection team members are obliged to respect laws and regulations of the inspected party, without prejudice to their privileges and immunities as inspectors. OSI team members may not interfere with internal affairs of inspected party except as needed to carry out the inspection mandate.
Immunity Abuse	In case of perceived abuse of these immunities & privileges, DG and inspected state party shall hold consultations to resolve and prevent repetition.
Point of Entry	Within 30 days after EIF, each state-party shall designate its points of entry, and supply the necessary information to the TS. Points of entry must be such that an inspection team can reach any area within that state-party within 24 hours from one (or more) designated point(s) of entry.
Air Travel	Inspection Team, for timely travel to the point of entry, may utilize nonscheduled aircraft when scheduled commercial flights not feasible. Within 30 days after EIF, each state-party shall inform TS of approved routes and standing clearance numbers for such unscheduled flights. Flights include team members and equipment.
OSI Equipment	Equipment needed for on-site inspections shall be approved by the Conference at its initial session. Each state-party may submit proposals for included equipment. Specifications for equipment shall be provided in the OSI Operations Manual. TS shall ensure that all types of approved equipment are available for an OSI when required. TS shall be responsible for maintenance and calibration. Permanently held equipment shall be in custody of TS.

CHART III-C. (Cont.)
Summary of Verification Provisions of the CTBT
Protocol on Monitoring, Data Collection, and On-site Inspections

Function	Provisions for Verification of Compliance with the CTBT
OSI Request	Each state-party may request an on-site inspection to clarify whether a nuclear explosion has been carried out in violation of Article 1 and to gather facts to assist in identifying any possible violator (Art. IV). Inspection request shall be based on information obtained by IMS and/or by NTM. OSI Request shall contain: estimated coordinates of event that triggered the request; proposed boundaries of areas to be inspected; state-party (or parties) to be inspected; probable environment and estimated time of event that triggered request; all data upon which request is based; results of consultation process (Art. IV); and proposed observer (if any).
OSI Mandate	INSPECTION MANDATE, shall contain: decision of Executive Council on the OSI request; name of state-party (parties) to be inspected; boundaries of inspection area; planned type of inspection activity; point of entry and transit or basing points; named head of OSI team; names of OSI team members, and observer(s); and list of equipment. DG may update the mandate when necessary, as per protocol (par. 42) and Art. IV.
Notification	DG will notify party to be inspected >24 hrs. prior to arrival of team at point of entry. Notification will include: inspection mandate; date & time of arrival of OSI team at point of entry; means of arrival; clearance number for non-scheduled aircraft; and list of equipment which DG requests inspectee to provide OSI team. Inspectee shall acknowledge notification by DG <12 hrs. after receipt.

CHART III-C. (Cont.)
Summary of Verification Provisions of the CTBT
Protocol on Monitoring, Data Collection, and On-site Inspections

Function	Provisions for Verification of Compliance with the CTBT
Preinspection Activities	Notifications and logistics for inspection team prior to arrival at point of entry and for transit to inspection area are specified in the Protocol, Paragraphs 45–55.
Conduct of OSIs	OSI team will began <72 hrs after arrival. OSI team has the rights and obligations to • determine how inspection is to proceed (consistent with OSI mandate and CTBT); • modify inspection plan as needed to execute OSI; • consider recommendations of inspectee; and • follow rules as provided (paragraphs 56 to 60, of the Protocol. Inspected state-party has right to • have representative accompany inspection team; • provide information and request collection of additional facts; • examine photographs, measurement products, samples, etc.; and • other rights and obligations specified (par. 61 of Protocol). OSI team members have right to communications with each other and TS during OSI Observer(s) has right to • be in communication with embassy (at Capital of inspectee) of requesting party; • have access within the inspection area (during the OSI); • be informed by the OSI team, and • make recommendations, during OSI.

CHART III-C. (Cont.)
Summary of Verification Provisions of the CTBT
Protocol on Monitoring, Data Collection, and On-site Inspections

Function	Provisions for Verification of Compliance with the CTBT
OSI Activities	OSI team may • conduct position finding from air and surface; • make visual observations with photography, video, multi spectral, infrared, etc., • measure radioactivity at surface and below surface; • obtain environmental samples and analysis of solids, liquids & gases at surface and below surface to detect anomalies; • conduct seismological monitoring for aftershocks; • conduct resonance seismometry and surveys to search for anomalies; • conduct magnetic and gravitational field mapping to detect anomalies; • conduct drilling to obtain radioactive samples for analysis; and • collect and remove samples from inspection area, as per par. 97 to 104 of Protocol. OSI team may conduct aerial overflight of inspection area to obtain general orientation and narrow down location options for ground based inspections. Overflight <12 hrs. Overflight procedures given in paragraphs 71 to 79 and 81 to 85 of protocol. Overflight equipment may include field glasses, video, and still cameras. An additional overflight may be conducted subject to agreement of inspectee and may include: multi-spectral imagery; gamma spectroscopy, & magnetic field mapping.

CHART III-C. (Cont.)
Summary of Verification Provisions of the CTBT
Protocol on Monitoring, Data Collection, and On-site Inspections

Function	Provisions for Verification of Compliance with the CTBT
Managed Access	OSI team has right to access the inspection area as provided in CTBT & Protocol. Inspected state-party has right and/or obligation to: protect sensitive installations; make final decision regarding access (to a location) subject to CTBT specifications; shroud sensitive equipment; restrict radiation measurements to purposes of CTBT; manage access to buildings and structures; declare restricted areas (<50 sq. km.), as per procedures in Pars. 90 to 96 in Protocol. Modalities for access subject to negotiation between OSI team and inspected party.
Post Inspection	Upon conclusion of inspection, OSI team and inspected party meet to review preliminary findings. OSI team provides written preliminary report of findings which includes lists of samples and other material taken from inspection area. Preliminary report shall be signed by the head of OSI team and countersigned by representative of inspected party (to acknowledge receipt). Meeting completed <24 hrs. after conclusion of inspection. Team then leaves inspectee territory promptly.

[a] The IMS detection threshold is expected to be 1-2 kT. Experts Group Report CD-NTB-WP238, Dec. 20, 1995.

Source: Reference 38.

Chapter IV

The NPT and Nonproliferation

Negotiation of the Nonproliferation Treaty (NPT)

The need to prevent the spread of nuclear weapons was evident from the earliest days of the nuclear era. The Baruch plan, proposed in 1946 by the United States while it still had a monopoly on the nuclear weapon (ch. II), sought to forestall nuclear arms proliferation by placing all nuclear resources under United Nations ownership with strict and verifiable international control. But this plan, and all other early efforts to achieve international limits or control of nuclear weapons, failed (ch. II). Four other nations tested nuclear weapons and became nuclear weapons states: the Soviet Union in 1949, the United Kingdom in 1952, France in 1960, and the Peoples Republic of China in 1964. It became increasingly apparent that early assumptions about the scarcity of nuclear materials and the difficulty of mastering nuclear technology were inaccurate. The potential for spread of nuclear weapons to other states was clear.[1]

The increasing use of nuclear energy for electric power also underscored the possibility of proliferation of nuclear weapons.[2] In the early 1960s, the development of peaceful uses of atomic energy, promised [3] at the end of the Manhattan project, led to important advances in nuclear technology and nuclear reactors. By 1966, nuclear reactors for electric power generation were operating or under construction in five countries, and it was estimated[2] that by 1985 more than 300 nuclear power reactors would be operating (or under construction) worldwide. Nuclear reactors produce plutonium along with the generation of power. Plutonium can be chemically separated and used in producing nuclear weapons. It was estimated that by 1985, the quantity of plutonium being produced would be sufficient to construct 15 to 20 nuclear bombs daily. If the diversion of nuclear materials from peaceful purposes were not prevented by an international system of safeguards, and if a growing number of nations came to possess nuclear arsenals, the risk of nuclear war as a result of accident, unauthorized use, or escalation of regional conflicts would greatly increase. The proliferation of nuclear weapons to many countries would add a grave new dimension of threat to international security.

A succession of initiatives by both nuclear and nonnuclear powers sought to check the likely proliferation of nuclear weapons. The effort to achieve a test ban (ch. III) indeed had as one of its purposes the inhibition of nuclear proliferation. In August 1957, the western powers (Canada, France, the United Kingdom, and the United States) submitted a "package" of measures[4] to the Subcommittee of the United Nations Disarmament Commission that included a commitment "not to transfer out of its control any nuclear weapons, or to accept transfer to it of such weapons," except for self-defense. Although the Soviet Union opposed proliferation, it claimed that this Western formula would allow an aggressor to use nuclear weapons "under cover of an alleged right of self-defense." The Soviets sought to couple a ban on transfer of nuclear weapons to other states to a ban on stationing nuclear weapons in foreign countries. This would of course have thwarted the US option of using tactical nuclear weapons to defend western Europe from Soviet attack with its massive ground forces.

During the period of time from 1960 to 1962, the United States and USSR each submitted general disarmament plans that included provisions banning transfer and acquisition of nuclear weapons, but Soviet proposals generally did not include safeguards. In January 1964, (shortly after the LTBT had entered into force) the United States outlined a program to halt the nuclear arms race in a message from President Johnson to the Eighteen-Nation Disarmament Committee (ENDC) of the UN. This program included a nondissemination and nonacquisition proposal and safeguards on international transfers of nuclear materials for peaceful purposes. The major nuclear powers were to accept that their peaceful nuclear activities were to undergo increasingly the same inspection they recommended for other states.[4]

A principal impediment for the next three years was the proposed multilateral nuclear force (MLF) then being discussed by the United States and NATO. The Soviets strongly objected and stated that no agreement on nonproliferation could be reached as long as the United States held open the likelihood of such nuclear-weapon-sharing arrangements in NATO. The Soviets contended that the MLF would give the

Federal Republic of Germany control of nuclear weapons. On August 17, 1965, the United States submitted a draft proposal that would oblige the nuclear weapon states (NWS) not to transfer weapons to the national control of any country that does not already have them. The nonnuclear weapon states (NNWS) would undertake to apply International Atomic Energy Agency (IAEA) Safeguards to their nuclear activities. The Soviet response of September 24 listed the MLF as the greatest proliferation danger and proposed prohibiting transfer of nuclear weapons directly or indirectly to NNWS. The Soviet draft included no safeguards provisions.

Despite the disagreements, the United States and Soviets agreed on the need for a nonproliferation agreement, and in the fall of 1966, the US and Russian cochairmen of the ENDC began private consultations to obtain an agreement. The United States presented the interpretation that the treaty would ban transfer of nuclear weapons and/or explosive devices, but not cover delivery systems, and it would not ban deployment of US-owned and -controlled nuclear weapons on the territory of nonnuclear NATO members. The Russians did not challenge these interpretations.[5]

On August 24, 1967, the United States and the Soviet Union were able to submit separate but identical texts of a nonproliferation treaty draft to the ENDC. These drafts underwent several revisions reflecting the concerns of the nonnuclear weapon states. After more discussions and revisions between the UN General Assembly and the ENDC, the General Assembly on June 12, 1968, approved a resolution commending the text of the treaty on the Nonproliferation of Nuclear Weapons and requesting that the depositary governments open it for signature. France abstained in the General Assembly vote but stated that, while France would not sign the treaty, it would "behave . . . as states adhering to the treaty."

During the course of the final negotiations, concerns of the NNWS involved provisions concerning safeguards, balanced obligations, and security assurances.[5] NNWS did not want International Atomic Energy Agency (IAEA) Safeguards (discussed below) to place them at a commercial disadvantage in developing nuclear energy for peaceful uses. Most NNWS held to the conviction that the NWS should commit to reducing their nuclear arsenals and seeking nuclear disarmament. Finally, the NNWS wanted security assurances so that they would not be at a military disadvantage or vulnerable to nuclear attack for having given up nuclear weapons.

The text[1] of the Treaty on the Nonproliferation of Nuclear Weapons (known as the Nonproliferation Treaty, or NPT) was opened for signature at London, Moscow, and Washington on July 1, 1968. The depositary governments included the USSR, the United Kingdom, and the United States. These three and over 70 other nations signed it on that date. The NPT entered into force on March 5, 1970, when the United States, United Kingdom, USSR, and over 50 other nations deposited their articles of ratification (or accession). By 1995, 178 nations had acceded to the treaty, France and China not joining until 1992. Table 3 lists the dates of signature and of ratification or accession of the states-parties to the NPT.

Summary Description of the NPT

The Preamble declares that the proliferation of nuclear weapons would seriously enhance the danger of nuclear war. The states-parties to the treaty undertake to cooperate in applying IAEA Safeguards on peaceful nuclear activities, agree to support research and development within the IAEA framework, support the principle that benefits of peaceful applications of nuclear technology (including peaceful benefits derived as by-products of development of nuclear explosives) should be available for peaceful purposes to all treaty parties, and agree that all treaty parties are entitled to participate in the exchange of scientific information relevant to peaceful uses of atomic energy.

The preamble also states the parties' desire to facilitate the elimination of all national arsenals of nuclear weapons "pursuant to a treaty on general and complete disarmament under strict and effective international control." The preamble further states that, in accordance with the UN Charter, states are to refrain from the threat or use of force against any other state, and are to promote the maintenance of international peace and security.

Article I states that each NWS party to the treaty undertakes not to transfer to any recipient nuclear weapons, other nuclear explosives, or control over such devices. NWS are not to assist or encourage any NNWS to acquire nuclear weapons or explosives.

Article II states that each NNWS party undertakes not to receive any nuclear weapon or nuclear explosive and not to otherwise acquire or manufacture such nuclear explosives.

Article III outlines measures to ensure the use of nuclear safeguards under the IAEA:

1. Each NNWS party to the treaty undertakes to accept safeguards to be negotiated with the IAEA under the IAEA's safeguards system for the exclusive purpose of verifying the fulfillment of the party's NPT treaty obligations. These safeguards procedures shall apply to fissionable material whether it is produced, processed, or used in any nuclear facility or outside the facility. These safeguards shall be applied to all fissionable material peaceful nuclear activities under the jurisdiction of the state.
2. Each NWS party undertakes not to provide source or special fissionable material (or related equipment) to any NNWS for peaceful purposes unless that material is subject to the safeguards required by this article.
3. These safeguards shall be implemented in a manner (Article IV) to avoid hampering the economic or technological development of the parties or peaceful international nuclear cooperation.
4. NNWS parties to the treaty shall conclude these safeguards agreements (either individually or together with other states) in accordance of the Statute of the IAEA. Negotiation of these agreements shall commence within 180 days of entry-into-force of the NPT. For states acceding after the 180-day period, safeguard negotiations shall begin on the date of accession. These safeguard agreements shall enter into force less than 18 months after initiation of the negotiations.

Article IV guarantees the right of all states-parties to research, develop, produce, and use nuclear energy for peaceful purposes. All the states-parties have the right to exchange information and equipment (with other states) for peaceful uses of nuclear energy.

Article V provides that each party to the treaty shall undertake measures to ensure (in accordance with the NPT), under appropriate international observation, to make available to NNWS parties any potential benefits of the application of peaceful nuclear explosions. NNWS parties shall be able to obtain such benefits through special agreements and an appropriate international body (with "adequate" representation of NNWS). Negotiations on this subject shall begin "as soon as possible" after NPT enters into force.

Article VI states that each of the parties to the NPT shall undertake to pursue negotiations in good faith on measures relating to the "cessation of the nuclear arms race" at an early date and to "nuclear disarmament, and on a treaty on general and complete disarmament under strict and effective international control."

Article VII provides that any group of states may conclude regional treaties to assure total absence of nuclear weapons in their territories.

Article VIII provides for an NPT amendment and procedure.

1. Any party may propose amendments. If requested by one-third of the parties, the Depositary Governments shall convene an amendment conference.
2. Any amendment must be approved by a majority of all the NWS party to the treaty and all other parties that, on the date the amendment is circulated, are members of the Board of Governors of the IAEA. The amendment shall enter into force (for each party that ratifies it) upon ratification by a majority of all parties including all NWS parties and all members of the Board of Governors of the IAEA. Thereafter, an amendment enters into force for any other party upon its ratification.
3. Five years after entry into force, a conference of NPT parties shall be held in Geneva to review operation and compliance. At five-year intervals thereafter, a majority of the parties may call review conferences with the same objective.

Article IX provides the following:

1. Any state may accede to the NPT at any time.
2. Ratification by signatory states shall be deposited with the United States, the USSR, and the United Kingdom, designated as the depositary governments.

3. The treaty shall be entered into force upon ratification by the three depositary states and forty other states. A NWS is defined as one that has manufactured and exploded a nuclear weapon (or any other nuclear explosive device) before January 1, 1967.
4. For states depositing their instruments of ratification after the NPT enters into force, it becomes applicable on the date of their accession.
5. The depositary governments shall promptly inform all state parties of the date(s) of each signature, date(s) of deposit(s) of instruments of ratification, the date of receipt of any requests for convening a conference, or other notices.
6. The treaty shall be registered pursuant to Article 102 of the UN Charter.

Article X provides the withdrawal clause: "Each party shall in exercising its national sovereignty have the right to withdraw from the treaty if it decides that extraordinary events, related to the subject matter of the treaty, have jeopardized the supreme interests of its country." It shall give notice of such withdrawal to all treaty parties and to the UN Security Council three months in advance. Such notice shall include a statement of the extraordinary events it regards as having jeopardized its supreme interests.

Article X also provides that twenty-five years after the treaty enters into force, a conference shall be convened to decide whether the treaty shall continue in force indefinitely, or shall be extended for an additional fixed period or periods. This decision shall be taken by a majority of the treaty parties.

Article XI establishes that texts in English, Russian, French, Spanish, and Chinese are equally authentic and shall be deposited in the archives of the Depositary Governments and transmitted to the signatory and acceding states.

Entry into Force of the NPT

The NPT was opened for signature July 1, 1968, and was signed on that date by the United States, the United Kingdom, the USSR, and 59 other nations. President Johnson submitted it to the US Senate on July 9, 1968, but prospects for early Senate ratification dimmed after the

Soviet invasion of Czechoslovakia in August. In February 1969, President Nixon requested Senate approval and in March the Senate gave its "advice and consent" to ratification. Other states-parties followed or had already ratified, and the NPT entered into force on March 5, 1970, with the deposit of the US and USSR instruments of ratification. By the end of 1970, about 80 nations had acceded to the treaty, and by 1995, 178 nations were party to the NPT, France and China (PRC) not joining until 1992. Major nations that have not joined include India, Pakistan, and Israel. Table 3 lists the members of the NPT.

Security Assurances

In the negotiations preceding the NPT signing, NNWS sought guarantees that renunciation of nuclear arms would not place them at military disadvantage and make them vulnerable to nuclear intimidation. But it was argued that the security interests of the various states and groups of states were varied and not identical. An effort to frame security assurances within the treaty to meet this diversity of interests and unforeseeable future contingencies would create inordinate complexities to negotiating the NPT itself.[6] To resolve the issue, the United States, United Kingdom, and USSR submitted a tripartite proposal that security assurances take the form of a UN Security Council resolution supported by declarations of the three parties. The resolution, noting the security concerns of NNWS wishing to join the NPT, would recognize that nuclear aggression or threat of nuclear aggression would create a situation requiring immediate action by the Security Council, particularly by the five permanent members. Following submission of the NPT to the General Assembly, the tripartite resolution was submitted to the Security Council. In a formal declaration, the United States asserted its intention to seek immediate Security Council action to provide assistance to any NNWS party that was the object of nuclear aggression or threats. The Soviet Union and United Kingdom made similar declarations. France abstained from voting on the resolution in the Security Council, stating that nations would not receive adequate security guarantees without nuclear disarmament. In 1978, and again in 1982, the United States reaffirmed its part of this security assurance.[6]

Verification

From the text of the NPT, Article III, we note that the principal mechanism for monitoring treaty compliance resides in the safeguards agreements negotiated between the IAEA and the treaty parties. The treaty seeks to prevent the spread of nuclear weapons materials to NNWS but only provides, through safeguards, for monitoring the inventories and flow of critical nuclear (fissionable) weapons materials at key locations such as production reactors. National technical means (NTM), as discussed in ch. III, were also available to individual parties at the time of NPT signing, but were not spelled out in the treaty text as a recognized means of verification, probably because most of the parties did not have the extensive NTM systems available to the superpowers. Because of the importance of safeguards to the NPT, we discuss the IAEA in some detail here.

The Creation of the IAEA

The IAEA was created[7] in 1957 following President Eisenhower's original[8] December 1953 proposal at the UN General Assembly for the "creation of an organization to promote the peaceful use of nuclear energy and to seek to ensure that nuclear energy would not serve any military purpose." This proposal gave impetus to a gradual change[8] taking place in American and global nuclear policies from one of secrecy and denial to one of openness, transparency, and international cooperation in developing nuclear technology for peaceful purposes, that is, "Atoms for Peace." One of the goals of the original proposal was to slow the nuclear arms buildup by siphoning off substantial quantities of nuclear materials (that is, enriched uranium) from the nuclear powers (United States, Russia, United Kingdom) to the control of the new international organization. United States support for this goal was not matched by other nuclear or industrial states (such as the USSR and Europe) who at first were more interested in obtaining nuclear weapons than curbing their spread.[8]

In 1954, the US Congress provided the legal basis[9] for "Atoms for Peace" by enacting the "Atomic Energy Act of 1954," which drastically amended the McMahon Act of 1946. The McMahon Act had created the US Atomic Energy Commission, but had imposed strict secrecy on the use of nuclear energy. The 1954 Act made it possible for the United States to share nuclear "know-how" for peaceful purposes and to offer nuclear research reactors to foreign countries to "strengthen ties with friends and allies and gain favor with developing countries." Under the 1954 Act, the United States negotiated agreements with other countries for the "cooperation in the peaceful uses of atomic energy," and by 1959 had negotiated such agreements with 42 countries.[8]

The initial Soviet reaction to Eisenhower's 1953 proposal was negative but in late 1954, the United States, United Kingdom, France, Canada, Australia, South Africa, Belgium, and Portugal (eight-nation group) began negotiations on a draft statute for the new agency. Ambassador Henry Cabot Lodge suggested[9] to the UN in November 1954 that, in view of Soviet objections, "it might be preferable for the new agency to act as a clearinghouse for requests rather than take custody of fissile material." In December 1954, the UN General Assembly unanimously approved (the principle) of the creation of the new agency (IAEA), and by July 1955, the Soviet Union (now led by Nikita Khrushchev) agreed to join the negotiations.

The United States proposed and the UN General Assembly agreed to hold the "First International Conference on the Peaceful Uses of Atomic Energy." It was held in Geneva from 8 to 20 August 1955. It became the largest gathering of scientists and engineers the world had ever seen with 1500 delegates and 1000 scientific papers. It confirmed to the world the feasibility of the countless uses of nuclear energy, particularly the generation of electricity.[9] The conference did much to persuade many nations to launch nuclear research programs, sharpened their interest in the proposed IAEA, lifted[9] the blanket of secrecy that had descended on nuclear research in 1939, and did much to restore the international character of science. It was the first time since WW II that Soviet scientists were able to attend a scientific meeting outside the USSR and meet their Western colleagues. Declassification of much previously secret nuclear science was encouraged.[10] A second comprehensive scientific conference was held in Geneva in 1958. The design, testing, and utilization of nuclear weapons themselves, along with production details of plutonium and enriched uranium, remained as the principle area of nuclear science classified secret by the United States, Russia, United Kingdom, and others.

In early 1956, the USSR, Czechoslovakia, Brazil, and India joined the eight-nation group and began final negotiations (as the twelve-nation group) on the IAEA statute,[11] finally approved October 23, 1956, by the Conference on the statute. The final draft maintained the IAEA's initially conceived function as a receiver, distributor, and safeguarder of nuclear materials. The statute was opened for signature October 26, 1956, to all states-members of the UN and remained opened for 90 days. The United States was designated the depositary government. The statute entered into force upon accession of at least 18 states (including at least three of the original "big five").

IAEA Functions

The IAEA's functions were broad. In summary, the IAEA was empowered[9,11] to do the following:

- Take any actions needed to promote research and practical applications of nuclear energy for peaceful purposes.
- Provide materials, services, and facilities for such research and practical applications, with due consideration to the needs of the underdeveloped areas of the world.
- Foster the exchange of scientific and technical information.
- Establish and apply safeguards to ensure that nuclear assistance or supplies, associated with the IAEA, would not be used to further military purposes.
- Apply such safeguards, if so requested, to any bilateral or multilateral arrangement.
- Adopt nuclear safety standards.

One clause (Article III.B.1) requires the IAEA to "conduct its activities in accordance with the principles of the UN . . . and to further the establishment of safeguarded world-wide disarmament . . . and agreements pursuant to such policies." The IAEA's main reporting link is to the UN General Assembly, but it is also required to submit reports to the UN Security Council if questions should arise within the Security Council's jurisdiction (Article III.B.4). It must also submit reports to the UN Economic and Social Council (ECOSOC) on matters relating to that body.

IAEA Structure

The statute[11] establishes a General Conference, a Board of Governors, and the Director-General. Their composition and powers (in accordance with the statute) are as follows.

General Conference. The conference consists of all members of the IAEA (who in turn may be any state-party to the United Nations who signs and agrees to the IAEA statute). It meets annually and in special sessions called by the Board of Governors or by a majority of members. It elects its president and other officers as required. Decisions pursuant to financial questions and the budget, amendments to the statute, and suspension of members failing to pay dues shall be voted on by a two-thirds' majority of voting members. Decisions on other questions shall be made by a majority of members present and voting. The conference may discuss any question within the scope of its statute. The general conference shall

- elect members of the Board of Governors in accordance with Article VI,
- approve states for membership in accordance with Article IV,
- suspend a member (Article XIV),
- approve IAEA budget (Article XIV), and
- approve reports and agreements between the IAEA and UN or other organizations; approve rules regarding borrowing power and acceptance of contributions; and approve amendments to the statute.

Board of Governors. Board membership is composed according to a formula[9,11] that divides the world into eight regions: North America, Africa, Latin America, Middle East and South Asia, Western Europe, Eastern Europe, Southeast Asia and Pacific. Five members (quasi-permanent) are the most advanced in nuclear technology (United States, United Kingdom, USSR, France, and Canada). Five members are most advanced in nuclear technology but not located in the same regions as the first five. In 1956 these were Brazil, India, South Africa, Japan, and Australia. Alternating seats were Czechoslovakia/Poland and Belgium/Portugal; and one rotated among the four Scandinavian nations. An additional ten members were elected for two-year terms by the Geneva Conference. In the past four decades, the Board of Governors has grown to 35 members, and the "first five" members have grown to ten and include China.[9] The General Conference elects the membership of the Board of Governors, consistent with the formula in the statute.

The Board of Governors has the authority[11] to carry out the functions of the IAEA, meets at the headquarters (Vienna) at times it determines, elects a chairman and other officers, establishes needed committees, prepares an annual report for the General Conference, and prepares IAEA reports as needed for the UN. The Board of Governors appoints the director general with approval of the General Conference.

Director General and Staff. The director general is appointed for a term of four years by the Board of Governors, with approval of the General Conference. As the chief administrative officer of the IAEA, the director general is responsible for the appointment, organization, and functioning of the staff, under the authority of the Board of Directors. He performs his duties[9,11] under regulations promulgated by the Board.

The staff shall include qualified scientific, technical, and other personnel as required to fill the IAEA objectives. According to statute guidelines, numbers of permanent staff should be kept at a minimum. Staff shall be recruited on the basis of efficiency, technical competence, and integrity, with importance given to wide geographical representation.

The Director General and staff shall not seek or receive instructions from any source external to the IAEA.

The IAEA statute[11] also provides[9] for exchanges of helpful information by members, supplying of materials by members, and provision of services and facilities by members. Procedures are provided for establishing research, development, and practical application projects, by members and/or the agency. The statute provides[11] for agency safeguards for any IAEA project.

The Board of Governors submits the annual budget to the General Conference using the procedures outlined in the statute. The Board of Governors shall apportion administrative expenses among the members on a scale fixed by the General Conference as guided by the principles adopted by the UN in assessing member states.

The Board of Governors, with approval of the General Conference, is authorized to enter into agreements with the United Nations and/or with any other organization. Procedures for such agreements are given in the statute.

First General Conference of IAEA

The first session of the IAEA's General Conference took place October 1 to 23, 1957, in Austria. The Conference approved all the documents from the very active preparatory conference (which met for several months earlier in 1957) and recommended that the Board of Governors give priority for future projects to nuclear activities benefiting developing countries. The Conference approved Vienna as the seat of the IAEA, and approved the board's appointment of Sterling Cole (former chair of the Joint Committee on Atomic Energy, US Congress) as the first permanent Director General. To accommodate the Soviets, Ambassador Pavel Winkler, of Czechoslovakia, had been elected as first chairman of the board. By October 23, 1957, the IAEA had grown to 59 member states.[12]

IAEA Operations

The IAEA's first tasks[12] were to establish its headquarters in Vienna and recruit qualified staff, and then begin establishing its programs. The relationship between the director general and the Board of Governors was often difficult. Cold War issues frequently spilled over into activities of the board, which also frequently sought to micromanage the IAEA, holding 156 meetings from October 1957 to June 1959. Despite difficulties, progress was made.[12] By mid-1958, all key staff had been appointed. The United States offered 20 to 30 consultants, a fellowship fund, a radioisotope laboratory and two mobile laboratories. In 1958, 13 member states offered 140 fully paid fellowships. By September 1958, almost all technical programs were under way, as were agreements with UN agencies (FAO, WHO, UNESCO, and ILO). In late 1958, the IAEA established a standing scientific advisory committee that played a large role in running IAEA's technical programs until 1988, when it made way for more specialized groups.

The headquarters laboratory was well supported and in its early years undertook

- analysis of radioactive fallout from nuclear weapons tests,
- preparation of international radioactive standards,
- calibration of equipment for measuring radioactivity,
- analysis in support of IAEA health, safety, and safeguards work, and
- services to member states in carrying out designated similar tasks.

In 1958, it appeared that the IAEA would be called on to verify the proposed test ban treaty, but this did not occur (see ch. III). The United States and other western nations insisted[12] that the IAEA should concern itself only with safeguarding "peaceful nuclear activities" despite the fact that the IAEA statute endorsed the principle of international inspection.

In 1959, the IAEA was able to get its first safeguards operations under way despite resistance from Russia and India. These safeguards were applied to three tons of natural uranium supplied by Canada to Japan. In 1961, the board approved the first rudimentary safeguards system for research reactors.[12]

As the IAEA evolved,[12] its budget[13] rose steadily from $3.5 M in 1958 to $251 M in 1995. IAEA technical assistance (to other nations and groups) rose from $0.5 M in 1958 to $63.5 M in 1995. The secretariat came to take the initiative for most of the IAEA technical work, but member states frequently came forward with their own proposals. The secretary general has become in effect the IAEA's chief executive.[12] In 1961, when Cole's term ended, Sigvard Eklund, a Swedish scientist of high reputation with extensive UN and IAEA involvement, was elected director general, a post he held for two decades. Under his leadership, political disputes were lessened and the IAEA grew in its scientific functions and competence.[12]

IAEA Safeguards and NPT Compliance

When the NPT entered into force in March 1970, the IAEA became the keystone of the nonproliferation regime.[12] As noted above, Article III of the NPT required that all NNWS accept IAEA safeguards to ensure that all fissionable materials in that state be used only for peaceful purposes. The IAEA's subsequent success in drawing up a radically new safeguards system and model agreement by consensus and in a very short time (April 1970 to March 1971) ensured that the agency would be able to promptly conclude such an agreement with each NNWS. To soften the discriminatory aspect of the NPT and encourage widespread adherence, the United States and the United Kingdom offered to place all their civilian nuclear plants under safeguards when such safeguards were put into effect in the NNWS. In view of the large number of US and UK plants, the IAEA devised a scheme for selecting particular US and UK plants for IAEA monitoring, to save resources. We note here that with advent of the NPT, the previous cold war controversies within the IAEA between the superpowers began to be replaced by differences[12] of opinion between the NNWS and the NWS. Even so, there was widespread support for this new nonproliferation regime.

Principles in the IAEA model safeguard agreement[14] agreed to in March 1971 included the following:

- NNWS should have a national nuclear material safeguards system that could supply information to be compared by IAEA inspections;
- NPT safeguards would apply to the entire fuel cycle of the state concerned, allowing verification of the flow of nuclear materials between facilities;
- IAEA inspectors, during routine inspections, look only at locations "declared" by the inspected state and at defined strategic points in the facility;
- the IAEA inspectors have the right to make their own measurements with IAEA instruments and not to rely only on the inspected states' instruments.

A dominating characteristic of the NPT safeguards regime is that separate safeguards agreements are negotiated by the IAEA staff with each state-party to the NPT. This has meant different procedures from case to case.[14] By June 1971, 29 such agreements were under negotiation. The five NNWS parties to Euratom[15] would not ratify the NPT until their agreement included unique provisions (aimed at reducing intrusiveness of IAEA inspections and thereby reducing IAEA verification effectiveness[14]). Japan requested similar consideration, as did the NNWS members of the Warsaw Pact.[14] The unique IAEA safeguard agreements were negotiated, and the five Euratom NNWS ratified the NPT in 1975, followed by Japan in 1976.

NPT safeguards are designed[16] to keep track of nuclear materials; to make sure they continue to be used for nonmilitary purposes; and to detect any diversion to military or unknown uses. These safeguards consist of a complex of interrelated measures: a system of checking and cross-checking the records of relevant facilities and reports of significant changes in location of nuclear materials; verification by surveillance of key locations by monitoring cameras, nuclear instrumentations, and so forth; physical inspections, sampling, and inspection by IAEA personnel; and use of seals and other techniques to ensure that all movement is reported. Safeguards look for losses in the fabrication process. Today, IAEA focuses on detecting the loss or diversion of more than a specific quantity of nuclear material with a certain probability. This quantity, called a significant quantity (SQ), is 8 kilograms for plutonium and 25 kilograms for highly enriched uranium, amounts considered sufficient for a nuclear weapon.

When fissionable material is in discrete forms such as fuel rods, accountability is straightforward. When it is in bulk form, such as liquids in pipe, accountability is very complex. Light water reactors, fast breeder reactors, research reactors, and fabrication facilities each present their own special characteristics or challenges for keeping track of material inventories. Some of these complexities are discussed in more detail in ref. 16. Nuclear instruments, many developed at Los Alamos, that may be used by IAEA inspectors are described by Keepin.[17]

Chart IV-A describes procedures for typical IAEA Safeguards Agreements with particular states or groups. There are several types of agreements, including those with NNWS, NWS, and special groups of states such as Euratom, which have their own safeguards procedures.

Finally, it should be noted here that the IAEA safeguards procedures are detailed and scientifically sound, and in general do a splendid job of keeping track of inventories of nuclear materials at declared and established facilities, but they do not in general verify the presence of deployed nuclear weapons and/or nondeclared stored nuclear weapons or components. In other words, standard IAEA safeguards agreements are not formalized arms control verification agreements of the same type as, for example in the INF and START treaties (ch. V, VII, and VIII), in which deployed nuclear weapons (with their delivery vehicles) are declared through a system of specified notifications and in which the status of these delivery vehicles is verified by comprehensive on-site inspections.

NPT Review Conferences

As provided in Article VIII, review conferences have been held every five years since entry-into-force to "assure the provisions of the treaty are being realized." The first such conference, held in Geneva in 1975, strongly reaffirmed support for the treaty by the parties. The conference observed that the parties had observed the principal nonproliferation requirements (Articles I and II) of the treaty. The conference noted the importance of[18,19] IAEA safeguards and urged all parties to complete their safeguards agreements. The conference urged common export requirements designed to extend safeguards to all peaceful nuclear activities.[18]

The 1980 Geneva Review Conference failed to agree on a final declaration but recommended that the third review conference be held.[19] The individual statements of the parties showed continued strong support for the NPT and its objectives.[18]

The third conference, held in Geneva in 1985, reaffirmed by consensus continued support for the NPT and strong endorsement of the IAEA and its safeguards system. It called for efforts to enhance safeguards effectiveness. It specifically urged NNWS not party to the NPT to make binding commitments not to acquire nuclear weapons. The conference expressed satisfaction that four of the five NWS had concluded safeguards agreements with the IAEA for its civilian programs, and made numerous technical suggestions for strengthening the regime. Evaluation of progress since 1970 revealed much criticism of progress toward disarmament goals of Article VI, and most parties supported immediate negotiations for a CTBT. The United States supported long-term efforts for a CTBT, but urged that highest priority be given to deep reductions in existing nuclear arsenals.[18,19]

The 1990 Review Conference occurred after implementation of the INF treaty (ch. V) but before signing of the START I treaty (ch. VII), and before accession to the NPT of China and France. Issues between the NNWS and the nuclear powers were more contentious, and the conference failed to reach a final consensus declaration, primarily because NNWS were not satisfied with efforts to end the arms race by the nuclear powers.[19]

Indefinite Extension of the NPT

The 1995 NPT Extension Review Conference (called for in NPT Article X, 25 years after entry-into-force) was particularly difficult.[20] Even though START I had entered into force the previous December (ch. VII); the United States and Russia had pledged to sign a CTBT (ch. III); and China and France had finally joined the NPT in 1992, after conducting a number of nuclear weapons tests; the NNWS were unhappy with the overall lack of progress by the nuclear powers to more fully reduce nuclear arsenals. Many NNWS wanted the nuclear states to renounce all nuclear weapons and make more rapid progress toward the goals of the NPT preamble. In addition, India and Pakistan had still not joined the NPT, and threats to go nuclear remained in Iran, Iraq, North Korea, and other NNWS. In spite of the many contentious issues that were heatedly discussed during the debate, the Conference, on May 11, 1995, took the decision accepted by consensus without a vote to extend the NPT indefinitely and without conditions.[20,21]

In addition, the delegates adopted agreements to strengthen the review process (mandating future review conferences), and the five NWS and other parties reaffirmed the treaty's disarmament goals. Despite anticipated future disputes over the contentious issues, the NPT remains as a principal international foundation for the future control, reduction, and elimination of the worldwide threat of use of nuclear weapons.[20,21]

Nuclear-Free Zones and Other Prohibitions

Treaty of Tlatelolco

Concurrent with negotiation of the NPT, and following the Cuban missile crisis, Latin American nations led by Brazil negotiated a nonproliferation treaty known as the Treaty of Tlatelolco, which prohibited the production, acquisition, or use of nuclear weapons by any means. Nuclear materials were to be used only for peaceful purposes.[22] The treaty established an agency for carrying out its terms, which included a general conference, a council, a secretariat, and a control system. The treaty, which provides for its parties to sign IAEA safeguards agreements, was signed in Tlatelolco, Mexico, in February 1967 by 20 Latin American states, effectively creating a nuclear-free zone. Treaty Protocol 1, signed by states outside the treaty zone, established denuclearization procedures for territories within the zone for which they are responsible. These states were the United States, United Kingdom, France, and the Netherlands. All four of these states signed and ratified Protocol 1 (France not until after 1990). Treaty Protocol 2, signed separately by the NWS, pledges each NWS not to contribute to violation of the treaty by its parties and not to threaten or use nuclear weapons against any of the parties. Protocol 2 was signed by the United States, United Kingdom, USSR, China, and France.

Despite Brazil's early initiatives for the treaty, the enduring rivalry between Brazil and Argentina prevented the fulfillment of the Treaty of Tlatelolco until the early 1990s.[22] Argentina did not sign the treaty in 1967, and Brazil and Chile did not complete their ratification. In the 1970s, both Argentina and Brazil became very interested in developing nuclear technologies for energy, and both developed a common front against the NPT regime.[22] In 1982, the military government of Argentina precipitated the disastrous Falkland Island war with the United Kingdom, which created tensions in the area. The Argentine public response was to return a civilian government to power, and Argentine-Brazilian cooperation began to improve. In the 1990s, they created the ABACC (Argentine-Brazilian Agency for Accounting and Control of Nuclear Materials). In its early inspections, ABACC emphasized facilities not previously subject to IAEA safeguards. By 1994, Argentina and Brazil had ratified the Treaty of Tlatelolco and Chile had declared its intention to adhere to it. Latin America's nuclear-free zone was nearing full entry in force (with only Cuba abstaining).[22] Brazil, Argentina, Chile, and Cuba delayed ratification of the NPT, having claimed it discriminated against their development of nuclear energy for peaceful purposes,[22] but by 1998, Brazil, Argentina, and Chile were members (see Table 3).

The Antarctic Treaty

In 1959, the United States and eleven other nations signed the Antarctic Treaty, which provided that Antarctica be used only for peaceful purposes.[23] The treaty prohibits any military activities or bases and specifically prohibits any nuclear explosions or disposal of radioactive waste. Military personnel are allowed to participate in scientific projects, however. All parties are entitled to designate observers to carry out inspections provided for in the treaty. Parties may also carry out aerial inspections. The twelve original signatories were the United States, the United Kingdom, the USSR, Argentina, Australia, Belgium, Chile, France, Japan, New Zealand, Norway, and South Africa. By 1990, 37 nations had ratified or acceded to the treaty. Argentina, Australia, New Zealand, the Soviet Union, the United Kingdom and the United States have all exercised the right of inspection. The United States conducted inspections in 1971, 1975, 1977, 1980, 1983, 1985, and 1989, all of which included Soviet facilities. US teams have also inspected facilities belonging to the United Kingdom, China (PRC), Argentine, Chile, Poland, France, Italy, New Zealand, and Germany. More than fifteen consultative meetings have been held by the treaty parties, in accordance with treaty Article IX, to exchange information and review operation of the treaty.

The Outer Space Treaty

In 1967, negotiations were completed on the "Treaty on Principles Governing the Activities of States in the Exploration and Use of Outer Space, Including the Moon and Other Celestial Bodies." The treaty was signed and entered into force October 10, 1967, after ratification by the United States, United Kingdom, and USSR, and by other nations. By 1990, 98 states had ratified or acceded to the treaty, including China (PRC) and France.[24]

The parties agreed not to install or place any nuclear weapon or other weapon of mass destruction in earth orbit, on the moon, or any other celestial body. They agreed to limit the moon and other celestial bodies exclusively to peaceful purposes, and prohibited the establishment of military bases and/or weapons testing of any kind.[24]

The treaty grants any state-party the right, by specific agreements to be negotiated, to observe space launches for space exploration. Such exploration is to be international in character. Each treaty party must notify the secretary general of the UN of the nature, dates, and places of its outer-space exploration events.

Seabed Arms Control Treaty

The "Seabed Arms Control Treaty" prohibits the parties from the emplacement of nuclear weapons, and other weapons of mass destruction, on the ocean floor and the subsoil thereof.[25] Verification is by NTM, and/or by "international procedures within the framework of the UN." The treaty was first signed in 1971, and entered into force in May 1972, when the United States, United Kingdom, USSR, and 19 other[22] nations had ratified it. By 1990, 140 states had ratified or acceded to the treaty.

Negotiation of Other Nuclear-Free Zones

Negotiations have been under way[26] or contemplated for nuclear-free zones (NFZ) in several additional areas of the world. These include (1) Africa; (2) Southeast Asia (in the context of the Association of Southeast Asia Nations (ASEAN); (3) South Asia; and (4) the Middle East. Obstacles to a NFZ in the Middle East are very great in view of the basic Arab/Israeli conflicts and tensions that have existed since the end of World War II, the common understanding that Israel already has nuclear weapons, and the violations of the NPT by Iraq discovered at the end of the Gulf War as discussed below. Chances for a NFZ in South Asia received a jolt when India and Pakistan each tested several nuclear weapons in May 1998, also discussed below.

Iraq Violates the NPT—the UNSCOM Experience

One of the outcomes of the Gulf War [27,28] of 1991 (Desert Storm) was the formal discovery[29–31] that Iraq, a member of the NPT since

1969, had been clandestinely violating that treaty. Even more startling was the fact that these violations had occurred despite Iraq's safeguards agreements with the IAEA.[32] The cease fire following the dramatic victory for the US-led Coalition action against Iraq involved several conditions. One of these (UN Security Council Resolution 687) required the Iraqi government to submit a full declaration of its nuclear materials and program, to surrender its nuclear-weapons-usable materials to the IAEA, to accept on-site inspections, and to accept future ongoing monitoring and verification. Iraq was subsequently less than forthcoming in compliance. The Security Council then passed resolution 707, calling on Iraq for full declarations and cooperation with the inspection teams. Finally, in Resolution 715, the Security Council reiterated its compliance demands and called for acceptance of the long-term compliance monitoring plans submitted by the UN Special Commission on Iraq (UNSCOM) and the IAEA. Iraq has continued to attempt to evade its obligations under these resolutions.[29]

During the first year (after the ceasefire), ten major inspections[29] were carried out by the IAEA with the assistance of UNSCOM and technical assistance[31] of the US OSIA and DOE laboratories. The first two inspections (May and June 1991) showed that Iraq was not forthcoming in its declarations, and that Iraq had been pursuing a major undeclared uranium enrichment program (in violation of the NPT). The third inspection (July 1991) identified Tuwaitha as the site of uranium enrichment and plutonium production. To the team, it appeared that all relevant facilities had been destroyed, but it was suggested that there were other undeclared facilities. By the sixth inspection (September 1991), conclusive evidence was obtained that Iraq had a major nuclear weaponization program. Documents discovered in the Iraqi Atomic Energy Design Center indicated extensive nuclear weapons design calculations, including implosion systems and five major weapons designs. During the seventh inspection (October 1991), Iraq finally acknowledged the existence of its nuclear weapons program. The Iraqi government said basic computations and high-explosive testing had been carried out, but that a practical implosion system was not yet developed. The next three inspections gathered additional details, gaining information on quantities of weapons-grade materials that had been accumulated.[29]

UNSCOM is headquartered in New York, has been led by Ambassador Rolf Ekeus from Sweden, reports directly to the Security Council, and operates a field office in Bahrain (Saudi Arabia) and a monitoring center in Baghdad.[31] It has four major components including a nuclear group, chemical-biological group, ballistic missile group, and a long-term monitoring group. The Commission has about 150 staff personnel who operate mainly from these three locations. From 1991 to 1996, UNSCOM and IAEA inspectors carried out 130 inspection missions in Iraq. They confirmed the destruction of over 60 SCUD missiles, thousands of chemical munitions, and numerous nuclear- and biological-weapons-related components and facilities. During the first three years, aerial inspections were carried out with US U-2 aircraft (high-altitude) and German and Chilean helicopters (low-altitude). These included 270 U-2 missions and 600 helicopter missions. Ekeus noted[31] that these aerial missions were an important part of the overall inspection process in Iraq. The United States has provided UNSCOM with over $200 million in funding (made available from "frozen" Iraqi assets in the United States) and has provided important technical assistance through the DoD and its OSIA.[31]

UNSCOM inspections had by 1996 uncovered evidence of critical aspects of Iraq's nuclear weapons program, but not enough to fully refute all of Iraq's denials.[31] It did collect a great deal of very persuasive "circumstantial" evidence used (with other evidence) to ferret out Iraq's hidden programs. The inspections were particularly effective in verifying the large amounts of equipment destroyed under terms of the cease fire. As part of the UNSCOM effort, IAEA inspectors were able to effectively monitor the "declared" programs.[32]

Strengthened Safeguards Systems

In response to the Iraqi clandestine undeclared programs, the IAEA Board of Governors approved a new Strengthened Safeguards System (Part 1, 1995; Part 2, 1997).[32,33] These measures include increased access to all declared nuclear locations (Part 1) and a new protocol (to the IAEA Safeguards Agreements) that includes access to all aspects of each state's nuclear fuel cycle, wide-area environmental monitoring, and short-notice/unannounced inspections (Part 2).[33] The new protocol needs to be signed by each participant who accepts them. Details of the Strengthened Safeguards System are given in Chart IV-A. Difficulties in implementing the Strengthened Safeguards System are noted in the GAO Report.[33]

The UNSCOM experience in Iraq has demonstrated the need for international force as well as verification to prevent a sovereign state with determined leadership from violating nuclear arms restrictions and threatening its neighbors.

Other Recent Threats to the NPT Regime

For a number of years, activities in several nations besides Iraq have been considered threats to the NPT regime. These nations have included South Africa, North Korea, Iran, Israel, India, Pakistan, and others.

South Africa

In early 1979, South Africa was believed to have conducted a nuclear test (only seen at the time by one US Vela satellite observation) and started construction of several nuclear weapons.[34] After a change in government policy in South Africa, South Africa joined the NPT (1991). Their clandestine program was disclosed to the international community (including their making of six nuclear bombs), their weapons program was dismantled, and South Africa's nuclear materials were placed under IAEA safeguards.[34]

North Korea

North Korea joined the NPT in 1985. From 1991 to 1994, disputes with the IAEA over allowed inspections resulted in severe tensions between the United States and North Korea.[35] Production of a few kilograms of plutonium was discovered, but with North Korean resistance, IAEA inspections were not sufficient to fully document their program. Special negotiations, involving Former President Jimmy Carter and Ambassador Robert Gallucci, led to a resolution of the crisis. Carter repudiated sanctions and North Korea agreed to freeze its plutonium production and allow IAEA inspectors to stay in place.[35]

Iran

Iran joined the NPT in 1970, but since the fundamentalist religious groups came to power in 1979 and the Iranian US hostage crisis of 1979–1980, relations between Iran and the West have undergone long periods of periodic crisis, contention, and volatility. Many believe that Iran has been trying to obtain nuclear weapons.[36] This concern has been particularly critical since the breakup of the Soviet Union and the fear that unaccounted nuclear weapons or nuclear materials will find their way to clandestine programs outside the former Soviet Union (FSU).[36]

Israel

Israel has long had the technical capability to initiate a nuclear weapons program, has never joined the NPT, and, given the constant state of tensions and crises with its Arab neighbors, is considered to have a strong incentive to create a nuclear deterrent.[37] Many observers and intelligence estimates have indicated or disclosed that Israel has an active nuclear weapons capability[38] Open disclosure of an Israeli nuclear weapons program would be cause enough for a new crisis in the Middle East.

Nuclear Tests by India and Pakistan

India conducted one test of a nuclear explosive in 1974, but no more for two decades. Then in May 1998, India conducted, and announced that it had conducted, several nuclear weapons tests in the tens-of-kiloton range.[39] Several days later, Pakistan announced that it had conducted[40] several nuclear tests in response to the Indian tests. Some of these tests, all underground, were observed by seismic stations that are part of the planned verification system for the CTBT.[41] India and Pakistan are both parties to the LTBT, but neither has ever joined the NPT. India and Pakistan have not signed the CTBT. These nuclear tests (noted in ch. III), an outcome long feared in view of decades of political conflict involving India and Pakistan, threaten the whole nonproliferation regime.[42] Events relating to these tests are still unfolding as this book is written.[43]

All of these threats to the nonproliferation regime, in the Middle East, South Asia, and Far East, will require enlightened leadership and response by the international community if the nuclear danger is to be diffused. The NPT remains a norm whose goals arms controllers strive to achieve, but the obstacles are formidable. We will discuss these issues further in ch. X.

References and Notes

1. "Treaty on the Nonproliferation of Nuclear Weapons," Arms Control and Disarmament Agreements," 1990 ed., US Arms Control and Disarmament Agency, Washington, DC (ACDA, 1990 Ed.). Background, pp. 89–97. Treaty text, pp. 98–102.
2. ACDA, 1990 ed., p. 89.
3. The data and knowledge of nuclear physics and fission together with the development of nuclear reactors, made public from the Manhattan Project, lent promise to an untold new source of energy for electricity for the peaceful benefit of mankind. Development of medical isotopes and other beneficial applications soon followed.
4. ACDA, 1990 ed., p. 90.
5. ACDA, 1990 ed., pp. 89–93.
6. ACDA, 1990 ed., pp. 93–94.
7. David Fischer, "History of the International Atomic Energy Agency–The First Forty Years," printed by the IAEA, Vienna, Austria, September 1997.
8. Ref. 7, ch. 1.
9. Ref. 7, ch. 3.
10. The author notes that basic nuclear physics, nuclear cross sections, nuclear experiments and theory (not critical to weapons design), and much other unclassified scientific information were published at Los Alamos and other AEC institutions beginning shortly after the end of World War II. The IAEA Geneva Conferences of 1955 and 1958 stimulated such publication. The accumulation, free exchange, and peaceful application of basic scientific information, consistent with US national security interests, has been a driving force at Los Alamos National Laboratory since 1946.
11. Ref. 7, Annex 1, IAEA Statute.
12. Ref. 7, ch. 4 and 5.
13. Ref. 7, Annex 3.
14. See ch. 8 in ref. 7. The model safeguard agreement of 1971 was INFCIRC/153 (IAEA Information Circular/153), titled "The Structure and Content of Agreements between the Agency and States Required in Connection with the Treaty on the Non-proliferation of Nuclear Weapons." Model agreements that preceded it were INFCIRC/26, 1961 and 1964 (covered reactor facilities), and INFCIRC/66, 1966 and 1968 (provisions for reprocessing plants and conversion and fabrication plants). Many features carried over from earlier to later models.
15. Ref. 7, pp. 243–245.

16. National Academy of Sciences, "Nuclear Arms Control, Background and Issues," National Academy Press, Washington, DC, 1985, ch. 8.
17. G. Robert Keepin, "Nuclear Fission and Nuclear Safeguards: Common Technologies and Challenges," 50th Anniversary Conference, National Academy of Sciences, Washington, DC, April 25–28, 1989.
18. ACDA, 1990 Ed., pp. 95–96.
19. Joseph F. Pilat and Robert E. Pendley, "1995–A New Beginning for the NPT," CNSS, LANL, Plenum Press, NY, 1995. Review Conference summaries are given in the Appendix, pp. 258–295.
20. Lewis A. Dunn, "High Noon for the NPT," *Arms Control Today*, Vol. 25, No. 6, July/August 1995, pp. 3–9.
21. J. M. Beier and S. Mataija, eds., "Proliferation in All Its Aspects, Post 1995: The Verification Challenge and Response," Symposium Proceedings, Center for International and Strategic Studies, York University, Toronto, Canada, 1995.
22. ACDA, 1990, ed., pp. 64–88. See also ref. 19, pp. 164–177.
23. ACDA, 1990 ed., pp. 20–30 (Antarctic Treaty).
24. ACDA, 1990 ed., pp. 52–63. (Outer Space Treaty).
25. ACDA, 1990 ed., pp. 107–117. (Seabed Treaty).
26. Pilat & Pendley, "1995—A New Beginning for the NPT," pp. 13–15.
27. James A. Baker, "The Politics of Diplomacy," G. P. Putnam's Sons, New York, NY, 1995. For the Gulf War, see ch. 19–24.
28. Colin L. Powell, "My American Journey," Random House, New York, NY, 1995. For the Gulf War, see ch. 18 and 19.
29. Steven Mataija and J. Marshall Beier, eds, "Multilateral Verification and the Post-Gulf Environment: Learning from the UNSCOM Experience," Symposium Proceedings, 11–14 March, 1992, Center for International and Strategic Studies, York University, Toronto, Canada (1992).
30. J. B. Poole and R. Guthrie, eds., "Verification 1995: Arms Control, Peacekeeping, and the Environment," Westview Press, Boulder, Colorado, 1995, ch. 17, Tim Trevan, "UNSCOM Activities in Iraq in 1994."
31. Edward J. Lacey, "The UNSCOM Experience: Implications for U.S. Arms Control Policy," *Arms Control Today*, August, 1996, pp. 9–14.
32. Fischer, "History of IAEA" pp. 115. For strengthened safeguards, see pp. 295–300.

33. GAO Report, "Nuclear Nonproliferation: Uncertainties With Implementing IAEA's Strengthened Safeguards System," GAO/NSIAD/RCED-98-184, US GAO, Washington, DC, July 1998. For new safeguards, see INFCIRC/540, IAEA, Austria, 1997.

34. Ref. 7, pp. 109–110, pp. 411–413. South Africa joined the NPT in 1991. President de Klerk of South Africa announced for the first time that South Africa had previously constructed six nuclear weapons, but had dismantled them in 1989. South Africa then placed all their fissile materials under IAEA Safeguards. The US has not officially recognized that a nuclear test occurred.

35. Leon S. Sigal, "The North Korean Nuclear Crisis: Understanding the Failure of the 'Crime and Punishment' Strategy," *Arms Control Today*, May, 1997, pp. 3–13.

36. Rodney W. Jones, Mark G. McDonough, with Toby F. Dalton and Gregory D. Koblentz, "Tracking Nuclear Proliferation: A Guide in Maps and Charts, 1998," Carnegie Endowment for International Peace, 1779 Massachusetts Ave. NW, Washington, DC, 20036, 1998, pp. 169–186.

37. Ref. 36, p. 209.

38. Ref. 36, pp. 205–209.

39. Johanna McGeary, "Nukes . . . They're Back," *Time*, May 25, 1998, pp. 35–42.

40. Kathy Gannon," Pakistan Detonates Nukes," Associated Press (*Albuquerque Journal*) 29 May 1998. Also see *Arms Control Today*, May 1998.

41. Irwin Goodwin, "Nuclear Devices Tested by India and Pakistan Perplex Scientists and Shake Prospects of CTBT," *Physics Today*, July 1998, pp. 45–46.

42. Ref. 36, pp. 111–143.

43. Strobe Talbott, "Dealing with the Bomb in South Asia," *Foreign Affairs*, Vol. 72, No. 2, March/April, 1999. An excellent review of the India/Pakistan problem, and US efforts to alleviate it.

CHART IV-A.
IAEA Safeguards Procedures Under the NPT

IAEA Safeguards	Provided through agreements by the IAEA Board of Directors with individual state parties, or other entities. May be applied to any bilateral or multilateral arrangement. Designed to ensure that fissionable materials under IAEA supervision are not used for any military purpose. May include analysis of nuclear power plant design, review of records and reporting systems, and use of agreed inspection procedures.
NPT Safeguards	Article III of the Nonproliferation Treaty (NPT) provides that NNW (nonnuclear weapon) parties shall agree to use of IAEA Safeguards for verifying the party's observance of its obligations under the NPT. These safeguards apply to all fissionable material activities under jurisdiction of the state.
INFCIRC/153	IAEA information circular that provides the basis for negotiating safeguards agreements between the Agency and NNW state parties to the NPT. First adopted in 1972, in Vienna. Provisions are listed below.
Agreement Guidelines	The Safeguards agreement shall include provisions for: • the Agency's right to ensure that fissionable materials are not used for nuclear weapons or nuclear explosive devices. Provide for the timely detection of diversion of significant quantities (SQ) of nuclear materials for nuclear weapons, explosives, or unknown purposes. • cooperation of the state party with the Agency • avoidance of undue interference in the states peaceful nuclear activities, particularly in the operation of facilities • precautions to protect industrial secrets & other confidential information

CHART IV-A. (Cont.)
IAEA Safeguards Procedures Under the NPT

Agreement Guidelines (Cont.)	• ensuring cost effectiveness • safeguarding the flow of nuclear material thru use of scientific instruments at strategic points • verification priority given to fuel cycles involving nuclear materials (such as Pu, HEU, etc.) from which nuclear weapons could readily be made
Accounting	The agreement shall provide that the state shall maintain a system of accounting and control of all nuclear materials subject to IAEA safeguards. Such safeguards shall enable the agency to verify that there is no diversion of nuclear material for nuclear weapons or nuclear explosive devices. The Agency's verification includes independent measurements & observations. The party shall provide the agency the information necessary for safeguarding the nuclear material.
IAEA Inspectors	The agreement shall provide that the state shall ensure that the inspectors can discharge their duties. The state shall approve the designations of inspectors to that state. The Agency shall propose alternates to inspectors not approved. Repeated refusals shall be referred to the IAEA Board for action. Immunities shall be granted agency staff needed to execute duties.
Costs	Each state party shall bear the cost of the agreed Safeguards. The Agency shall bear the cost of additional measuring or sampling requested. Provision is made for third party liability for nuclear damage.
Request for Action by State	Agreement shall provide for request by the IAEA for action by the state deemed urgent to ensure the verification
Interpretations	Agreement shall provide for Agency/state consultations on questions arising from interpretations of the agreements.

CHART IV-A. (Cont.)
IAEA Safeguards Procedures Under the NPT

Amendments	Amendments require agreement by both the state and the Agency.
EIF	Entry-into-force of the agreement shall be the date Agency receives notice from state that agreement is ratified.
National Accounting	IAEA shall make full use of state's national accounting system which shall be based on a structure of material balance areas, and shall include: • a system for determination of quantities of nuclear material received, shipped, produced, lost, or in inventory • evaluation of accuracy • procedures for evaluating differences in receiver/shipper measurements • procedures for taking physical inventory • procedures for evaluation of unmeasured losses • records system for inventory for each material balance area • provisions to ensure accounting procedures are being operated correctly • specified reports to the Agency
IAEA Inventory	The Agency shall establish a unified inventory based on the initial state report and all subsequent reports and verification activities. Copies available to state.
Design Information	Design information about existing and new facilities (such as nuclear reactors) shall be submitted to the IAEA by the state as provided in the agreement. Shall include the description, character, purpose, capacity and geographic location of the facilities. Shall include description of form, location, and flow of nuclear materials. Include description of features relating to material accountancy, containment and surveillance.

CHART IV-A. (Cont.)
IAEA Safeguards Procedures Under the NPT

Reports	INFCIRC/153 details a comprehensive system of reports, to be spelled out in the agreement, that the state must provide to IAEA. These include the inventory, accounting, and design information noted above. Special reports are required for unusual incidents involving significant loss or possible unauthorized removal of nuclear materials.
Inspection Types	The agreement shall provide for IAEA inspections as noted below. Types & Purposes of Inspections are: Ad Hoc Inspections to: • confirm initial inventory reports • identify and verify changes • verify quantities of nuclear material before transfer into/out of the state Routine Inspections to: • verify that reports are consistent with records • verify location, identity, quantity, and composition of all nucl. material • identify possible causes of unaccounted material Special Inspections: • to verify information contained in special reports • additional inspections deemed necessary when routine OSI insufficient
Inspection Rights	The agreement shall enable the IAEA inspectors to: • examine records • make independent measurements of all subject nuclear material • verify proper functioning of instruments & control equipment • apply surveillance and containment measures • observe sample at key measurement point • make arrangements with the state for additional measurements if needed • use its own measuring equipment and apply its own tamper proof seals

CHART IV-A. (Cont.)
IAEA Safeguards Procedures Under the NPT

Inspection Access	The agreement shall provide IAEA inspection access rights for: • any location where initial report indicates nuclear material present • any location where nuclear material is reported being prepared for shipping • strategic points listed in subsidiary agreements, only for routine inspections Access may be limited in agreed special cases. Special inspections may require special agreements.
Frequency/Intensity	Routine inspections shall be kept to the minimum needed for Safeguards. If a facility inventory has <5 kG (nuclear material), routine inspections ≤1/yr. The Agreement shall specify inspection frequency at each facility subject to guidelines given in INFCIRC/153.
Inspection Notice	Agency shall give advance notice to states >24 hrs for ad hoc inspections >24 hrs for routine inspections time specified by consultations for special inspections The agreement may provide for unannounced inspections and random samples
Designation	The Director General shall provide relevant personnel information about the IAEA Inspectors to be used in the state. INFCIRC/153 provides procedures for this designation, acceptance by state, and for the conduct of inspectors.
Inspection Results	The agreement shall provide that the IAEA inform the state, at specified intervals, as to results of inspections and the conclusions drawn.

CHART IV-A. (Cont.)
IAEA Safeguards Procedures Under the NPT

Strengthened Safeguards	INFCIRC/540 (Model Protocol between states and IAEA for Safeguards.) Adopted by the IAEA in 1997 in response to violations in Iraq. Known as "Strengthened Safeguards System" (93+2). IAEA negotiates new Safeguards Agreements with individual states, based on this Model Protocol. Such states must be prepared to accept the new requirements in this Model Protocol. Features of new Model are given below.
Applicability	Art. 1 of the Model states "In case of conflict between provisions of Safeguards Agreement (with individual state) and this Protocol, the provisions of this Protocol shall apply."
Info Provision	The state shall provide Agency with: • location & description of all nuclear fuel-cycle research activities • map of each site and description of each building on each site • description of operations for each location • specification of location and status of U & Th mines and concentration plants • other information regarding status of source materials (see INFCIRC/540) • additional dates for such reports are specified
Access	Agency shall have access to: • any location referred to in Art. 5 (Protocol/540) • any location (in Art. 5) to confirm declaration of decommissioned status Agency shall give 24 hrs. advance notice of inspection of above sites, except in case of regular inspection, Agency may give >2 hrs. notice for exceptional inspection for design information.

CHART IV-A. (Cont.)
IAEA Safeguards Procedures Under the NPT

Inspections (Art. 6)	Inspection activities at above sites (Art. 5) may include visual observation, environmental sample collection, radiation detection, application of seals, etc.
Other Provisions	Managed access, state requests for verification, protection of sensitive info, inspector designations, communications, and other details are in INFCIRC/540.

Sources: NPT (Ref. 1).
Fischer, "History of the IAEA," (Ref. 7), includes Statute of the IAEA.
Information Circulars, IAEA, Vienna, Austria.
INFCIRC/153 (1972).
INFCIRC/540 (1997).

Chapter V

The INF Treaty

The INF Threat

In the early 1970s, the Soviets achieved rough parity with the United States in the deployment of strategic range nuclear vehicles (ICBMs, SLBMs, and bombers). [1,2] By 1976, the Soviets began a rapid production of a new intermediate-range mobile missile, the SS-20, each of which contained three nuclear-armed reentry vehicles (RVs) to replace much older SS-4 and SS-5 single-warhead missiles.[1–3] By the mid-1980s, the Soviets were to have 650 SS-20s, capable of delivering 1950 nuclear warheads. These intermediate-range nuclear force (INF) deployments, not covered by the ongoing strategic-range SALT negotiations (ch. II), represented a form of break-out from the SALT limits. Combined with the Soviet deployments of heavy ICBMs (SS-18s, 10 WHs each) and other modern Soviet strategic missiles (ch. II), the Soviet SS-20 deployments added a new dimension to the hair-trigger dangers of the nuclear arms race.

By the mid-1980s, the total Soviet theater-range missile force consisted of 1752 ballistic missiles that could deliver a total of 3121 nuclear warheads.[2] These were divided between intermediate-range (1000 to 5500 kilometers; SS-20s and SS-4s) and shorter-range (300 to 1000 kilometers; SS-23s and SS-12/22s) missiles. These Soviet missiles were within 18 minutes of flight time from Western European capitals.

The newer Soviet deployments came at a time when NATO's longer range nuclear deterrent, mainly US and UK aircraft stationed in Britain, were being rendered less credible by age and by improved Soviet air defenses.[4] The US/NATO response to the SS-20 deployments was complicated by the competing European points of view that (1) reassurance that the United States coupled itself to Europe's defense with theater nuclear forces and (2) apprehension that theater nuclear forces might actually be used in anything resembling classic military combat.[4] Many Europeans also perceived a paradox, that US theater nuclear forces in Europe could be used to keep the war on European soil without committing strategic forces to a US/Soviet ICBM exchange.

Obviously, European views on the desirability of US theater (and tactical) nuclear forces have fluctuated over the years depending on the current political climates. The presence of significant numbers (~325,000 in 1988) of US conventional force personnel along with the very substantial US business investments in Europe has been central to European confidence in the joint US/NATO strategic relationship, which included a strategy of "flexible response" to maximize Soviet uncertainty about the nature of NATO's nuclear response to any attack.[4]

In November 1979, after a series of planning group meetings, the NATO ministers unanimously adopted a "dual track" strategy to counter the SS-20 deployments.[1] One track called for arms control negotiations between the United States and the USSR to reduce INF forces to the lowest possible level. The second track called for deployment in Western Europe, beginning in 1983, of 464 single-warhead US ground-launched cruise missiles (GLCMs) and 108 modern Pershing II single-warhead ballistic missiles. In late 1983, the GLCM and Pershing II deployments proceeded on schedule despite a vigorous Soviet propaganda campaign against them aimed at European public opinion.

INF Treaty Negotiations

At first the Soviets refused to enter into INF negotiations until the new US deployments were revoked, but by late 1981 formal talks began. President Reagan then offered to eliminate all the GLCMs and Pershing IIs if the Soviets would dismantle all its SS-20s, SS-4s, and SS-5s (known as the zero-zero offer).[1] The US positions involved careful consultations with NATO and the requirements for effective verification. In 1983, the United States emphasized its preference for the zero option, but agreed on the concept of an interim agreement based on equally low values for each party. The Soviets "walked out" in late 1983 and there were no INF negotiations in 1984. During this time, US deployment of Pershing IIs and GLCMs continued on schedule.

In early 1985, Secretary of State Shultz and Foreign Minister Gromyko agreed to separate but parallel negotiations on INF, strategic arms (START), and defense and space issues as part of a new bilateral forum. The interrelationship of each of the three areas would be considered. Negotiations would be conducted by a single delegation for each side, divided into three groups, one for each of the three areas. Formal talks resumed in March. US GLCM deployments continued.

As noted in ch. I and II, Mikhail Gorbachev came to power in 1985, and arms control agreements became much more likely. President Reagan and General Secretary Gorbachev held their first summit in November 1985 in Geneva.[1] They issued a joint statement calling for an interim accord on INFs. The United States proposed a limit of 140 launchers in Europe for each side and proportionate reductions in Asia with collateral restraints on shorter range missiles. In January 1986, Gorbachev proposed a three-stage program to ban nuclear weapons by the year 2000 including elimination of all US and Soviet INF missiles in Europe. In February the United States added to its previous proposal a statement that all INF weapons would be eliminated by the end of 1989. The United States also submitted an outline for comprehensive verification.

At the Reykjavik (Iceland) summit in October 1986, Reagan and Gorbachev agreed to INF missile ceilings of 100 each, none of which were to be deployed in Europe. Gorbachev also agreed (for essentially the first time) to an intrusive on-site verification regime. In February 1987, the Soviet Union agreed to reach a separate INF agreement, not tied to the START or Space negotiations. In March, the United States tabled a draft treaty text which encompassed the Reykjavik agreements and included a comprehensive verification regime. In July, the Russians agreed in principle to some of the provisions of the US draft treaty including on-site observations of missile eliminations. But in a major shift, they included inclusion of US-owned nuclear warheads on the West German owned Pershing IA missile systems. After the NATO foreign ministers council supported global elimination of all INF missiles and "shorter-range" missiles, Gorbachev agreed (July 22, 1987) to a "double global zero" treaty to eliminate all INF missiles and shorter-range missiles. The United States agreed to limit short notice OSIs to declared INF facilities. On August 26, Chancellor Kohl announced that Germany (FRG) would dismantle its 72 Pershing IA missiles and not replace them, if the United States and USSR agreed to the foreseen INF treaty.

In September, the two sides agreed in principle to the complete treaty. On December 8, 1987, President Reagan and General Secretary Gorbachev signed the INF treaty at a summit in Washington, DC. The complete treaty package[1] includes protocols on eliminations and inspections. It also includes a Memorandum of Understanding (MOU) which provides data on all the missiles to be eliminated.

Description of the INF Treaty

The "Treaty between the United States and the Union of Soviet Socialist Republics on the Elimination of Their Intermediate-Range and Shorter-Range Missiles" (INF treaty) calls for the elimination of all the parties' ballistic and ground-launched cruise missiles with ranges of 500 to 1000 kilometers (shorter-range) and 1000 to 5500 kilometers (intermediate-range). The INF treaty and its associated documents have been given and described in detail by ACDA[1] and the Senate Foreign Relations Committee (SFRC).[2] The treaty provided for the elimination of 1752 Soviet missiles and 859 US missiles. The treaty and its protocols provided for comprehensive on-site inspections (OSIs) and verification, unprecedented in arms control negotiations with the Soviet Union. Table 4 lists the numbers and types of missiles to be eliminated, and Charts V-A and V-B summarize the elimination and verification procedures. We provide here an article-by-article description.

Article I sets forth the basic requirement for each party to eliminate its intermediate and shorter range missiles, and not have such systems thereafter.

Article II defines terms used in the treaty. It specifically defines an intermediate-range missile as a ground-launched ballistic missile (GLBM), or a ground-launched cruise missile (GLCM), having a range capability that is greater than 1000 km but less than 5500 km. A shorter-range missile is defined as a ground-launched GLBM or GLCM having a range capability of more than 500 km but less then 1000 km. GLBMs and GLCMs are defined as being weapons-delivery vehicles. Deployment areas and missile support facilities are defined.

Article III defines the existing types of missiles covered by the INF treaty. For the United States, these are the Pershing II, the BGM-109G

(GLCM), and the Pershing IA (shorter range). For the USSR these are the SS-20, SS-4, and SS-5; and the shorter-range SS-12 and SS-23.

Articles IV and V require that the parties eliminate all treaty-applicable missiles, launchers, support structures and equipment within three years of entry into force (EIF). Equitable time phases and stages for removal to elimination facilities are provided.

Article VI prohibits production and flight testing of treaty-applicable missiles, but launching of intermediate-range missiles for destruction purposes is allowed. Definition and exception are made so that the Russians can continue to produce the SS-25 mobile ICBM (covered in the START treaties).

Article VII further defines treaty-applicable missiles. A GLBM or GLCM not listed in Article III shall be counted as having a range equal to the maximum for which it has been tested (assumed observable by the other side by NTM). GLBMs developed solely to intercept aircraft or incoming missiles are exempt from the treaty. Launchers for launching GLBMs or GLCMs are defined.

Counting for components for GLBMs and GLCMs is defined. GLCMs are defined separately from other cruise missiles.

Article VIII specifies locations allowed for treaty-applicable missiles and launchers. Allowed areas shall only be in deployment areas, support facilities, elimination facilities, or in notified transit. The allowed areas are specified in the MOU.

Article IX sets forth the obligations for notifications and data exchanges related to eliminations.

This article provides for the MOU, which lists all missiles, launchers and other equipment covered by the treaty possessed by the parties as of November 1, 1987. Types and locations are listed, and updates of the MOU are to be provided at EIF and each six months thereafter. Article IX describes seven specific types of elimination notifications each party is to provide the other after EIF. These are listed in Chart V-A. All such notifications are to be made through the Nuclear Risk Reduction Center (NRRC) of each party (see ch. VI).

Article X sets forth the basic obligations for eliminations. These are listed in Chart V-A. Elimination procedures are specified in the Protocol on Eliminations and summarized in Chart V-A.

Article XI provides for the rights and obligations for the use of on-site inspections (OSIs), and includes the type and purposes of each kind of inspection. We list these in Chart V-B. The Protocol on Inspections, INFT, gives detailed procedures for the on-site inspections, also listed in Chart V-B.

Article XII provides for the use of national technical means (NTM)[5] to help ensure treaty compliance and prohibits concealment or interference with the use of NTM.

Article XIII provides for the establishment of a Special Verification Commission (SVC) to meet at the request of either party to resolve compliance questions and improve treaty effectiveness.

Article XIV requires the parties not to assume international obligations that conflict with the treaty.

Article XV provides unlimited duration of the treaty, but provides each party's "right of withdrawal" for "extraordinary matters that jeopardize its supreme interests." Article XVI provides the process for amending the treaty. Article XVII provides for its EIF upon ratification.

Implementation of the INF Treaty

Ratification and EIF

Following the December 1987 signing, the INF treaty was submitted by President Reagan to the US Senate, January 25, 1988. Senate consideration lasted four months.[2,3] Three Senate committees, the Senate Foreign Relations Committee (SFRC), the Senate Armed Services Committee (SASC), and the Senate Select Committee on Intelligence (SSCI) held extensive hearings on the treaty. Administration witnesses included Secretary of State George Shultz, INF treaty Ambassador Maynard Glitman, ACDA Director William Burns, Secretary of Defense Frank Carlucci, JCS Chairman Admiral William Crowe, Special Presidential Advisor Paul Nitze, and Ambassador Max Kampelman, all supporting the treaty. Members of the Senate requested formal answers to over a thousand questions, all of which were answered by the administration.[6] The Senate had available the confidential record of the negotiations, made available by the administration with confidentiality arrangements.

During the administration's preparations to implement the treaty, concerns about certain aspects of the verification arose. These concerns were alleviated by "clarifications," signed May 12, 1988, by Ambassador Glitman and Soviet Col. General N. Cherov.[7] This agreement was made available to the Senate before final ratification.

The final Senate resolution of ratification contained two conditions: (1) the May 12 agreements[7] would be treated as if part of the treaty itself; and (2) Senate approval was based on the administration's presentation of the meaning of the treaty, and any other interpretation would require further Senate action. The Senate ratified the INF treaty on May 27, 1988, and the two parties "exchanged instruments" entering the treaty into force on June 1, 1988.

Establishment of Notification and Inspection Agencies

Before signing the INF treaty, US Secretary of State George Shultz and USSR Foreign Secretary Eduard Shevardnadze signed an agreement establishing the Nuclear Risk Reduction Centers (NRRCs) on September 15, 1987.[8] The NRRCs are highly efficient, dedicated-channel electronic communications centers located in each party's capital (see ch. VI). The NRRCs handle the large volume of notifications sent formally from each party to the other as required by the INF treaty, the START treaties, and numerous other treaties signed subsequent to the signing of the INFT. The US NRRC, located on the fourth floor of the State Department Building in Washington, and its Russian counterpart in Moscow, were used, for example, to transmit the detailed data exchanges of INFT-relevant missile deployments between the parties as required after EIF of the INF treaty, and each six months thereafter (Chart V-A). The NRRCs also have been used to transmit all of the notifications required by the treaty and listed in Charts V-A and Chart V-B.

Recognizing the large number of annual on-site inspections that would be required by the INF treaty, and by the START treaty then being negotiated, President Reagan, on January 26, 1988, directed the secretary of defense to establish a new separate operating agency within the Department of Defense (DoD). This was done immediately, and the On-Site Inspection Agency (OSIA) was created under the jurisdiction of the assistant secretary of defense for acquisition, as described in ch. VI. The first director of OSIA was Brig. General Roland Lajoie, a Soviet specialist with broad military and diplomatic experience, appointed February 1, 1988. Because of the interagency nature of the OSIA task, the principal deputy director is appointed by the director of ACDA, the first one being George L. Ruechkert, an INF treaty negotiator with broad foreign service and Soviet experience (ch. VI).

After establishing the OSIA, the United States engaged the Soviets in extensive discussions on the use of inspection equipment to forestall practical difficulties once the treaty came into force. Also, a host of logistical problems associated with conducting and/or hosting inspections were addressed by the OSIA and its Soviet counterpart. The two inspection agencies met for technical talks in February, March, and May, 1988, and worked out a number of implementation procedures.[6]

Implementation Activities and Inspections

After treaty EIF on June 1, 1988, implementation was brisk. To complete the initial baseline data exchange and achieve the baseline inspections on schedule, it was necessary for the Special Verification Commission, Article VIII (see next section), to reach agreement on a number of details.[9] This was done, the sides exchanged the required baseline data, and baseline inspections began July 1, lasting for two months. The data to be confirmed included numbers of each party's INF missiles, launchers, support structure and support equipment at all missile operating bases and missile support facilities, as well as certain technical characteristics.

The United States conducted baseline inspections at 133 facilities in the Soviet Union and Eastern Europe. The Soviets conducted baseline inspections at 18 facilities in 10 locations in the United States and at 12 facilities in the basing countries.

Closeout inspections (Chart V-B) began during the baseline period. Closeout inspections are conducted within the 60 days following the notified scheduled date of elimination of INF missile operating bases and missile support facilities. These OSIs help verify that facilities have been eliminated and that all INF activities have ceased at these locations. As of August 30, 1988, the United States had confirmed that 23 Soviet INF facilities had been eliminated.[6]

Elimination inspections (Charts V-A and B) also began during 1988. Soviet inspection teams were present at Longhorn, Texas, to observe the elimination of Pershing missile stages. They were also present at Davis-Monthan Air Force Base in Tucson, Arizona, to observe elimination of US GLCMs. US inspectors observed Soviet elimination of SS-20 missiles at Kansk, Chita, and Kapustin Yar, and other treaty-limited items (TLIs) at Sarny, Lesnaya, Sarykozek, Stankovo, and Jelgava.[6]

In 1988, the continuous monitoring provisions of the treaty were initiated to ensure each side that production of Soviet SS-20 missiles and US Pershing II missiles had ceased. The Soviet PPCM (portal perimeter continuous monitoring) activity (Chart V-B) was set up at Hercules Plant No. 1 at Magna, Utah, and the US PPCM monitor was established at Votkinsk, Russia.[6] Each side is permitted to have up to 30 inspectors present at the site to observe shipments leaving the plant, to use remote sensors to conduct necessary measurements, and to use direct physical inspection and other measurements of cargoes that could contain treaty-limited items (TLIs).

Special Verification Commission (SVC)

The SVC, established in treaty Article VIII, began its work shortly after June 1, 1988. ACDA provided the US component of the SVC with logistical, administrative, and technical support.[6] DOE and DoD provided technical advisors.[9]

From June 7 to July 15, the SVC convened in Geneva and agreed on a text for procedures of the SVC itself. Work began on an MOA covering detailed implementation procedures under the treaty, including the early technical agreements worked out before entry into force (above.). Much of the MOA text was agreed on by the end of the first session.[6]

Because of the haste in getting the treaty signed, details of logistics and procedures, including the actual equipment to be used during baseline and other inspections, were delayed until the SVC could meet to address these issues. The urgency in the first meeting was to complete action on the updated baseline data exchange (required by July 1) and to complete all other work required for conducting the baseline inspections so they could commence on July 1. This was accomplished.[9]

A second session of the SVC took place September 12 to October 28, and the third session took place November 28 to December 21, 1988. The completed procedures for the SVC were signed. The sides made further progress on the MOA and many issues, but some problems persisted,[9] such as inspection rights at continuous monitoring sites, the inspection of bases that were converted for use "as a base associated with GLBM or GLCM systems not subject to this treaty" (Art. X. 9), and precise actions required to eliminate transporters and transporter erector launchers, and other TLIs.

Continuous monitoring at Votkinsk (and Utah) provided special problems.[9] The Soviets wanted to move an item "large enough to contain a TLI" from Votkinsk and there was no procedure in place to inspect the item. The Russian word (in the treaty) for "contain" can mean either carry or contain. As a result, the Soviets insisted on inspection rights for large flatbed trucks departing the Utah site. The major issue between the sides was the US demand to either look inside the SS-25 canisters (or other missiles) departing Votkinsk inside closed railroad boxcars or, in lieu of that, to x-ray the contents. The United States wanted to prove that no TLI was inside the boxcar and the Soviets considered the x-ray (or direct look) of SS-25s (to be covered by START) as too intrusive. Agreement was finally reached a year and a half later, and the United States was permitted to take tightly controlled, slit x-ray pictures of the boxcars with a device known as CargoScan. An agreed statement on Votkinsk was completed and signed.[6,9]

Another issue was how to inspect SS-25 canisters located on transporters at converted missile bases. The SS-20s (to be eliminated by the INFT) and the strategic range SS-25 (a mobile ICBM covered by START) had similar external dimensions. The SS-20 contained three nuclear warheads and the SS-25 only one. The United States wanted to use neutron and gamma-ray detectors to distinguish them. The Soviets finally agreed to permit use of neutron monitors and to permit the United States to perform a "baseline inspection" on both SS-20s and SS-25s in order to distinguish them from outside the canisters. These inspections were carried out on July 4, 1989.[9] Final procedures were agreed by late 1989.

During these and subsequent meetings of the SVC, other technical issues were also discussed, and some trial inspections were carried out by members of the SVC and/or their technical advisors.[9]

Completion of Eliminations under the INF Treaty

Following the baseline period, the eliminations of missiles and related equipment, along with the on-site inspections (20 per year for each side), proceeded for the three-year elimination period. By November 1990, US inspectors had witnessed the elimination of 1780 missiles and their launchers. These included 6 SS-5s, 718 SS-12s, 238 SS-23s, 80 SSC-X-4s, 149 SS-4s, and 90% of their 650 SS-20s.[10] By January 1990, the United States had eliminated 100% of its Pershing IAs, and by January 1991 had eliminated 181 of its 234 Pershing IIs and 315 of its 443 GLCMs.[10] Further details of the inspections and eliminations under the INF treaty are given in ch. VI.

By mid-1991, all treaty-prohibited forces had been eliminated or accounted for.[11] A significant violation of the treaty by the Soviets was discovered after the Eastern European (Warsaw Pact) satellites of the USSR obtained their freedom from Soviet domination.[12] About 70 unreported SS-23s had been transferred to East European governments before 1988 and were considered by the United States to be a violation of the INF treaty. These were subsequently accounted for and transferred back to Russia for elimination. That this number of previously unreported missiles was discovered illustrates that the INF treaty verification regime was not perfect. One has to ascribe "error bars" to any verification regime. The fact that these 70 SS-23s were considered significant is a tribute to the degree of completeness of the eliminations achieved under the INF treaty. After 1991, inspections continued at the rate of less than 15 per year through 1996, and will continue at less than 10 per year until 2001.

The INF treaty first demonstrated that the United States and the former USSR could reach a major nuclear arms control agreement on the reduction of nuclear deployments and carry out its implementation and on-site verification. Implementation of the INF treaty spearheaded the creation of the NRRCs and the OSIA, paving the way for verification of future nuclear treaties, particularly START. The treaty did indeed eliminate all the SS-20s as deployed in 1988, removing a major threat to nuclear stability.

The INF treaty is clearly a major achievement in the history of nuclear arms control.

References and Notes

1. "Treaty Between the United States and the USSR on the Elimination of Their Intermediate-Range and Shorter-Range Missiles (INF treaty)," Arms Control and Disarmament Agreements, US ACDA (1990 Ed.), Washington, DC; background pp. 345–349; Treaty Text, Protocol on Eliminations, Protocol on Inspections, MOU, etc., pp. 350–459.
2. "The INF Treaty," Report of the SFRC, exec. report 100-15, US Senate, April 14, 1988.
3. "The INF Treaty," SFRC hearings, Part 2, February 1–5, 1988, US Senate Hearing Doc. 100–522, Pt. 2. See p. 486 for alarming 1976 report on SS-20.
4. Ref. 2, pp. 11–22.
5. William C. Potter, Ed., "Verification and Arms Control," Lexington Books, D.C. Heath & Co., Lexington, MA, 1985. For NTM, see ch. 1, 2, and 6.
6. "Annual Report to Congress, 1988," US ACDA, Washington, DC, March 14, 1989.
7. Agreed Minute, signed May 12, 1988, by Ambassador Glitman and Col. Gen. Chervov, ref. 6, pp. 26–27. The document clarified (1) the smallest item subject to inspection; (2) provisions relating to second stages of Pershing II missiles; (3) restatement of the right to inspect the entire inspection site; (4) an understanding regarding what shipments would be subject to inspection when exiting the Votkinsk PPCM; (5) restatement of right to use inspection equipment; (6) provisions for measuring and weighing a sample TLI (treaty limited item); (7) procedures for confirming contents of launch canisters immediately prior to elimination; (8) dimensions of missile stages; and (9) exchange of additional photographs.
8. ACDA, 1990 Ed., pp. 336–344. NRRC agreement.
9. Delmar Bergen, DOE/LANL technical advisor to the SVC (1988–1990), private communication.
10. ACDA Annual Report to Congress for 1990, ACDA, Washington, DC, March 20, 1991.
11. ACDA Annual Report to Congress for 1991, ACDA, Washington, DC, June 2, 1992, pp. 34–36.
12. James A. Baker, III, "The Politics of Diplomacy," G. P. Putnam's Sons, New York, NY (1995).

CHART V-A.
INF Treaty
Data Exchanges, Eliminations, and Related Notifications

Data Exchanges (INF Treaty, Art. IX; Ref. 1):

The Memorandum of Understanding (MOU) lists, by categories, all intermediate-range and shorter-range missiles, launchers, and related support equipment, covered by the treaty and possessed by the parties on November 1, 1987. Within 30 days after entry-into-force (EIF), the parties shall provide each other with the updated inventories (baseline data) according to the categories of the MOU. Each six months thereafter, the parties are to provide each other the changes and their updated inventories by MOU categories. These data exchanges, as well as all other notifications (such as below) are to be provided through each party's Nuclear Risk Reduction Center (NRRC), established by agreement in September, 1987, and described in ch. VI. The notifications will continue through the duration of the treaty, which is unlimited (unless amended otherwise).

Types of Notifications of Eliminations (INF Treaty, Art. IX; Ref. 1):

1. Notification (>30 days in advance) of scheduled date of elimination (close out) of a specific deployment area, missile operating base or missile support facility.
2. Notification (>30 days in advance) of changes in the number or location of elimination facilities.
3. Notification (>30 days in advance) of scheduled date of initiation of elimination of intermediate-range and shorter-range missiles, stages of such missiles, launchers of such missiles, and support equipment. These notifications shall include: number and type of missile, elimination site, location from which such missile is moved (to elimination facility), the point-of-entry (POE) and transit times to be used by inspection team (when applicable).
4. Notification (>10 days in advance) of scheduled date of the launch, or date of initiation of series of launches, of intermediate-range missiles for the purpose of their elimination. These notifications shall include: type of missiles to be eliminated; location of the launch(es); and the POE and transit times for the inspection team (when applicable).

5. Notification (<48 hours after occurrence) of changes in inventory of missiles, etc. resulting from eliminations (Article X). Include number and type of items, and date and location of eliminations.

6. Notification (< 48 hours after completion) of transit of intermediate-range or shorter-range missiles, launchers, and/or training missiles/launchers. Notification shall include: number of missiles or launchers; points and times of departure and arrival; mode of transport; and location and time at least once every four days during the transit.

7. Notification (<10 days in advance) of scheduled date and location of launch of research booster system (Art. VII, Par. 12, INF treaty).

Elimination Obligations (INF Treaty Art. X; Ref. 1):

1. Each party is to eliminate its missiles, launchers, and support structures in accordance with the Protocol on Elimination.

2. Verification of the eliminations shall be carried out in accordance with Art. XI of the treaty and the Protocol on Inspections.

3. Missiles (intermediate-range), launchers, and support equipment from deployment areas to elimination facilities, shall be removed in complete deployed organizational units. For the United States, these units are Pershing II batteries and BGM-109G flights. For the USSR, these units are SS-20 regiments (of two or three battalions).

4. Elimination of missiles, launchers, and support equipment shall be carried out at facilities specified in the MOU or as otherwise notified; unless eliminated In Situ, by accidental destruction, or by Static Display (see Articles IV and V, Protocol on Elimination). Support structures are eliminated In Situ.

5. Each party may eliminate <100 missiles (intermediate-range) by launching, <6 months after EIF.

6. INF treaty applicable missiles, tested prior to EIF but never deployed and not listed as existing types in Article III, shall be eliminated <6 months after EIF in accordance with the Protocol on Elimination.

   These are: for the United States the Pershing IB, and for the USSR the RK-55 (SSC-X-4).

7. Missiles, launchers, and support equipment shall be considered to be eliminated upon the completion of the procedures in the Protocol on Elimination, and provision of the specified notification.

8. Each party shall eliminate its deployment areas, missile operating bases and missile support facilities. Conditions for such elimination include:

   (a) all INFT applicable missiles, launchers, and support equipment have been removed;

   (b) all relevant support structures have been eliminated;

   (c) all activity related to production, flight-testing, training, repair, storage, or deployment of such missiles has ceased there.

   Such areas and facilities shall be considered eliminated following inspection (pursuant to par.4, Art. XI, INF treaty), or >60 days after the specified notification.

9. A party may convert a missile operating base listed in the MOU for use as a base associated with GLBM or GLCM systems not subject to this treaty, then the party shall notify the other party, <30 days prior to initiation of the conversion, of the scheduled date and purpose.

Elimination Procedures (Protocol on Eliminations, INFT; Ref. 1):

I. Items of Missile Systems Subject to Eliminations are

1. For the United States

Pershing II:	missile, launcher, launch pad shelter
BGM-109G(GLCM):	missile, launch canister and launcher
Pershing IA:	missile and launcher
Pershing IB:	missile

2. For the USSR

SS-20:	missile, launch canister, launcher, transporter vehicle, fixed structure
SS-4:	missile, transporter, missile erector, launch stand and propellant tanks
SS-5:	missile
SSC-X-4:	missile, launch canister and launcher
SS-12:	missile, launcher and transporter vehicle
SS-23:	missile, launcher and transporter vehicle

3. For both parties: all training missiles, stages, launch canisters, launchers.

4. For both parties: all stages of intermediate-range and shorter-range GLBMs.
5. For both parties: all front sections of deployed INFT relevant missiles.

II. Procedures at Elimination Facilities

1. Parties fulfill these requirements to ensure reliable determination of type and numbers of items to be eliminated (above).
2. Elimination procedures are subject to on-site inspections (OSIs) provided in Article XI, INFT and the Protocol on Inspections.
3. Prior to missile arrival at elimination facility, the nuclear warhead and guidance system are removed.
4. Each party shall select the particular technological means necessary to implement the elimination procedures required in paragraph 10 and enable the treaty prescribed OSIs.
5. The initiation of elimination of items subject to elimination shall be start of procedures of Par. 10 & 11.
6. Immediately prior to initiation of elimination, inspector shall confirm and record type and number of items which are to be eliminated.
7. A missile stage being eliminated by burning shall not be instrumented for data collection. The missile stage shall be subject to continuous observation during the burning.
8. The completion of elimination procedures of this protocol (except for training missiles) shall be recorded and cosigned by representative of inspection party and by host.
9. The parties agree that all missiles and RVs shall be eliminated 15 days prior to the (three year) elimination time prescribed in articles IV and V.
10. Specific procedures for each specific type of missile (listed above) are detailed in this section of the protocol. Examples include:

    Pershing II: missile stages eliminated by burning or explosive demolition solid fuel, rocket nozzles and motor cases crushed, flattened, or exploded front section crushed or flattened

BGM-109G: cruise missile airframe cut longitudinally into 2 pieces wings and tail severed from missile (not at joints) front section crushed or flattened

SS-20: missile stages all burned or explosively demolished
solid fuel, rocket nozzles and motor cases crushed or explosively demolished
front section crushed or flattened
launch canister explosively demolished, or cut in two pieces & crushed
erector launcher cut into two equal pieces (not at joints)
mountings of erector launcher cut off launcher chassis, other cutting.

All other missiles: eliminated by similar procedures, where Par. 11 is for training missiles.

III. Elimination by Launching

Pursuant to Article X (INFT), up to 100 missiles may be eliminated by launching, within six months after EIF. They are subject to OSI (Art. XI, INFT). Just prior to each elimination-launch, an inspector shall confirm by visual observation the type of missile to be launched. All such missile launches shall be from designated elimination facilities to designated impact areas. Such launches shall be one at a time, >6 hrs. between launches. All missile stages shall be ignited, and no party may transmit or receive data from the missile except that needed for safety. The missile shall be considered eliminated after completion of the procedures, including the notification of completion.

IV. Elimination In Situ

1. Support structures (listed in Sect. I) shall be eliminated In Situ, and shall be subject to OSI. The superstructure of the fixed structure shall be removed from its foundation and demolished. The base (foundation) shall be excavated. The base shall remain visible by NTM until after the OSI.
2. Propellant tanks for SS-4s shall be removed from launch sites.
3. Training missiles, stages, and launch canisters, not eliminated at elimination facilities, shall be eliminated In Situ. Specific procedures, similar to above, are provided.

V. Other Types of Elimination

1. Loss or Accidental Destruction. An item to be eliminated but destroyed as result of accident, may be considered eliminated following the specified notification (above).
2. Static Display. Up to 15 missiles, launch canisters, etc., may be eliminated by Static Display. Such missiles, etc, shall be rendered useless, placed on display for 60 days with specified notification. An OSI is provided.

CHART V-B.
INF Treaty On-Site Inspections (OSIs)—Rights and Procedures

Inspection Rights & Obligations (INFT Article XI, Ref. 1)

1. The right of on-site inspections (OSIs) are established to ensure verification of treaty compliance.
2. The inspection right is established on the territory of both treaty parties and other basing countries.
3. Each party has right to conduct baseline inspections to verify the MOU data exchanged at EIF (baseline data). Such inspections may include all missile operating bases, support facilities, and elimination facilities specified in MOU, and are conducted for: 30 days $< t < 90$ days, where t = time from entry-into-force (EIF) of the treaty.
4. Each party may conduct an OSI (close out inspection) to verify the elimination of missile operating bases and support facilities, within 60 days after scheduled elimination date. One such inspection per eliminated facility.
5. Each party may conduct OSIs to determine the inventories of missiles, launchers, and support equipment according to the MOU categories. These OSIs may be conducted at 90 days $< t <$ 13 years, where t = time from EIF. The yearly quotas are:

   20 OSIs/yr for first 3 years.
   15 OSIs/yr for next 5 years.
   10 OSIs/yr for last 5 years.

   These OSIs may be at missile operating bases, missile support facilities (other than elimination facilities and production facilities), and former missile operating and support facilities eliminated pursuant to Art. X. No more than one half of OSIs may be in any one basing country.
6. The parties may inspect, by continuous monitoring, the portals of any facility of the other party used for final assembly of a GLBM outwardly similar to solid-propellant GLBMs listed in Art. III., or any agreed former such production facility. Such monitoring may occur from 30 days after treaty EIF until 13 years thereafter.

   The inspected party shall ensure that the monitoring party is able to establish such monitoring system (permanent portal continuous monitoring, PPCM) within six month after EIF.

The facilities to be inspected by continuous monitoring (PPCM) were agreed as:

For the United States:	Hercules Plant No. 1, Magna, Utah
For the USSR:	Votkinsk Machine Building Plant, Udmurt, Russia

7. Each party has the right to conduct OSIs of the elimination processes provided in Article X and the Protocol on Eliminations. Inspectors shall determine that specified processes are completed.

8. Each party has the right to conduct OSIs to confirm that the process of elimination has been completed pursuant to the Protocol on Eliminations.

Procedures for On-Site Inspections (OSIs)—Protocol on Inspections, INFT, Ref. 1.

I. ***Definitions.*** Terms like "inspected party," "inspecting party," etc. are clearly defined. Points of entry (POE) are defined. Includes: Washington, D.C, San Francisco, CA; Brussels, Frankfurt, Rome, Schiphol (Netherlands), RAF Greenham Common (UK), Moscow, Irkutsk (Russia), Schkeuditz Airport (GDR), Ruzykne Airport (Czechoslovakia). "In-country period" means time from OSI team arrival at POE to departure thru POE. "In-country escort" means persons specified by inspected party to accompany and assist inspectors

Ten definitions in all.

II. ***General Obligations.*** Each party shall facilitate inspection by the other party. Each notes agreements by basing countries.

III. ***Pre-inspection Requirements***

1. Inspectors/aircrew members are designated by each party in accordance with paragraphs 3 & 4.

2. Each party provides other with list of inspectors and aircrew members (<200), by 1 day after EIF.

3. Inspectors/aircrew must be citizens of inspecting party; must be accepted by inspected party.

4. Each party may amend its lists of inspectors.

5. Within 30 days of receipt of list, host party provides visas and documents needed for entry.

6. Inspectors and aircrew members shall be accorded privileges and immunities (see Protocol Annex).
7. Inspectors and aircrew members are obliged to obey laws and regulations of inspected party. May be removed for failure to do so.
8. Inspected party must provide standard diplomatic clearance for airplanes of party transporting inspectors.

IV. Notifications. Shall be made through the Nuclear Risk Reduction Centers (NRRCs).

1. Notification of intent to conduct OSI shall:

   Pursuant to Art. XI, par. 3, 4, & 5:

   - be made 16 hrs. prior to arrival at POE
   - list POE, date and time of arrival at POE
   - list date and time when inspection site will be specified
   - list names of inspectors and aircrew

   Pursuant to Art XI, par. 7, 8

   - be made 72 hrs. prior to arrival at POE
   - list POE, date and time of arrival at POE
   - list the site to be inspected and type inspection
   - list names of inspectors and aircrew

2. Notification of inspection shall provide time of inspection (t), measured after arrival at POE:

   Pursuant Art. XI, P4,5 $4 < t < 24$ hrs.
   Pursuant Art. XI, P3 $4 < t < 48$ hrs.

3. Inspecting party provides (thru NRRC) flight plan into POE, >6hrs, before flight departure.
4. Inspected party approves flight plan, >3hrs prior to OSI team departure.
5. Either party may change point(s)-of -entry with five months notice.

V. Activities at Point-of-Entry (POE)

1. In-country escort meets inspector team at POE
2. Inspectors commence their official duties at POE.

3. Inspection equipment is exempt from customs.
4. Inspection equipment examined at POE may be impounded if not required for OSIs; inspection equipment may be stored at POE in tamper proof containers.
5. Inspected party provides meals, lodging, work space, etc.
6. Inspected party provides parking, security, protection.
7. Inspection team enters country through POE closest to site to be inspected.

VI. General Rules for Conducting Inspections

1. Inspectors are bound by these rules.
2. Inspectors do not disclose information (about OSI) without agreement of both parties.
3. Inspectors do not interfere with site activities.
4. OSI must conform with treaty Article XI.
5. In-country escort has right to accompany inspectors at all times.
6. Inspectors may travel within 50 km. of site (for leisure activities only) with escort approval.
7. OSI team provided continuous telephone contact with their embassy.
8. Representative of the inspected site are included in the escort team.
9. Inspectors may bring on-site: documents, linear measuring devices, cameras, weighing devices, radiation detector, other agreed equipment.
10. Escort may observe OSI equipment (for Art. XI, P3, 4, 5, 7, 8).
11. Measurements at inspected site are certified by OSI team and escort.
12. Inspectors may request clarification of ambiguities and report if unsatisfied.
13. Inspectors must observe site safety regulations.
14. OSI team follows pre-inspection procedure within 1 hr. of arrival at site; OSI starts within 1 hr.

15. Inspection Team consists of n members:

    n <10 for Art. XI, P3, 4, 5.
    n <20 for Art. XI, P7, 8.
    n <30 for Art XI, P6 (PPCM).

16. Inspecting party must provide notification if it intends for team to conduct another OSI before leaving country.

VII. Procedures for On-site Inspections (OSIs) pertaining to treaty Art. XI, P.3, 4, 5. (To verify initial MOU data exchange and subsequent data exchanges*)*

1. Inspected party implements site movement restrictions (<1 hr. after OSI site specified) Missiles, launchers, etc. not to be moved from site during OSI.
2. Inspected party transport OSI team to site (<9 hrs after specification).
3. If site within a basing country, aircrew of inspected party may include reps. of basing country.
4. Limits to OSIs conducted at one time: 10 OSIs for case of verifying initial data base (first 90 days); one OSI for subsequent cases.
5. Boundaries of the sites subject to OSIs are given in the MOU.
6. Escort informs OSI team leader, upon arrival, of numbers of missiles and launchers at the site. Escort provides diagram of the site.
7. OSI team may inspect entire site, subject to paragraphs 8-14 of this section.
8. A missile, stage, or launcher may be observed only visual, but may include measurement of dimensions. A container large enough, but declared not to contain an INFT limited missile, may be weighed and/or its interior observed visually to determine it does not contain missile, or stage. If such container is launch canister associated with a missile not subject to INFT, but declared by inspected party to contain such a missile, it shall be subject to visual inspection, linear measurement, and use of radiation detectors.
9. A container smaller than needed to contain missile or stage may be observed only externally.

10. Within a structure, a space large enough to contain missile, but demonstrated to satisfaction of OSI team not to be accessible to an INFT missile or stage, is not further inspected. If such demonstration may be made at entrance to an enclosed space, such space shall not be further inspected.

11. OSI team may patrol site perimeter during the inspection.

12. OSI team may inspect any likely vehicle.

13. OSI team may station subgroups at building exits during OSI.

14. Inspected party must demonstrate that a shrouded object, which is larger than an INFT limited object, is not in fact a missile or stage subject to INFT. Do this by partial removal of shroud, visual observation, weighing, or radiation measurements. (see par. 14, Sect. VII)

VIII. Inspections of Eliminations.

1. Upon arrival, escorts give OSI team site elimination schedule Inspectors observe specific elimination procedures Inspectors may determine if missile to be eliminated is truly a missile (of declared type) prior to the elimination.

2. Inspections of eliminations subject to Protocol on Eliminations.

IX. Portal Perimeter Continuous Monitoring (PPCM)—Pursuant to treaty Art. Xl, Par. 6.

1. Inspected party shall maintain agreed perimeter around periphery of any facility at which final assembly of a GLBM (as specified in Art. III) occurs, and shall designate a single portal through which vehicles (one road, one rail) may pass which can contain a treaty limited GLBM.

2. Art. VII, P. 10, shall apply to the GLBM.

3. There shall be no more than two other exits from the facility; shall be monitored by sensors.

4. Inspection party may continuously monitor the designated portal, and the other exits.(may establish PPCM system)

5. Inspected party shall provide needed utilities, site preparation, & transportation, telephone lines, radio equipment, etc., needed for PPCM.

6. Inspection party may construct facilities (as specified) outside the PPCM site.
7. Inspection party shall not, in carrying out PPCM, interfere with inspectee's access to facilities.
8. Inspected party shall not interfere with installed equipment or restrict access to the PPCM.
9. Inspection party may use its own two-way radio system between members of PPCM team.
10. Aircraft not permitted to land within PPCM perimeter, except for emergencies and prior notification.
11. Shipments exiting the portal, large and heavy enough to be an intermediate-range GLBM, shall be declared as such by the inspected party and its size and weight indicated.
12. The inspection team may measure and weigh any vehicle (including rail cars) believed large enough to contain a relevant missile or largest stage, to determine if it is large and heavy enough. All vehicles not large and heavy enough may pass through without further delay.
13. Vehicles exiting the portal that are large and heavy enough, but declared not to contain such or missile or stage, shall be subject to:

    – visual inspection of the interior of the vehicle
    – if inside vehicle there are containers large enough to contain such a GLBM, the inspected party must demonstrate that such containers do not contain a relevant GLBM or stage.

14. A vehicle exiting the portal and declared (by inspected party) to contain a missile or missile stage as large or larger (or as heavy or heavier) than a GLBM specified by Art. III, is subject to:

    – inspectors shall preserve integrity of the missile or stage
    – measuring equipment shall be placed only outside the canister or container;
    – measuring equipment shall be as specified in this protocol;
    – measurement certified by escort
    – inspectors may weigh and/or measure such canister or container and image contents

- interior viewing (<8 times/yr):
  - i. front end (or cover) of canister (or container) shall be opened
  - ii. missile (or stage) shall not be removed
  - iii. length and diameter measured to ascertain that missile (or stage) is not an intermediate-range missile (or stage) GLBM of inspectee and that the missile has no more than one stage similar to an existing INFT relevant GLBM
- inspecting party has right to inspect any other shrouded objects inside this vehicle.

X. OSI Cancellation. If an OSI can not be carried out due to a unforeseen circumstances, a delay or "force majeure," it may be canceled and not count as an inspection (against the quotas).

XI. Inspection Report. (See section XI, Protocol on Inspections)

1. OSI team leader provides written report to escort within 2 hours after OSI completed. It shall include type of inspection, number of missiles, stages, etc. (subject to INFT) observed, measurements recorded and copies of photographs taken.
2. PPCM reports shall be provided monthly by the team leader, and shall include numbers of vehicles inspected, inspectee's declarations, results of measurements, and copies of photographs.
3. Inspected party may include written comments in the report.
4. Parties shall resolve, when possible, ambiguities contained in the report. Report shall be signed by the OSI team leader and by member of the in-country escort.

Chapter VI

Verification for Nuclear Arms Control

As noted in the previous chapters, verification of compliance for arms control treaties for each party to each treaty depends on a variety of mechanisms, including the national technical means (NTM) available to each party, notifications specified by the treaty, on-site inspection rights for each party as provided by the treaty, and cooperative measures. The United States has long developed its NTM capabilities. In the first three decades of the nuclear arms race, NTM represented the only means the United States had to verify or measure the declared nuclear weapons capabilities of most other nonallied nations, particularly the USSR. With the signing of the INF treaty, the United States created the On-Site Inspection Agency (OSIA) to carry out allowed on-site inspections of the arms control treaties. As noted in ch. V, the United States also established the Nuclear Risk Reduction Center (NRRC) to facilitate exchanges of notifications and data with the former Soviet Union (FSU) and other parties as needed. We note that other parties to the various treaties have their equivalent verification agencies, but in this chapter we discuss the development of these verification mechanisms by the United States.

National Technical Means (NTM)

In the 1950s, US NTM consisted primarily of intelligence means (such as the CIA), radar sites on the periphery of the Soviet Union, aircraft sampling of debris (radioactive fallout) from Soviet nuclear tests, seismic stations outside the Soviet Union, photographs from clandestine, high-altitude U-2 flights over the Soviet Union, and related activities. With the advent of the US space program and the development of satellite photography and other technological advances, the US ability to conduct effective verification by NTM increased substantially. We have already noted the development and value of Vela satellites to detect aboveground nuclear tests (ch. III).

Reconnaissance Satellites

By the 1970s, US NTM consisted of an extensive network of technological capabilities, collection systems, and other intelligence and analytical resources.[1,2] The use of photo reconnaissance satellites was first officially declassified by President Johnson in 1965. The satellite systems have sophisticated optical imaging sensors, infrared (heat sensitive) and other radiation sensors, radar, and electronic listening devices for observing signals from the other party's radars and communications.[3] Such sensors are augmented by appropriate sensors on aircraft and ships. The term "national technical means" was referred to in the ABM treaty (SALT I, ch. II) but was left undefined so that each party would have maximum flexibility in its development and use. Reconnaissance satellites have had major advantages over high-altitude aircraft (such as the U-2 and SR-71), including unlimited range; broader, more rapid coverage; and lack of vulnerability to the other party's air defenses.[4]

Both low and high orbits are used for surveillance satellites. Low-altitude orbits are best for observing features with fine resolution. US satellites are generally in orbits 100 to 500 miles high. Lower orbits have more atmospheric drag, which limits the time the satellite may remain in orbit. Satellites in low orbit circle the earth every 90 minutes and, tilted at optimum inclination, can cover the Soviet Union in about six passes during an eight-hour period. Satellites in high-altitude geosynchronous orbits are in the best position for stationary monitoring. Such satellites, at altitudes as high as 22,000 miles, can continually monitor most Soviet territory. Equipped with infrared sensors, they can give early warning, within about five minutes, of any ICBM launch.[3]

US satellite capabilities are extensive. Television pictures and photographs from above 100 miles altitude may search wide areas. Film taken by the satellites may be jettisoned in pods and retrieved by planes able to catch the package in parachutes. When developed, the film permits a much more detailed look at chosen targets. Some satellites take enhanced color and infrared television pictures and provide real-time information to the ground after passing over the Soviet Union. Because of their multispectral capability (RF-uwave-infrared-visible-UV-x-ray-gamma ray)[3] they can distinguish certain features such as camouflage, which are not apparent in normal light. High-resolution satellites, operating as low as 80 miles altitude, take detailed pictures that clearly show objects as small as windows on buildings, but can stay in orbit a shorter time. Image resolutions as fine as 10 centimeters are available.[3]

Satellite surveillance has limitations such as technical failures, during which key sensors are not available at critical times, or cloud cover that obscures visible observations during certain periods. Many treaty-verification problems take long enough to develop that the necessary observations may be obtained,[3] but verification of some activities, such as mobile missile movements, must be accounted for in the treaty provisions.

Electronic Intelligence

The process of collecting, intercepting, and analyzing electronic intelligence is politically sensitive, very technical, and highly classified. Diverse types of radio signals provide information that is useful in verification. Direction-finding techniques can aid in locating a broad range of emitters. Radar returns and observations can enable analysts to determine many missile and aircraft parameters, including size, weight, payload, speed, and maneuvers. Phased array (line of sight) radar, such as Cobra Dane on Shemya Island, Alaska, has given information on Soviet missile tests such as missile size and weight, as well as number and type of reentry vehicles (RVs).[3] The large radars are supplemented by RC135 electronic surveillance aircraft (derived from Boeing 707) crammed with side-viewing radar, electronic listening devices, and infrared detectors. An assortment of photo and electronic eavesdropping satellites have supplied the United States with up to half its usable intelligence.[3] These were supplemented with ground stations around the world, as well as shipboard facilities.

Other Sources

Information provided by human sources (for example, spies, recent émigrés, and visitors)[3] can provide clues about activities that merit closer examination by NTM. Such information can provide advance warning but is often fragmentary and sometimes misleading. Since the intelligence community often cannot reveal such "sources," such information may not be usable to prove "noncompliance," but its existence may be a deterrent to "cheating."

Data Analysis

Analysis of data sent back by NTM observations is crucial. The wealth of information obtained from satellite imagery and other sources requires painstaking analysis. The techniques for interpreting aerial pictures began during World War II and have evolved greatly since then. Modern computers have carried the process to a high technological level.[5]

Computer enhancement of images includes

- building multicolored single images out of several pictures taken in different spectral bands,
- restoring shapes by adjusting for angle of view,
- adjusting for amounts of contrast,
- extracting particular features while removing background, and
- enhancing shadows.

Computers are learning to recognize patterns. For example, the computer can be programmed to recognize changes in ICBM fields and identify construction of new launch silos.

The whole process of analyzing data, storing data, and cataloging the information depends heavily on the use of computers. Because computer technologies have developed so rapidly in recent years, one expects NTM capabilities to also increase rapidly.

US NTM was capable enough that, as early as 1979, Secretary of Defense Harold Brown was able to tell the US Senate that he was confident that the SALT II treaty (which limited deployed ICBMs, submarine-launched ballistic missiles [SLBMs], and bombers, but not warhead counts; ch. II) could be adequately verified even though we did not have the right of on-site inspection.[6] As the START treaties were negotiated and signed, NTM was considered[7] a key element of the verification regime even though unprecedented on-site inspections were negotiated.

Nuclear Risk Reduction Centers (NRRCs)

In anticipation of extensive use of notifications in the INF treaty (ch. V) and the START I treaty (ch. VII), US Secretary of State George Shultz and Soviet Foreign Minister Eduard Shevardnadze signed an agreement in Washington, DC, September 15, 1987, to establish a Nuclear Risk Reduction Center (NRRC) in each party's capital, and to establish a special facsimile communications link between these two centers.[8]

These NRRCs became operational on April 1, 1988. The US center is located on the 7th floor of the State Department Building, Washington, DC, and is staffed by the US State Department. The Russian center is located in Moscow and staffed by Russians. The centers are intended to supplement existing means of communication and provide direct, reliable, high-speed systems for transmitting notifications and communications at the government-to-government level. The centers communicate by direct satellite links that can rapidly transmit full texts and graphics.[9] Their capability is similar to, but separate from, the modernized "hot line" which is reserved for heads of state. The assistant secretary of state for political-military affairs, appointed by the president, has served as the director of the US NRRC. The NRRC staff[9] is divided between a staff component and a 24-hour watch operation. Staff members represent the NRRC at interagency meetings, prepare NRRC policy positions, and assist in planning for future treaty implementation. The watch operation is composed of both Foreign Service and Civil Service officers, including those with Russian and OSCE language proficiencies. These officers come from throughout the foreign affairs community.

The NRRCs do not replace normal diplomatic channels of communication or the "hot line," nor are they intended to a have a crisis management role. The principal function of the NRRCs is to exchange information and notifications as required under certain existing and future arms control and confidence-building agreements. Their use is called for in the INF treaty, START I, and START II treaties (ch. V, VII, and VIII), each of which contains a considerable list of specified notifications between the parties.[10]

The NRRC agreement has two protocols. Protocol I identifies the notifications the parties initially agreed to exchange, including[8] ballistic missile launches required under the 1971 "Agreement on Measures to Reduce the Risk of Outbreak of Nuclear War," and under the 1972 "Agreement on the Prevention of Incidents on and over the High Seas."

The NRRC Agreement provides that the list of notifications transmitted through the centers may be altered by agreement between the parties as relevant new agreements are reached (for example, the INFT, START I, and START II). Since the agreement was signed, the parties have additionally agreed to exchange, through the centers, inspection and compliance notifications, required under the INF treaty, notifications under the Ballistic Missile Launch Notification Agreement,[8] notifications required by the START treaties,[10,11] and other information.[12]

The NRRC agreement, in Protocol II, establishes[8] the technical specifications of the communications and facsimile links, the operating procedures to be employed, and the terms for transfer of and payment for equipment required by the system. The NRRC agreement is of unlimited duration and calls for regular meetings at least once a year between representatives of the national centers to discuss operation of the system.

The breakup of the Soviet Union in 1991 required NRRC links to be established with Belarus, Ukraine, and Kazakhstan (ch. VII). A link with OSCE countries was added in 1991. NRRC is now exchanging notifications for the CFE treaty, the Open Skies Treaty, and US nodes for the Chemical Weapons Convention (CWC). The US NRRC now operates, 24 hours a day, seven separate communications systems linked with 50 countries. In 1997, NRRC sent or received about 15,000 international arms control messages. The NRRC has served as a dependable means of exchanging information, is relied upon as an integral player in arms control implementation, and supports communications requirements for nearly 20 arms control treaties and agreements.[13]

The On-Site Inspection Agency (OSIA)

As noted in ch. V, the INF treaty was signed December 8, 1987, introducing for the first time significant on-site inspections into the regime of US and Soviet arms control agreements. On January 15, 1988, President Reagan signed National Security Directive 296 instructing the secretary of defense to establish a new organization responsible for INF treaty inspections. Eleven days later the secretary of defense established the OSIA, a separate operating agency reporting to the undersecretary of defense for acquisition.[14–16]

Creation of the OSIA

The first charter for the OSIA stipulated two principal responsibilities:

- to manage and coordinate the US INF treaty on-site inspection (OSI) activities in the USSR and Eastern European INF sites (E. Germany and Czechoslovakia), and
- to manage and coordinate all US activities related to the Soviet Union's OSIs of the US INF facilities in the United States, Belgium, the Federal Republic of Germany, Italy, Netherlands, and the United Kingdom.

On February 1, 1988, Brigadier General Roland Lajoie, US Army, was appointed the first director of OSIA. General Lajoie was a Soviet specialist who had commanded a battalion at Ft. Bragg and served liaison assignments in Berlin, France, and the USSR. By February 8, the initial cadre of about 40 military officers and noncommissioned officers arrived at OSIA headquarters, drawn from all branches of the service and including a few civilians from other government agencies. The temporary offices were at Buzzard Point, an area in southeast Washington, DC. The first principal deputy director, appointed by ACDA, was George L. Rueckert, a career diplomat and experienced INF negotiator. The secretary of state nominated Raymond F. Smith as OSIA's first deputy director for international negotiations, and the FBI director selected Edward J. Curran as OSIA's first deputy director for counterintelligence. This diversity of experience in the agency's leadership was reflected in the initial cadre of inspectors and escorts.[14] We note here that the initial structure for the OSIA had no separate Congressional funding and was funded by internal agency transfers, mostly within the

Department of Defense (DoD). The interagency task force that recommended the organizational path, which creation of the OSIA followed, considered the resources required to carry out the intense and difficult mission, and recommended putting OSIA within the DoD (rather than under the State Department or ACDA) because of the personnel and logistical capabilities of DoD.[17]

The INF treaty mission largely determined the OSIA's initial organizational structure. The operations directorate was responsible for planning, training, and conducting on-site inspection and escort missions. The directorate consisted of an inspections division (to conduct US inspections of Soviet forces) and an escort division (to coordinate escort of Soviet inspectors at US INF facilities).

The complexity of the initial OSIA mission is demonstrated by the fact that the Soviets had 130 INF missile sites in the USSR and Eastern Europe, and the United States had 31 such sites in Western Europe and the US.

Preparing for Inspections under the INF Treaty

The INF treaty entered into force on June 1, 1988. Thirty days later, baseline inspections were to commence and be completed 60 days after that, following the procedures outlined in ch. V and Chart V-B. This was a unique and challenging task for such a new and diverse agency.[14] The United States had to have escort teams ready to meet Soviet inspectors at seven entry points, two in the United States and five in Europe. The OSIA prepared to conduct the five types of inspections (ch. V) provided by the treaty. These OSI types were baseline, elimination, close-out, short-notice, and portal perimeter continuous monitoring (PPCM). OSIA initially established field offices in Frankfurt, Germany, and a gateway field office near Tokyo, as well as an Arms Control Implementation Unit in the US embassy in Moscow.

The OSIA prepared to conduct more than 150 OSIs during the first treaty year.[14] Under the treaty, an OSI team was composed of a team chief, a deputy team chief, two linguists, and six specialists. These ten-member teams are used for baseline, short-notice (inventory), and close-out inspections. Inspection teams for eliminations are allowed 20 members, and PPCM teams are allowed 30 members. The treaty stipulated that the OSI teams would be drawn from a list of 200 persons submitted by the inspecting party and approved by the host party. An additional pool of 200 portal monitoring inspectors would be similarly established. The air crews responsible for flying the inspectors and escorts to the designated points of entry (POEs) were limited (by the treaty) to a similarly approved third pool of 200 members.[14]

The several months before treaty EIF were busy for US national security interagency personnel, which included OSIA, ACDA, NRRC, and the State and Defense Departments.[18] With its quickly recruited personnel, OSIA organized and trained its inspectors and conducted mock inspections to prepare the way for the intense inspection period that was to follow.[19] Officials from ACDA, OSIA, DoD, Department of Energy (DOE), and the State Department prepared extensive testimony for the US Senate treaty ratification process (ch. V). Arrangements were needed with appropriate officials of West Germany and other NATO parties to host Soviet inspections. Agreements were needed with the Soviets on treaty interpretations involving a variety of details relating to the inspections. The Special Verification Commission (SVC) called for in the treaty (US delegation chaired by ACDA) was established June 6, 1988. Coordinating activities of US agencies involved in NTM, relative to the verification of treaty implementation, were required.

Baseline Inspections under the INF Treaty

Baseline inspections began July 31, 1988, and continued for 60 days. Baseline inspections were conducted to verify the numbers of missiles, launchers, support structures and equipment, and provide other data, as given in the Memorandum of Understanding (MOU) of the treaty (ch. V). Inspectors had the right to inspect the entire site, including the interior of structures, canisters, and covered objects with dimensions as specified in the treaty. Characteristics such as length, diameter, and weight of missiles, launchers, and other treaty-limited items (TLI) specified in the MOU were to be checked for each type of TLI.

Both Soviet and US military services committed considerable resources to preparing each site for a baseline inspection. At many Soviet sites, temporary living quarters were rehabilitated for the use of US inspectors. At six Soviet elimination sites, new facilities were constructed for US inspectors. At US INF bases, temporary housing was set aside for Soviet inspectors. To carry out the baseline inspections, the

OSIA organized and trained 20 of the 10-member teams. In late June, 12 of these teams deployed at the forward gateway fields.

General Lajoie was a member of the first US inspection team, led by Lt. Col. Lawrence Kelley.[14] The team flew to Moscow on July 1, 1988. Following the procedures (ch. V, Chart V-B), the US NRRC sent a notification 16 hours in advance giving the date and time of arrival at the Moscow POE, and the date and time when Col. Kelley would specify which INF site would be inspected. They were met by the host escort team members, who were with them the whole time they were in the USSR, expediting passage through customs and arranging transportation, hotels, and meals. After the four-hour minimum time, Kelley declared the SS-20 base at Richitsa, Belarus, as the inspection site. With their escorts, the inspection team members arrived there within the specified nine hours. They proceeded immediately to the one-hour pre-inspection briefing given by the site commander, who presented them with a site diagram showing the locations of INF treaty TLIs. The US team proceeded to conduct the inspection, accompanied throughout by Soviet officials who were knowledgeable about the INF treaty. Though allowed 24 hours by the treaty, Kelley declared the inspection complete within 8 hours, and prepared the inspection report in English and Russian.

The inspection report stated which TLIs had been observed and counted. Following a brief ceremony, this first inspection team left the site for Moscow, and went on to Frankfurt to prepare another OSI. By July 5, 10 US teams were conducting baseline inspections of Soviet INF sites. Some Soviet sites required more than the specified 24 hours for the inspection because of their size.

During this intense baseline inspection period, the OSIA also initiated continuous portal monitoring (PPCM) at Votkinsk. The first Soviet missile elimination occurred July 22 at Kapustin Yar, with a US inspection team present. During the baseline period, the OSIA also conducted 16 close-out inspections (which in some cases were accomplished with a baseline OSI). During this eight-week period, Soviet inspectors conducted similar baseline inspections of US INF bases and initiated a PPCM at Magna, Utah.

The baseline inspections were impressive.[20] During the 60-day period, OSIA teams conducted 114 inspections encompassing 129 Soviet INF sites. Soviet inspectors conducted 31 baseline inspections at 21 US INF sites. The two parties observed a recorded total of 7,681 TLIs listed in the MOU. These inspections also established the technical data (standard length, diameter, height, and weight) for all INF missiles and launchers (and associated equipment) for each type of INF missile for each party.

During this period, the international media followed the implementation process with much interest, the INF treaty being the first major brake on the cold war arms race. Lt. Col. Kelley told TASS, "It is clear to us that the Soviet side is interested in facilitating our inspections. Excellent conditions were created for our work and we are quite satisfied." In an extensive interview[20] following the baseline inspection period, General Lajoie said ". . . . We can go to specific sites . . . and return with more confidence than before concerning compliance at that site. But it's not an anytime/anywhere regime. . . . We now have more knowledge about Soviet forces. . . . I think on-site inspections have a very positive role to play in arms control." At the very least, the OSIA demonstrated a major logistical accomplishment during the baseline inspection period.

Continued OSIA Inspections for the INF Treaty

As implementation of the INF treaty continued in 1988, 1989, and 1990, OSIA continued to carry out the prescribed short-notice, elimination, and close-out inspections; to operate the PPCM at Votkinsk; and to host Soviet inspectors at US facilities. In February 1989, OSIA relocated to facilities at Dulles International Airport, where it is today. In July 1989, the OSIA received its first Joint Meritorious Unit Award, for the year 1988. During 1989, the Soviets eliminated their last SS-11 missile, their last SS-5, and their last (declared) SS-23 missile.

In early 1990, the United States began installing the nondamaging Radiographic Imaging System (CargoScan) [21] at Votkinsk to image ICBMs exiting the factory and verify that they were not SS-20s, which are prohibited by the INF treaty. Soviet officials objected to various operating procedures, and events ensured that they could not be resolved by the local parties. In March, Secretary of State James Baker lodged an official protest, leading the two countries to send official delegations to Votkinsk to negotiate the dispute. This led to resolution of the dispute, and the US Votkinsk team began imaging rail cars with CargoScan.

Eliminations and OSIs for the INF treaty continued into 1991, during which time the three-year elimination period was completed. On May 12, 1991, OSIA inspectors observed Soviet elimination of the last SS-20. By July 1991, all declared INF-treaty-limited missiles had been eliminated[22] for each side, as discussed in ch. V. The short-notice (inventory) OSIs and the PPCM inspections have continued yearly as called for in the treaty, and will continue through the year 2001.

Expansion of the OSIA

In May 1990, President Bush ordered expansion of the OSIA and assigned the agency responsibility for planning inspection procedures for several proposed treaties: the Conventional Armed Forces in Europe (CFE) treaty, the Strategic Arms Reduction Treaty (START), the Threshold Test Ban Treaty (TTBT), the Peaceful Nuclear Explosions Treaty (PNET), and several chemical weapons agreements.[15] The TTBT and PNET protocols were subsequently completed and ratified, and the TTBT and PNET entered into force in December 1990, as discussed in ch. III. Also, in June 1991, the National Security Council tasked the OSIA with inspection duties for the Vienna Document of 1990, which called for on-site monitoring of large-scale military exercises. In January 1991, Major General Robert W. Parker became the new OSIA Director, as Major General Lajoie departed for a new assignment.

The CFE treaty entered into force in November 1992. In July 1992, the OSIA began its baseline inspections for the treaty, which took place during a 120-day period preceding EIF.[15] As part of its inspection of reductions under the CFE treaty, OSIA began inspecting former Warsaw Pact equipment in Zossen-Wuensdorf, Germany, in August 1992. OSIA inspections in Eastern Europe and hosting of FSU (former Soviet Union) parties to the CFE treaty continued through 1996.[15] The multilateral Organization for Security and Cooperation in Europe (OSCE) became intimately involved in the CFE verification regime, and the

US OSIA worked closely with the OSCE both in hosting and conducting inspections.[15]

In August 1994, the OSIA conducted a trial inspection of the Pochep chemical-weapons storage facility in Russia, conducted under Phase II of the Wyoming Memorandum of Understanding (1989). The last of the five Phase II US inspections in Russia took place in December.[15] The Chemical Weapons Convention (CWC), signed by President Bush in January 1993, led to further chemical-weapons-related inspections by the OSIA in subsequent years. In 1996, the DoD delegated management of CWC implementation and management to the OSIA.[15]

The Open Skies Treaty, first signed in 1992, was ratified by the United States in August 1993. The US Open Skies Treaty aircraft (OC-135B) was delivered to the US Air force for use by the OSIA in conducting trial Open Skies Treaty overflights.[15] The OSIA has participated in a number of Open Skies Treaty trial missions to test logistics and sensors. These have included historic successful missions over Russia.[16]

In July 1991, the DoD designated the OSIA as its executive agent for supporting the United Nations Special Commission on Iraq (UNSCOM). As noted in ch. IV, the OSIA provided logistical support to the IAEA in conducting these inspections.

OSIA Inspections under the START I Treaty

The START treaty was first signed in July 1991, as discussed in ch. VII. Signing was followed by the viewing of treaty-specified on-site exhibits of technical characteristics of ICBMs, SLBMs, heavy bombers, and ALCMs (one of each SNDV type). START I finally entered into force in December 1994. After the specified initial data exchange, the baseline inspections between the parties were conducted from March 1, 1995, through June 28, 1995. During the baseline period, the OSIA conducted 73 inspections at 50 sites in the FSU, and hosted FSU teams on 36 inspections within the United States.[15,16] This represented a momentous codification of the strategic nuclear deployments of the nuclear superpowers and verified the modest but significant reductions that had taken place before treaty EIF.

The OSIA grew to play an indispensable role in the security of the United States, and all nations, by helping codify and verify the nuclear deployments of the United States and the FSU, and by contributing to the verification of nearly all the multilateral worldwide arms control agreements to which the United States is party.

Directors[15,16] of the OSIA have been

- Maj. General Roland Lajoie USA February 88–January 91
- Maj. General Robert W. Parker USAF January 91–July 93
- Brig. General Gregory G. Govan USA July 93–July 95
- Brig. General Thomas E. Kuenning USAF July 95–July 97
- Brig. General John C. Reppert USA July 1997–1998

Verification and Implementation Review

In a thorough review and analysis of US arms control agreements over the past decades, Allan Krass[23] has described the roles of NTM, on-site inspections, and other measures to verify compliance with the agreements by the parties. Krass includes a detailed description of US management of its verification agencies and processes. As Krass reports, an Arms Control Interagency Working Group under the National Security Council has coordinated the overall arms control implementation process with appropriate subcommittees on verification and compliance, nuclear testing, START I implementation, INF treaty implementation, and CFE treaty implementation. Each of these subcommittees involves participation by the DoD, ACDA (now under the Department of State, DOS), DOE, and DOS.

As discussed above, NTM involves input from both technical observations (such as satellites) and from the intelligence community (such as the CIA). The DoD is the primary operating agency for obtaining verification data from such sources as NTM and inspections from OSIA. These extensive verification data (from NTM and OSIs) have been analyzed by the ACIS (Arms Control Intelligence Staff), a small agency created within the CIA but which represents several DoD intelligence agencies. ACIS directly advises the National Security Council (NSC) and participates with ACDA in ACDA's annual compliance report.[23]

The Defense Threat Reduction Agency (DTRA)

Following an initiative put forward by the secretary of defense, elements of the Office of the Secretary of Defense Staff, the Defense Technology Security Administration, the Defense Special Weapons Agency, and the On-Site Inspection Agency consolidated to form DTRA.[24] This consolidation took place on October 1, 1998. The agency is authorized 2088 military and civilian personnel and has an FY 99 budget of $1.8 billion. DTRA is creating[24] the intellectual infrastructure for a "new approach to deter and counter the worldwide proliferation of weapons of mass destruction (WMD)." The DTRA will provide operational and analytical support for nuclear stockpile stewardship duties and technical support for nuclear weapons in DoD custody. The agency will focus DoD efforts to prepare and respond to chemical or biological attacks on US or friendly forces, including overseeing the development and implementation of special weapons technologies. These technologies provide US commanders with (1) options for targeting hardened structures and (2) enhanced ability to assess battle damage. The agency will implement on-site arms-control inspections, escort, and monitoring activities; support arms control confidence-building activities; and develop treaty-verification monitoring technologies.

DTRA will monitor international transfers of US technologies that could be misused to support WMD. The DTRA will implement the Cooperative Threat Reduction Program (Nunn-Lugar, see ch. IX). The DTRA will conduct vulnerability assessments to protect military and civilian personnel from terrorist acts and will also lead DoD efforts to support operational forces and field systems to counter WMD proliferation.

The DTRA director reports to the undersecretary of defense for Acquisition and Technology. The director's advisors include senior officials from DOE, DOS, and the FBI. DTRA is located at Dulles International Airport with field offices in Alexandria and Arlington, VA; Albuquerque, NM; San Francisco, CA; Johnson Atoll; Frankfurt, Germany; Moscow, Russia; and other overseas locations. Dr. Jay C. Davis, a nuclear physicist at Lawrence Livermore National Laboratory who has experience as a UN science advisor, was appointed director of the DTRA, which began formal operations October 1, 1998.

References and Notes

1. Richard A. Scribner, Theodore J. Ralston, and William D. Metz, "The Verification Challenge," Project of the American Association for the Advancement of Science in Cooperation with The Center for International Security and Arms Control, Stanford University, Birkhauser, Boston, MA, 1985.
2. William C. Potter, Ed., "Verification and Arms Control," Lexington Books, DC Heath and Co., Lexington, MA, 1985.
3. Ref. 1, ch. III.
4. Ref. 3, p. 49. In 1960, Gary Powers was shot down over Soviet territory while photographing Soviet military activities from the U-2 he was piloting.
5. Ref. 1, ch. IV.
6. Ref. 1, Harold Brown/SALT II hearings. Also see "The SALT II Treaty," SFRC exec. rept. 96-14, Sect. VII.C, "Verification," November 19, 1979, US GPO, Washington, DC.
7. "The START Treaty," SFRC exec. rept. 102-53, Sect. V, "Verification and Compliance," September 18, 1992, US GPO, Washington, DC.
8. ACDA, 1990 Ed., pp. 336–344.
9. Col. Harold W. Kowalski, "The US Nuclear Risk Reduction Center," NRRC Information Release, US DOS, March 30, 1998. Also see notes from AFCEA Lectures on Arms Control, Fairfax, Virginia, April 1992; lecture on "Nuclear Risk Reduction Center (NRRC)," Colonel Harold W. Kowalski, Jr., staff director of NRRC.
10. See ch. V and VII for discussion of INF treaty and START notifications.
11. See ch. VII for effect of Lisbon Protocol on NRRC notification requirements.
12. Use of NRRC in CFE, Open Skies Treaty, and other arms control agreements, noted in ref. 9.
13. NRRC information release, 1998, ref. 9.
14. Joseph P. Harahan, "On-Site Inspections Under the INF Treaty," US On-Site Inspection Agency, US GPO, Washington, DC, 1993.
15. M. Sgt David M. Willford, USAF, "A Brief History of the On-Site Inspection Agency," OSIA, US DoD, PO Box 17498, Dulles International Airport, Washington, DC, 20041-0498.
16. Richard M. Cole, Ed., "On-Site Insights: 10th Anniversary Commemorative Edition," OSIA, Dulles International Airport, Washington, DC, 20041-0498.

17. See Harahan, ref. 14, pp. 14–23 for early history of establishment of OSIA.
18. Ref. 14, interagency preparations.
19. Ref. 14, mock inspections.
20. Ref. 14, baseline inspections and results.
21. Ref. 15, pp. 22–23; and ref. 14, see CargoScan.
22. The eliminations under the INF treaty were essentially completed by 1991, as discussed in ch. V.
23. Allan S. Krass, *The United States and Arms Control: The Challenge of Leadership*, Praeger Publishers, Westport, CT (1997). Ch. 4 describes in some detail the management and coordination of NTM, inspections, analysis, and compliance decisions by the US government and its agencies.
24. DTRA Fact Sheet, "Defense Threat Reduction Agency," November 13, 1998, Office of Public Affairs, DTRA, 45045 Aviation Drive, Dulles, VA, 20166-7517; "The Defense Threat Reduction Agency," brochure, Office of Public Affairs, DTRA, Dulles, VA; Dick Cole, "Defense Threat Reduction Agency Director Selected," On-Site Insights, Vol. 10, No. 5, May 1998, OSIA, Dulles International Airport, Washington, DC.

Chapter VII

The START I Treaty

The Soviets' dangerous buildup of modern ICBMs with multiple independently-targetable reentry vehicles (MIRVs) and their concurrent deployment of threatening new intermediate-range missile forces (INF) in the late 1970s and early 1980s, as discussed in ch. I, represented a dangerous threat to the United States and Europe.[1] Recognizing the perceived inability of the SALT II treaty to provide effective and verifiable limits to MIRVs with their multiple nuclear warheads, discussed in ch. II, President Reagan proposed a new strategic arms reduction treaty (START) in 1982.[2] His proposal was accompanied by actions and proposals to strengthen US strategic offensive and defensive capabilities.[1]

START I Negotiations

As with the INF treaty (ch. V), Mikhail Gorbachev's accession to power in the USSR in 1985 allowed START to progress. Negotiations on START were conducted by Reagan and Gorbachev in 1985 at Geneva and in 1986 at Reykjavik.[3] At the Reykjavik summit, the two sides agreed on specific limits of 1600 strategic nuclear delivery vehicles (SNDVs, ICBMs, SLBMs, and heavy bombers) and 6000 accountable strategic deliverable warheads. They also agreed on the principle of on-site inspection. Other details were more difficult. The two sides had different force structures, so the issues of sublimits were difficult. Counting rules (such as how many warheads to attribute to a bomber) were introduced to achieve parity. Gorbachev had agreed to the idea of inspections, but it was not until the INF treaty had been signed that the United States could be sure the Soviets would really sign a treaty limiting deployments with effective verification.

At the Washington Summit in 1987 (where the INF treaty was signed), Gorbachev and Reagan agreed to several sublimits: no more than 4900 warheads on ICBMs and SLBMs combined, and no more than 1540 warheads on 154 heavy ICBMs (SS-18s). The history and issues leading to these agreements were reviewed by Garrity.[2]

In January 1985, the United States and the Soviet Union had agreed[3] to resume nuclear arms control under the single format of "Nuclear and Space Talks" (NST) as a result of Soviet concern over the US Strategic Defense Initiative (SDI). The INF and START treaties were subsequently negotiated separately, however.

In 1989, George Bush became president, and with Secretary of State James Baker, continued START negotiations. At the September 1989 meeting of Baker and Shevardnadze at Jackson Hole, Wyoming, the two sides agreed to have mobile missile sublimits and to restrict the mobiles to specific areas. At the 1990 summit meeting of Bush and Gorbachev, the sublimits, as well as the handling of SLCMs (sea launched cruise missiles), had been agreed on.[4,5] Much work remained, including decisions about the specifics of on-site inspections, the notifications protocol, and so forth. Just weeks before the final signing, the two sides were debating provisions such as downloading limits. Issues discussed and resolved during the START I negotiations are reviewed in Chart VII-A.

Finally, in Moscow on July 31, 1991, George Bush and Mikhail Gorbachev signed START, subsequently known as the START I treaty.[6,7] The voluminous treaty reduces deployed strategic delivery vehicles (ICBMs, SLBMs, and heavy bombers) from about 2500 to 1600 for each side. It reduces accountable strategic deployed warheads from about 10,200 to 6000 for each side. Accountable warheads are those defined in the treaty using specified counting rules. They are defined in Chart VII-B. The treaty's data exchange, notification, verification, and on-site inspection procedures were the most comprehensive ever negotiated for a treaty limiting nuclear weapons.[6,7]

The Lisbon Protocol

More effort was required. In December 1991, the USSR broke up into 15 independent republics.[4] Four of these nations contained the strategic nuclear forces covered by START I. These were Russia, Kazakhstan, Belarus, and Ukraine. The critical question as to the legal status of the treaty and the obligations of each of these FSU parties was decided in Lisbon, Portugal, in May 1992. After intense negotiations, Secretary of State James Baker obtained agreement, and the foreign ministers of these four states and Baker signed the Lisbon Protocol[4,8] on May 23. Under the protocol, added to the START I treaty, these four FSU states pledged to assume the obligations of the former USSR under the treaty. Kazakhstan, Belarus, and Ukraine were further pledged to become nonnuclear weapons parties to the NPT. Russia would remain a nuclear weapon state-party to the NPT. The four FSU parties were to make "arrangements among themselves" as necessary to carry out their treaty obligations and provide for implementation of the verification procedures. The protocol called for the four FSU parties to participate with the United States in the Joint Compliance and Inspection Commission (JCIC). The Lisbon Protocol was added to the START I treaty package and submitted to the US Senate and the parliaments of the four FSU states for ratification. The US Senate and the Russian Parliament ratified START I promptly in the Fall of 1992, but, because of problems in Ukraine, it was not until December 1994 that the treaty entered into force (see later section on ratification of START I).

Description of the START I Treaty

As noted previously, START I limits the deployments of each side to 1600 strategic nuclear delivery vehicles (SNDVs) and limits each side to 6000 accountable warheads on these vehicles. The treaty provides for a reduction of deployed heavy ICBMs (Soviet SS-18s) from 308 (with 3080 nuclear warheads) to 154 (with 1540 warheads). Together with other prohibitions, sublimits, and counting rules, the treaty is designed to reduce the number of most threatening deployments capable of a first strike. The limits, prohibitions, sublimits, counting rules, and other restrictions are given in Chart VII-B. The July 1991 strategic nuclear deployments for the United States and USSR are given in the START I Memorandum of Understanding (MOU). The MOU lists the numbers and locations of each type of deployed strategic-range nuclear weapons (ICBMs, SLBMs, and heavy bombers) at each deployment site.

The full text of the START I treaty as signed in 1991 including the treaty, protocols, annexes, MOU, and related agreements, letters, supporting documents, and declarations, are given in ACDA's START I compilation (280 pages), ref. 6. The full treaty text, protocols, and other documents listed in the President's Message delivering the START I treaty to the US Senate (November 1991) are given in ref. 7, which includes the administration's article-by-article analysis. The President's Message submitting the Lisbon Protocol to the US Senate as an amendment to the START I treaty is given in ref. 8.

Upon entry into force (EIF), the treaty provided for initial and then semiannual data exchanges as detailed updates to the inventory given in the MOU. The treaty establishes 82 types of notifications relating to deployments, data updates, movements, dispersals, missile tests, eliminations, and other activities relating to the strategic offensive arms subject to treaty limitation. These notifications are summarized in Chart VII-C. The treaty also establishes cooperative measures such as open displays (with notification) of mobile missile launchers and bombers and prohibitions of interference with national technical means (NTM) of verification. The notifications and cooperative measures are summarized in a previous report on START.[9]

Most notably, the treaty and its protocols establish 12 types of on-site inspections (Chart VII-D) to verify the deployment data given in the MOU and in subsequent notifications. The OSI procedures are described in Charts VII-D, VII-E, VII-F, and VII-G. These procedures are also summarized in detail in refs. 9 and 10. Figure VII.1 illustrates the time line for the conduct of OSIs. The inspection procedures benefit from experience with the INF treaty (ch. V). These OSI procedures combine with NTM and the notification requirements to form what is the most comprehensive verification regime ever negotiated for nuclear weapon limitations.

START I established, in Article XV, a Joint Compliance and Inspection Commission (JCIC) to promote the objectives and implementation of the treaty. The JCIC protocol spells out the procedures for the composition and meetings of the commission. Regular and special meetings of the JCIC may be called at the request of either party. Special or urgent concerns may be brought up at these meetings. The provisions for alleviating concerns include a procedure for a site visit with special right of access. The Lisbon Protocol (described above), signed ten months after the START I treaty was signed, provided for the JCIC to become a five-party body with the United States and with Russia, Ukraine, Kazakhstan, and Belarus assuming the obligations of the former Soviet Union.[8,11]

START I Ratification and Entry into Force (EIF)

With advent of the Lisbon Protocol,[11–13] formal EIF of START I required ratification by the five parties through their appropriate constitutional processes. This turned out to be a long and difficult process.

United States

The US Senate Foreign Relations Committee (SFRC) held hearings on START I after the treaty's initial submission to Congress in November 1991 and held additional hearings after the Lisbon Protocol was signed in May 1992. The final report of the SFRC[14] included recommendations of the Senate Armed Services Committee (SASC) and was submitted in September 1992, endorsing the treaty. After a 2-day debate, the Senate voted 93 to 6 to ratify START I October 1, 1992. This process, key testimony, and the ratification resolution are summarized in ref. 13.

Russia

Almost concurrent with US Senate action, the Supreme Soviet of the Russian Federation (the Russian Parliament of 1992) considered START I and passed a resolution of ratification on November 4, 1992. A condition of the Russian resolution was that EIF of START I "follow accession of Belarus, Kazakhstan, and Ukraine to the Treaty on Nonproliferation of Nuclear Weapons," and follow agreements by Belarus, Kazakhstan, Ukraine, and Russia on procedures for implementation. As we shall see, this condition on the timing of NPT accession delayed the EIF of START I because of objections to NPT accession within Ukraine. The Russian parliamentary resolution for START I ratification is highlighted in Appendix B.

During late 1992 and 1993, concerns continued about the basic stability of the Russian government and other governments within the former Soviet Union (FSU). The Russian government was then considered by many observers to be in grave danger of coming apart.[15]

However, this has not happened, despite subsequent crises.[16] Yeltsin retained the power of the presidency, and Russia affirmed its electoral processes under a new constitution.[17] Kazakhstan, Belarus, and Ukraine retained their governmental stability, and progress was made toward START implementation.

Kazakhstan

In August 1992, the Supreme Soviet of the Republic of Kazakhstan consented to the ratification of START I as amended by the Lisbon protocol.[18] After internal discussions leading to Kazakhstan's non-nuclear status, the Kazakhstan Parliament agreed to accession to the NPT in 1993.[18]

Belarus

On February 3, 1993, the Parliament of Belarus voted 218 to 1 (60 abstentions)[19] to ratify START I. After additional discussions leading to Belarus's nonnuclear status, the Parliament agreed to the accession to the NPT in 1993.[19]

Ukraine

The greatest impediment to START I entry into force came from Ukraine. During 1993, President Kravchuk of Ukraine continued to support the Lisbon Protocol (which he had signed), including the pledge for Ukraine to join the NPT as a nonnuclear weapons state. However, severe economic problems, including high inflation, and related problems within Ukraine, led to constant political strife between Kravchuk, Premier Kuchma, and the Ukrainian Rada (parliament). In November the Rada passed a START I ratification resolution[20] that included several declarations clearly unacceptable to both the United States and Russia.

To alleviate the situation, Presidents Clinton, Yeltsin, and Kravchuk met in a summit in Moscow on January 14, 1994, and signed the Trilateral Agreement,[21] providing financial inducements for Ukraine to properly ratify START I and join the NPT. The Trilateral Agreement provided for Russia to compensate Ukraine the equivalent of up to one billion dollars (US) in return for the approximately 1800 nuclear warheads to be transferred from Ukraine to Russia as part of the

START I agreement and Ukrainian accession to the NPT. The Russian compensation was to be in the form of nuclear fuel assemblies badly needed by Ukraine for its nuclear power industry. The US contribution to the Trilateral Agreement included the earmarking of $60 million, which would be transferred from the United States Enrichment Corporation (USEC)[22] to Russia to facilitate the conversion of highly enriched uranium (HEU) from nuclear warheads into fuel rods for the Ukrainian power plants. President Clinton reaffirmed the US commitments under the Nunn-Lugar program, including $175 million to provide Ukraine with technical assistance in carrying out the nuclear arms control agreements. In the Trilateral Agreement, Presidents Clinton and Yeltsin affirmed that the US and Russian commitments[23] to provide for the security of nonnuclear NPT members would particularly apply to Ukraine as soon as Ukraine had joined the NPT.

The Ukrainian Parliament voted to approve the Trilateral Agreement on February 3, 1994, and voted to remove the 13 negative conditions from its November 1993 ratification of START I. This resolution of ratification was considered acceptable by the other parties, but in a separate action the same day, the Rada failed to muster sufficient votes to adhere to the NPT despite the urgent pleas of President Kravchuk to ratify.[24]

During 1994, Ukrainian internal politics were volatile; a parliamentary election took place in the spring[25] and a presidential election in July, during which Leonid Kuchma emerged as the new president.[26] Kuchma then supported NPT accession and arranged to meet with President Clinton in Washington, November 21 and 22, to clarify and strengthen Ukraine's relationship with the United States [27]

On November 16, 1994, after an emotional appeal by Kuchma, the Ukrainian Parliament overwhelmingly passed an acceptable resolution of ratification of the NPT.[28]

Entry into Force

On December 5, 1994, in Budapest, Hungary, President Clinton and the presidents of Russia, Ukraine, Belarus, and Kazakhstan met and jointly signed the final necessary documents, and START I finally entered into force.[29] Their meeting in Budapest was facilitated by a previously planned European summit on security. Before the final START I signing, Presidents Clinton and Yeltsin, along with Prime Minister Major of the United Kingdom, signed security assurances requested by Ukraine.[29]

The formal entry into force of START I enabled full implementation of the treaty, including the baseline data exchange, subsequent force reductions, notifications, and verification, as described in the next section.

Implementation of START I

A. The JCIC and Early START I Implementation Actions

The JCIC organized and first met in October 1991 as a bilateral body under START I as signed on July 1, 1991. With the advent of the Lisbon Protocol, the JCIC became a five-party body and met and signed a five-party agreement in Geneva, October 23, 1992,[30] to provide formally for the participation of Russia, Ukraine, Kazakhstan, and Belarus. This agreement amended the original JCIC protocol with procedures allowing the representatives of these four FSU states to participate with the United States in the commission. The provisions of this five-party JCIC applied provisionally until START I entered into force, and it has been meeting periodically to resolve issues pertaining to implementation of the treaty.

The JCIC resolves compliance questions, agrees on additional provisions to improve treaty effectiveness, clarifies ambiguities, and determines how to deal with any new kind of strategic weapon declared by a party.

An agreement on Early Exhibitions of Strategic Offensive Arms was signed separately by Secretary of State Baker and Foreign Minister Bessmertnykh on July 31, 1991, as part of the START I package.
It enabled each party to inspect one of each type of ICBM, SLBM, air-launched cruise missile (ALCM), and heavy bomber of the other party. These early exhibitions[31] were carried out between September 1991 and March 1992, adding to the confidence of the parties in the viability of the treaty.

The JCIC held two sessions in 1993, and agreements[32] were reached on the following:

- provision of tapes and analysis of telemetric data;
- procedures for confirmation of dimensions of SLBMs;
- technical specifications for US equipment used for portal perimeter continuous monitoring (PPCM);
- added points of entry for the non-Russian parties for START inspection aircraft and inspectors;
- use of an additional type of inspection aircraft;
- definitions for restrictive zones for submarines during certain SLBM base inspections;
- exhibition of the characteristics of the silo-based variant of the SS-24 at its Pavlograd, Ukraine, production facility; and
- exhibition of a new variant of the road-mobile RS-12M (follow-on to SS-25) at its plant in Votkinsk, Russia.

The JCIC continued to meet in 1994[33] and 1995.[34]

Chart VII-H lists by date and subject the 35 specific agreements and 21 joint statements agreed upon by the five-party JCIC in sessions from October 1992 through December 1995.[35] Each of these agreements and joint statements, ranging in length from one paragraph to several pages, clarifies or amends the detail of START I treaty documents such as the Inspections Protocol, the Notifications Protocol, the Telemetry Protocol, the JCIC Protocol, the MOU, and/or other START I agreement documents.

The JCIC agreements helped pave the way for the baseline data inspections carried out the first several months after START I entry into force and have played a significant role in the subsequent inspections and the general determination of treaty compliance by the parties.

B. START I Data Exchanges and On-Site Inspections

START I provides for extensive specified exchanges of data involving all the treaty-limited items. The MOU, which is part of the START I package signed July 31, 1991, lists the inventories of all types of ICBMs, SLBMs, and heavy bombers at each location of each of the parties. Table 5 lists the overall strategic deployments listed in the July 1991 MOU[36] for the United States and the USSR. When START I entered into force in December 1994, the five parties exchanged their inventory data according to the same categories as in the 1991 MOU, and a site-by-site comparison could be made. Tables 6 through 10 show the overall strategic deployments given from 1994 to 1999.[37] The inventories shown in these tables count a warhead as being an accountable item as long as its delivery vehicle (ICBM, SLBM, or bomber) is still in place, even though the warhead may have been removed. Removing a delivery vehicle from the START I count requires its removal by means of the elimination and/or conversion procedures given in the treaty. These procedures are spelled out in the treaty along with the appropriate notification requirements and on-site inspection procedures (see Chart VII-F for a summary).

In comparing Tables 5 through 10, we note that total countable warheads for the FSU were 10,271 in July 1991 and 9584 in December 1994, decreasing to 7362 in January 1999. For the United States these warhead counts were 10,563 in July 1991 and 8824 in December 1994, decreasing to 7958 in January 1999. By comparing the tables in detail, one can observe the types of weapon systems that have been reduced or eliminated. It is important to note that the reductions are well under way and that the system of notifications and exchange of data is working well.

These data exchanges are important because they give US agencies a database against which to compare information obtained by NTM and by on-site inspections. In the spring of 1995, the FSU deployments reported in the December 1994 data exchange (Table 6) were checked by over 70 on-site baseline data inspections[38,39] at 50 sites by teams from the US OSIA using the START I baseline data inspection procedures. Similar inspections were conducted on US territory by teams from the FSU.

Since completion of the baseline data inspections in July 1995, the other on-site inspections have continued as prescribed by the treaty, including data update inspections, reentry vehicle (RV) inspections, and others as needed.[38]

In its 1995 annual report, the Arms Control and Disarmament Agency (ACDA) evaluated compliance by the four FSU parties to

START I and stated, "The United States is confident that these reductions were accomplished in an irreversible manner."[34]

We note that Table 7 shows that deployment reductions are occurring more rapidly than required by START I (see Chart VIII-A, 3-year START I phase). In January 1996, one year after entry into force, the FSU reported 8625 total accountable warheads. START I allows up to 9150 such warheads by December 1997. US reductions are similar.

START I, now in force for more than 4 years, has demonstrated a practical and workable verification regime with its system of notifications and data exchanges that are verified by OSIs[39] and other means. In its report for 1997, ACDA[40] continued to report effective FSU compliance with START I.

References and Notes

1. Caspar W. Weinberger, "Secretary of Defense Annual Report to Congress, FY 1984," DoD, February 1, 1983, US GPO, Washington, DC.
2. Patrick J. Garrity, "The U.S.-Soviet START Negotiations: Status and Implications," Center for National Security Studies (CNSS) Paper No. 7, Los Alamos National Laboratory report LA-11280-MS, April 1988.
3. Garrity, "START Negotiations," pp. 2–3.
4. James A. Baker, "The Politics of Diplomacy," G. P. Putnam's Sons, New York, NY, 1995.
5. David B. Thomson, "START: A Status Report, September 1990," CNSS Briefing, Vol. 1 No. 6, September 28, 1990, (Los Alamos National Laboratory report).
6. "START: Treaty Between the United States of America and the Union of Soviet Socialist Republics on the Reduction and Limitation of Strategic Offensive Arms," Arms Control and Disarmament Agreements, 1991, US Arms Control and Disarmament Agency, Washington, DC, 280 pp. Includes the complete treaty text, protocols, MOU, and other related documents exchanged at signing.
7. "Message from the President of the U.S. Transmitting the START Treaty, Signed at Moscow on July 31, 1991, Including the Treaty Text, Annexes on Agreed Statements and Definitions, Protocols on Conversion or Elimination, Inspections, Notifications, Throw-Weight, Telemetry, JCIC, and the MOU," 102nd Congress, 1st Session, US Senate Treaty Doc. 102-20, November 25, 1991. Includes the complete text of the treaty and the related treaty documents. The MOU gives the complete inventories of deployed strategic nuclear weapons and treaty-limited items by category and location as reported at treaty signing. The president's message (1101 pp.) also includes an article-by-article analysis of the treaty text and the transmittal letters by President Bush and Secretary of State Baker.
8. "Message from the President of the United States to the US Senate Transmitting the Protocol to the START Treaty, Signed at Lisbon, Portugal, on May 23, 1992," US Senate Treaty Document 102-32, June 23, 1992.
9. David B. Thomson, "The Strategic Arms Reduction Treaty and Its Verification," CNSS, Los Alamos National Laboratory report LA-12364 (July 1992).
10. David B. Thomson, "The START Treaties: Implementation and Status," Center for International Security Affairs (CISA), Los Alamos National Laboratory report LA-UR-97-2045 (May 1997).

11. Linton F. Brooks, "Strategic Nuclear Arms Control: Status and Prospects," CNSS Briefing, Vol. 5, No. 1, Los Alamos National Laboratory report (March 25, 1994), LA-UR-94-952.
12. James A. Baker, "The START Protocol," ref. 4, pp. 658–665.
13. David B. Thomson, "The START Treaties: A Status Report," CNSS briefing, Vol. 4, No. 1 (April 26, 1993), LA-UR-93-1381.
14. "The START Treaty," SFRC, exec. report 102-53, September 18, 1992, (U.S. Senate).
15. Peter Reddaway, "Russia on the Brink?" *The New York Review of Books*, January 28, 1993, pp. 30–35.
16. In the early fall of 1993, President Yeltsin dissolved the Russian Parliament in an action that involved military action, including the surrounding of the Parliament building by the army.
17. A new constitution was adopted by Russian voters in December 1993. See Sonni Efron, Moscow "Constitution Vulnerable after Tepid Turnout," *Los Angeles Times*, December 13, 1993. LEXIS-NEXIS. For text of this constitution, see transcript by federal news service, Washington, DC, November 9, 1993.
18. The Kazakhstan government ratified START in 1992 and ratified the Treaty on the Nonproliferation of Nuclear Weapons (NPT) following a parliamentary vote of 238 to 1 in favor in late 1993. See Richard L. Berke, "Kazakhstan Signs a Pact on A-Arms," *New York Times International*, December 14, 1993.
19. Rostislav Khotin, "Belarussian Parliament Ratifies START I Treaty," Reuters World Service, Dateline: Minsk, Belarus, February 4, 1993. Belarus acceded to the Treaty on the Nonproliferation of Nuclear Weapons (NPT) in July, 1993, US DOS dispatch, August 9, 1993, Vol. 4, No. 32, p. 565.
20. Spurgeon M. Keeney, "The Rada Throws Down the Gauntlet," *Arms Control Today*, December 1993, p. 2.
21. Dunbar Lockwood, "U.S. Reaches Understanding with Ukraine, Russia on Denuclearization," *Arms Control Today*, Vol. 24, No. 1, January/February 1994, pp. 19–23. In an annex to the Trilateral Agreement, the three presidents stated that the first 200 warheads would be transferred to Russia and the equivalent fuel rods supplied to Ukraine by November 1994, in time to meet urgent winter fuel needs.
22. The USEC is a quasi-public corporation under the auspices of the DOE formed to facilitate the US-Russian agreement to transfer weapons-grade uranium to nonweapons nuclear fuel.

23. In the negotiation of the NPT, the nuclear weapons state members agreed to provide security assurances (through the UN Security Council) to any nonnuclear NPT member threatened by nuclear weapons. "Arms Control and Disarmament Agreements," 1982 ed., US ACDA, pp. 82–98.
24. Robert Seely, "A-Arms Pact Approved in Ukraine," *The Washington Post*, February 4, 1994. See also White House Press Conference report on the meeting of President Clinton and President Kravchuk (of Ukraine), March 4, 1994.
25. F. Stephen Larrabee, "Ukraine: Europe's Next Crisis?" *Arms Control Today*, Vol. 24, No. 6, July/August 1994, pp. 14–19.
26. Dunbar Lockwood, "Kuchma Reverses Field on NPT, Ready to Seek Vote in Parliament," *Arms Control Today*, Vol. 24, No. 7, September 1994, pp. 25–32.
27. "Joint Summit Statement by President Clinton and Ukraine President Kuchma," and fact sheet, Office of the Press Secretary, the White House, November 22, 1994.
28. James Rupert, "Ukraine Joins Treaty Curbing Nuclear Arms," *The Washington Post*, November 17, 1994.
29. START I enters into force, December 1994. See "The White House, Office of the Press Secretary, Budapest, Hungary, December 5, 1994, White House News Conference, (Budapest Congress Center and the Helia Hotel, Budapest), December 5, 1994; background briefing, Office of the Press Secretary, the White House, December 5, 1994; Also see NY Times News Service, Jane Perlez, "START Treaty Allowed to come Into Force," Budapest, Hungary, December 5, 1994. The security assurances were pledges by the US, UK, and Russia to respect the territorial integrity of Ukraine and refrain from economic coercion.
30. ITAR-TASS World Service, Moscow, October 23, 1992, JPRS-TAC-92-032, November 4, 1992, p. 17.
31. See testimony of Major General Robert W. Parker, director of US On-Site Inspection Agency (OSIA), SFRC hearing on START, U.S. Senate Doc. 102-607, June 30, 1992, pp. 168–191.
32. "Annual Report to Congress for 1993," US ACDA, Washington, DC.
33. "Annual Report to Congress for 1994," US ACDA,, Washington, DC.
34. "Annual Report to Congress for 1995," US ACDA, Washington, DC.
35. Text of JCIC Agreements, 1992–1995, released by Bureau of Public Affairs, ACDA, 1996.

36. "Memorandum of Understanding (MOU) on the Establishment of the Data Base," signed July 31, 1991, as part of the START treaty package; see ref. 6.
37. Table 6 is obtained from the data exchanged and transmitted by the parties according to the categories of the START treaty and the MOU (see refs. 6 and 36) for the US, Russian Federation, Ukraine, Republic of Kazakhstan, and Republic of Belarus, effective December 5, 1994, at the time of START I entry into force. Table 7 is obtained from the data transmitted by the parties according to the categories of the START treaty and the MOU for the US, Russian Federation, Ukraine, Republic of Kazakhstan, and Republic of Belarus, effective January 1, 1996. Table 8 was obtained from the data transmitted by the same parties, effective January 1, 1997. Table 9 was obtained from the data transmittal by the parties, effective January 1, 1998. Table 10 was obtained from the data transmitted by the parties January 1, 1999. For each data exchange and as agreed by the parties, three months after transmittal, these data were released by the Bureau of Public Affairs, US Arms Control and Disarmament Agency (ACDA).
38. "On-Site Insights," Vol. 7, Nos. 4, 6, and 7; July, p. 14; August, p. 8; and September 1995; US OSIA, Washington, DC. Baseline data inspections occurred from March 1 through July 1, 1995. The US conducted 73 such inspections on FSU territory.
39. Brig. General Gregory G. Govan (OSIA director, 1993–1995), "An In-Depth Look at On-Site Inspections," an interview by Jack Mendelsohn and Sarah Walkling, *Arms Control Today*, September 1995, pp. 15–19.
40. "Annual Report to Congress for 1997," (issued July 7, 1998), ACDA, Washington, DC.

CHART VII-A.
Some START I Issues During Negotiations

START PRINCIPLE

At Geneva, 1985, the United States and the USSR agreed to cut strategic nuclear arms by nearly 50%. Strategic delivery vehicles are defined as capable of reaching one of the parties from bases on the home soil of the other (intercontinental capability).

OVERALL LIMITS

At Reykjavik, 1986, the sides agreed to specific overall limits of no more than 1600 strategic nuclear delivery vehicles (ICBMs, SLBMs, and heavy bombers) for each side; and no more than 6000 accountable nuclear warheads on these strategic range vehicles. At this time, the sides each had just over 10,000 such warheads deployed. The sides agreed to the general principle of reducing first-strike capabilities with remaining weapons being for deterrence or retaliation. The stated goal of each side was to reduce the dangers of any nuclear war occurring since such a war would cause untold devastation. The sides also wanted to reduce the high costs of the arms buildup, so the new ceilings, lower than SALT II, were to be achieved by eliminations. Nevertheless, some new production and modernization was underway in both the United States and the USSR with the MX ICBM (for the United States) and the SS-24 and SS-25 rail and road mobile missiles (for the USSR). Replacement and some modernization was allowed in the final treaty signed in 1991.

BALLISTIC MISSILE LIMITS

Both sides agreed that strategic-range ballistic missiles were among the most threatening weapons. In Washington, 1987, both sides agreed to ballistic missile sublimits:

- No more than 4900 warheads on ICBMs and SLBMs combined
- No more than 1540 warheads on 154 heavy ICBMs (SS-18, the only defined "heavy")

MAJOR WEAPON-TYPE ISSUES

Heavy ICBMs

Large deployments and high throw-weight of Soviet heavy ICBMs (SS-18s, 10 MIRVed warheads each) were viewed by the United States as dangerously threatening because they were specifically designed to destroy US ICBM sites and other hard targets giving them high first strike capability. The Soviet, fixed silo-based, MIRVed ICBMs could also be destroyed by a US attack. Thus, such weapons could lead to crisis instability which may occur if one or both sides believe a decisive advantage is gained by striking first, or if a party believes the other side is about to strike first. Heavy ICBMs are defined as any ballistic missile with a launch weight and throw weight greater than the SS-19 (which in 1990, and thereafter, included only the SS-18). In 1987, the Soviets agreed, for START I, to cut SS-18 deployments in half (from 308 SS-18s to 154). In START I it was also agreed to prohibit new-type heavy ICBMs and prohibit any heavy SLBMs. In START II (1993), the Russians agreed to reduce SS-18s to zero.

Mobile ICBMs

In 1982, the United States had insisted that mobile ICBMs (such as the Soviet road mobile SS-25, 1 RV each; and Soviet rail mobile SS-24, 10 MIRVed warheads each) were too difficult to verify by NTM and should be banned. The Soviets, with much investment in these newer weapons, insisted on keeping them. By the September 1989 foreign ministers meeting (Jackson Hole, Wyoming) the sides had agreed there would be a sub limit of warheads on mobiles, limited allowed areas for deployment, and on-site inspections within deployment areas. The final START I treaty provided specific allowed deployment areas (Chart VII-B, and OSI procedures Chart VII-E) for mobile ICBMs, and provided a sub limit of 1100 warheads deployed on such mobiles.

Bomber and ALCM Limits

At the 1987 Washington Summit, the parties agreed that nuclear armed heavy bombers would each count as one SNDV and that each bomber would count as only one warhead (against the 6000 WH limit) if loaded with gravity bombs or SRAMs but not ALCMs. The United States regarded bombers with only gravity bombs or SRAMs as stabilizing compared to ICBMs; thus, the counting rule of one such bomber counts as only one warhead against the 6000 WH limit, regardless of the number of bombs on board. In the final treaty, the sides agreed on rules that provided an ALCM-equipped-bomber sub limit of 150 for the United States, and 180 for the USSR (Chart VII-B). This was to encourage the USSR to use more of their 1600 SNDV total in bombers rather than ICBM and SLBM deployments, further reducing first-strike capabilities. An agreed counting rule is that each US ALCM-equipped bomber will count as 10 WHs (against the 6000 limit) and only 8 per ALCM-equipped bomber for the USSR, regardless of the number on board. This recognizes the differences in designed ALCM capacities for the two parties. An additional sublimit is ≤20 ALCMs for any bomber for the US, and ≤12 for any bomber for the USSR (Chart VII-B). The range above which an ALCM would be considered a "long- range" ALCM and counted as such in START I was negotiated to be 600 km.

SLCMs

At Jackson Hole, September 1989, Shevardnadze[4] dropped the previous USSR insistence that sea-launched cruise missiles (SLCMs) should be numerically limited within the treaty and subject to "on-board" inspection. The US Navy strongly objected to such inspection of US naval vessels since it had plans for deploying thousands of non-nuclear cruise missiles (as used in the 1991 Gulf War) as well as a limited number of nuclear armed SLCMs. The compromise was to use declaratory limits for the SLCMs that are separate from the 1600/6000 limit. In the final treaty package[6,7] SLCMs are dealt with by separate declarations by each of the two parties that declare the number of SLCMs, of range greater than 600 km, possessed by the party. These declarations are to be exchanged annually, and neither party is to possess more than 880 such nuclear armed SLCMs. At treaty EIF, each side was to provide the other confidential information as to the particular types of naval vessels capable of carrying such SLCMs. The declarations also provide that each party annually receive from the other confidential information as to the number of shorter range nuclear armed SLCMs (range between 300 and 600 km.) deployed on its naval vessels. These confidential data exchanges began with treaty EIF and continue annually for the duration of the treaty. Verification of the declaratory limit of 880 SLCMs is by NTM, with cooperative measures suggested by the agreement language. This agreement was a major step towards achieving START I.

ABM Systems (SDI)

Following agreement at Jackson Hole,[4] by June 1990 the USSR had dropped its insistence that START I would only be acceptable if the US would accept strict limits on strategic defense research (SDI). This issue had been contentious at the Reykjavik Summit (1986) and later became an issue in Duma consideration of START II (ch. VIII).

DEPLOYMENT ISSUES

Phased Reductions

By June 1990 the sides had agreed to reduce to the agreed limits within seven years of EIF, with reductions taking place in three phases with agreed levels at the end of each phase.

Warhead Sublimits

As of 1990, the United States wanted an ICBM sublimit of ~3300 warheads. The USSR wanted a similar sublimit for SLBM warheads. The final treaty only provided a combined sublimit of 4900 warheads on ICBMs plus SLBMs, along with the mobile and heavy ICBM sublimits (Chart VII-B).

Throw-Weight Limit

By June 1990, the sides agreed to limit total throw-weight to 50% of the USSR value, but the USSR wanted to use their value at the time of signing, giving them a higher value than their value for an earlier time. The final treaty limited throw-weight at 3600 metric tons.

Modernization

By June 1990 the sides had agreed that new types of heavy ICBMs and new types of ICBMs and SLBMs with more than ten RVs would be banned. Otherwise, modernization and replacement of existing strategic arms would be allowed. Final language was not ready for the 1990 summit but was given in the treaty in 1991 (Chart VII-B).

Nondeployed Missiles

By June 1990 the parties had agreed that there would be number limits on non deployed missiles for any type of missile that had been launched from a mobile launcher, but no limits on non deployed missiles of other types. Non deployed mobile ICBMs are to be stored separately and outside allowed mobile missile areas. The number of non deployed mobiles was not agreed till final signing (Chart VII-B). No provision deals with nuclear warheads themselves.

Rapid Reload

Rapid reload capability was prohibited because the US regarded this as particularly threatening and amenable to aggressive strategies.

VERIFICATION ISSUES AND DETAILS

Eliminations

By June 1990, the parties had agreed that TLI eliminations would be verified, but many details of the OSIs were not resolved until the July 1991 signing.

Challenge Inspections

The June 1990 Joint Summit Statement specified that short notice OSIs would be used to help verify inventories, but treaty language was not agreed until the final months (or weeks) before signing.

Suspect Sites

Suspect site inspections were discussed until final treaty signing. The USSR agreed only that each party has the right to determine by OSI that covert assembly of mobile ICBMs is not occurring at a facility declared as not producing mobiles. These OSIs may take place only at any of three (for each party) facilities so designated in the MOU. In the final treaty, no OSI procedure is given for sites, not declared in the MOU, that may become suspect as harboring deployed SNDVs. In START, such cases require NTM for detection and discussion in the JCIC for resolution. The JCIC Protocol does provide for a site "visit with special right of access" that addresses such concerns.

Mobile ICBMs

By June 1990, the sides had agreed that mobile ICBMs would be deployed only in specified areas of limited size. The size of the areas and OSI procedures were negotiated in the months before signing.

Nuclear Armed ALCMS and Bombers

Wording for distinguishing between nuclear and nonnuclear armed ALCMs and bombers was discussed and negotiated during the final months before signing.

CHART VII-B.
START I Limitations[6]

Principal Treaty Limits	
Strategic nuclear delivery vehicles (SNDVs)	1600 (ICBMs, SLBMs, bombers) ("Strategic" means those of intercontinental range. All such arms are limited, whether WHs are nuclear or not. See article-by-article analysis, ref. 7.)
Heavy ICBMs	154
Total nuclear warheads	6000 (accountable deployed strategic nuclear warheads)
Ballistic Missile warheads	4900 (ICBMs and SLBMs)
Warheads on heavy ICBMs	1540
Warheads on mobile ICBMs	1100
Throw-weight in metric tons	3600 (aggregate total for all deployed ICBMs and SLBMs)
Definitions and Counting	
SNDV	ICBM and associated launcher, SLBM and associated launcher, heavy bomber (nuclear armed)
Accountable warhead	Any nuclear warhead deployed on an ICBM, SLBM, mobile ICBM, or ALCM with a range greater than 600 kilometers. A heavy bomber armed only with gravity bombs or SRAMs counts as only one warhead.
Heavy ICBM (or SLBM)	Any ICBM with throw-weight greater than that of the Soviet SS-19 (4350 kilograms); this applies only to the Soviet SS-18 and to no US missiles.
Bomber counting rules	The first 150 US (180 for the USSR) bombers armed with ALCMs will count as having only 10 ALCMs (for US) or 8 ALCMs (for USSR), regardless of the number on board. Above the 150/180 bomber limits, each bomber will be counted as having the actual number of ALCMs for which it is equipped.

CHART VII-B. (Cont.)
START I Limitations[6]

Definitions and Counting

Major Prohibitions:	No new-type heavy ICBMs No heavy SLBMs or launchers No mobile launchers of heavy ICBMs; no rapid reload of ICBM launchers No long range ALCMs with multiple warheads No new-type ballistic missiles with >10 RVs

Additional Sublimits

For deployed nuclear systems	No more than 20 ALCMs for any US bomber No more than 16 ALCMs for any USSR bomber No more than 10 RVs per ICBM or SLBM
For nondeployed mobiles	No more than 250 ICBMs of types flight tested from mobile launchers (up to 125 of these may be rail mobile)
For nonnuclear heavy bombers (HBs)	Up to 75 HBs may be removed from the SNDV and warhead (WH) counts if converted to nonnuclear weapons only. There may also be no more than 20 test HBs.

Other Features

Nondeployed WHs	There is *no* limit on the total number of nondeployed warheads.
Declaratory limits (SLCMs)	Nuclear armed SLCMS do not count in the total SNDV/WH counts (1600/6000) but are limited by separate declaratory limits of 880 for each side, to be declared annually, not subject to on-board inspection. SLCMs are counted if the range is >600 km.

CHART VII-B. (Cont.)
START I Limitations[6]

Other Features (Cont.)

Downloading	There may be no more than 1250 "empty spaces," reducing the START RV count on ballistic missiles with specified MIRV capabilities. See Sect. 5, Art. III of treaty. RV platform replacements specified. The US may download MM III plus only two other types. Russia may download the SS-N-18 plus only two other types. A downloaded MM III, or any other missile reduced more than two RVs must have a new RV platform with the old one destroyed. Only missiles with same number of RVs (WHs) may be deployed at any one ICBM or SLBM base. For any ICBM or SLBM, may not download by more than 4, from the number attributed at date of treaty signature. May not download new types of missiles.
Modernization	Modernization of strategic nuclear forces may be undertaken by each side except as specifically prohibited.
Heavy ICBM reductions	The Soviets will eliminate 22 SS-18 heavy ICBMs each year for the first 7 years of the treaty to reduce to the 154 limit. Heavy ICBMs may not be downloaded.
Duration and timing	The sides will reduce their deployments in three phases over 7 years (to agreed levels at the end of each phase—see Chart E) to reach the final START deployment limits. The treaty will remain in force for 15 years unless superseded. It may be renewed thereafter at 5-year intervals.
Reduction methods	Deployment reductions will be achieved by eliminations and/or conversions as spelled out in the protocols.

CHART VII-B. (Cont.)
START I Limitations[6]

Other Features (Cont.)

Restricted Areas (road-mobile missiles)	Deployed road-mobile missiles and launchers shall be deployed only in restricted areas of 5 sq km or less, which may contain up to 10 mobile ICBMs of only one type. Each restricted area must be in a specified deployment area of 125,000 sq km or less. Such deployment areas may contain one ICBM base, one maintenance facility, and one or more specified restricted areas. No more than 15 percent of the road-mobile missiles may be outside the restricted areas at one time except during an operational dispersal.
Restricted Rail Garrisons (rail-mobile missiles)	Deployed rail-mobile launchers and missiles shall be based only in rail garrisons. A rail garrison is an area in which one or more parking sites for rail-mobile launcher trains may be located. No point on a portion of track located inside a rail garrison shall be more than 20 km (along the track) from any exit/entrance for that rail garrison. Each party is limited to seven rail garrisons, and no more than 20 percent of the rail-mobile missiles may be outside the garrisons at one time except during operational dispersals.
Dispersals	The treaty provides for exercise dispersals and strategic exercises during which mobile missiles may be moved outside their restricted areas for training, maintenance, and major strategic exercises (only once a year).

CHART VII-B. (Cont.)
START I Limitations[6]

Other Features (Cont.)	
Dispersals (Cont.)	The treaty also allows for operational dispersals involving all their mobile missiles. These dispersals may be conducted if either party considers the survivability of its strategic forces at risk. The other party must be notified within 18 hours of the initiation of the dispersal. Such dispersals are to be used only rarely and in a crisis. Upon completion, all inspections and cooperative measures that could have otherwise occurred are to be allowed, plus two additional cooperative measure displays.

CHART VII-C.
Summary of START I Notifications

Treaty Article VIII and the Protocol on Notifications spell out the 82 types of specific notifications on deployments, movements, and missile tests that are called for in START I.[6,7] An additional 22 types of notifications are spelled out in the Protocol on Inspections and Continuous Monitoring. All notifications are exchanged through the NRRCs (ch. VI). Each party provides the same type notifications to the other party. Nearly all of the notifications involve time limits.

The types of notifications are grouped into ten categories, as follows:

1. Inventory Data

   Provides for data exchanges of inventory data of deployed TLIs (treaty-limited items; ICBMs, SLBMs, heavy bombers, ALCMs, launchers, etc.). Within thirty days of EIF, each party must provide current deployment data for each category of data given in the MOU. This includes the number, type, and location of each type of TLI (ICBMs, SLBMs, bombers, bombers with ALCMs, launchers, etc.). Second notification provides that each six months thereafter updated data for each category in MOU shall be provided. Third notification provides for notification of any change in deployed TLI inventory within five days of occurrence. A total of 18 types of notifications report updates or changes to previous data or other MOU conditions.

2. Movements of ICBMs or Bombers

   These involve general movements of ICBMs and heavy bombers among deployment locations, test sites, assembly facilities and air bases. These may contribute to understanding of movements observed by NTM. For example, <48 hrs after completion, party must notify transit of nondeployed BMs, mobile launch canisters after tests, etc. Other notifications involve beginning/completion of exercise dispersals of mobile ICBMs and bombers, etc. There are 17 types of such notifications.

3. Notifications of Throw-Weight Data

   These involve ICBM and SLBM flight tests. For example, <7 days in advance, must provide notification of the each new-type ICBM/ SLBM , including throw weight demonstrated in first seven tests and other data. There are four types of such notifications.

4. Conversions/Eliminations

   Each TLI to be eliminated, or converted to non-treaty-limited status (such as converting nuclear armed bomber to nonnuclear armed) involves options which are specified in the Protocol on Eliminations and Conversions. Seven types of notifications are involved in specifying the chosen options for the TLIs to be removed from the inventory count by elimination/conversion.

5. Notifications for Cooperative Measures to Enhance NTM

   The verifying party may request a display of specific mobile missiles or heavy bombers at specified bases at specified times. A party must notify the other, within 24 hours, of the exit of a submarine from a covered facility in which conversion of SLBM launchers was carried out. There are five types of such notifications.

6. Flight Tests of ICBMS/SLBMS and Telemetric Information

   Notice of any flight test of an ICBM or SLBM must be provided, including launch date, launch area, RV impact area, telemetry broadcast frequencies, plans for encryption, etc. There are five kinds of these notifications.

7. New-Type Strategic Offensive Arms

   There are 16 types of notifications concerning development of new types of strategic offensive arms (ICBMs, mobile ICBMs, SLBMs, bombers, ALCMs, etc.). For example, each party must provide notice, <48 hrs in advance, of planned exit from production facility of first prototype of new type or new kind of ICBM or SLBM. Must include length, diameter, weight, calculated throw-weight, and name/location of the production facility.

8. Change of Notification on Movements or Conversion/Elimination

   Two types of these notifications.

9. OSIs and PPCM

   Notifications concerning on-site inspections and Portal Perimeter Continuous Monitoring (PPCM) activities, including notice of short notice OSIs, are given in detail in Section III of the Protocol on Inspections and Continuous Monitoring. OSIs are summarized in detail in Charts VII-D, E, F, and G. There are 22 types of notifications on OSIs and PPCM.

10. Operational Dispersals

    Each party may conduct operational dispersals of its strategic forces (see Chart VII-B). The party conducting the dispersal must notify the other party as provided by one or more of seven types of notifications in this section. For example, a party must provide notice <18 hrs. after start of operational dispersal of its mobile ICBMs, including the date, time, and reason for the dispersal.

Notification Regime

Most, or all of the notification types listed above and specified in the Notifications Protocol serve as important triggers to the various monitoring and verification mechanisms. Movements or tests of ICBMs, etc., may be observed by NTM satellites or detectors in response to the notification. The verifying party will frequently have the option to request open displays at specific missile or bomber bases at strategic times. Decisions to conduct OSIs may be made in response to certain notifications and in coordination with the inflow of information from NTM. Taken together, the 82 types of notifications, obtained through the efficiently operating NRRCs, provide a valuable addition to the overall START verification regime.

CHART VII-D.
Types of Inspections Defined in START I

Article XI of the START I treaty, and its Protocol on Inspections and Continuous Monitoring spell out the general categories of on-site inspections (OSIs) and Portal Perimeter Continuous Monitoring (PPCM). OSIs and PPCMs are allowed at facilities designated in the Memorandum of Understanding (MOU).[6,7]

The types of OSIs and PPCMs are summarized here.

Baseline Data Inspections

Conducted to validate the initial inventory data exchange and make baseline measurements (missile dimensions, etc.) of TLIs. The baseline inspections (conducted in 1995 as described in Chapter VII text) were conducted at ICBM bases, SLBM bases, bomber bases, storage and other facilities specified in MOU.

Data Update Inspections

Conducted to confirm accuracy of existing TLI inventories as provided in the regular exchanges of updated data called for each six months after EIF (Chart VII-C, Notifications). May be conducted at ICBM, SLBM, and bomber bases and other facilities listed in the MOU, as above. There may be as many as 15 data-update OSIs per year.

New Facility Inspections

When new facilities are listed in notifications, they are subject to OSIs to confirm numbers and types of TLIs specified.

Suspect Site Inspections (SSI)

Inspecting party has right to conduct inspections to confirm that covert assembly of mobile ICBMs or first stages of mobile ICBMs is not occurring at a suspect site not specified as producing mobile ICBMs. These inspections may be conducted only at agreed sites listed in the MOU (three for each side). Each SSI counts against the quota of 15 data-update inspections per year.

Reentry Vehicle (RV) Inspections

OSIs are permitted to confirm that the number of RVs (1 warhead each) deployed on ballistic missiles are as stated in the MOU and subsequent notifications. This is done by removing the shroud (RV cover) and allowing observations of the front-end of the missile using procedures that prevent the inspectors from seeing the details of the warheads or bus. There may be up to ten RV inspections per year.

Post-Exercise Dispersal Inspections

OSIs may be conducted after an allowed and notified dispersal exercise of mobile ICBMs to determine that the specified number of mobiles have returned to the base, and to determine that the total at the base does not exceed the number allowed and specified.

Conversion or Elimination Inspections

Conversions or eliminations for mobile ICBMs and launchers, heavy bombers, or SLBM launchers are carried out at specified conversion/elimination facilities. After notification of a scheduled conversion or elimination, NTM and/or OSIs may be conducted by the inspecting party to observe the elimination or confirm the conversion to treaty allowed uses. In START I, elimination of ICBM silo launchers is conducted on-site with advance notification and observed only by NTM (see Chart VII-F).

Close-Out Inspections

Conducted to determine that treaty limited activities have ceased at a site declared to be eliminated or converted to allowed uses. The OSI will confer the appropriate change of status.

Formerly Declared Facility Inspections

After a period of close-out inspections for an eliminated/converted facility, the inspecting party may conduct up to three formerly declared facility OSIs per year to confirm this status.

Technical Characteristics Exhibitions for ICBMs and SLBMs

Each side must conduct an exhibition of the technical characteristics (length, diameter, shape, weight, and other observable features listed in the MOU, etc.) for one of each type and variant of ICBM, SLBM, and mobile ICBM launcher limited by START. The other party may conduct an OSI for each exhibition to confirm the declared characteristics.

Distinguishability Exhibitions for Heavy Bombers and ALCMs

Each party must conduct exhibitions for heavy bombers, former heavy bombers, and long-range nuclear-armed (strategic) ALCMs. The other party may conduct OSIs to confirm the data, given in the MOU and subsequently, as to the distinguishing features of heavy bombers equipped for strategic ALCMs, heavy bombers equipped only for nuclear armaments (bombs and SRAMs) other than strategic ALCMs, and long-range nuclear-armed ALCMs. These OSIs also are to confirm the maximum number of ALCMs for which each type heavy bomber is actually equipped.

Baseline Exhibitions for Nonnuclear Heavy Bombers

Each party must conduct baseline exhibitions of all types of heavy bombers equipped for nonnuclear armaments, training heavy bombers, and former heavy bombers specified in the initial data exchange.

The other party may conduct inspections of these bombers to confirm that such bombers satisfy the requirements for conversion to nonnuclear weapons use as given in the conversion/elimination protocol.

Perimeter Portal Continuous Monitoring (PPCM)

Each party may conduct PPCM at mobile-missile production facilities to confirm the number of mobile ICBMs produced that exit the facility. Using TV cameras, infrared sensors, and other equipment, the inspectors establish continuous monitoring of the perimeter of the entire facility or site, and observe all candidate TLIs entering or leaving the facility. PPCM of production facilities may continue as long as the facility is active and the treaty is in effect.

CHART VII-E.
On-Site Inspections of Deployments (START I)

Weapons Site	Type of Inspection[a]	OSI Observations/Techniques
ICBM silo base	Baseline data, data update, new facility, and close-out	Observe ICBM locations at site; observe selected silos and ICBMs; measure dimensions as needed; observe inside containers as needed; obtain photographs;[b] compare data with reference data[c]
ICBM mobile-missile site (road-mobile, rail-mobile)	Baseline data, data update, new facility, and close-out	Host has moved mobile missiles to be within restricted areas; for OSI, inspection team posts perimeter monitor; team observes, reads tags, and counts declared ICBMs; team observes selected missiles and launchers and measures dimensions as needed; team observes inside containers as needed; team obtains[b] photographs; team compares data with reference data[c,d]
SLBM submarine base	Baseline data, data update, new facility, and close-out	Host displays requested submarines by type; team counts submarines by type; host opens specific tubes on request; team measures SLBM dimensions; team obtains photographs[b] as needed; team compares data with references[c]
ICBM and SLBM bases; mobile-missile bases	RV inspections	Team selects ICBM/SLBM at site; missile is moved by host for observation and front section prepared (as team observes); host opens shroud; team counts RVs

CHART VII-E. (Cont.).
On-Site Inspections of Deployments (START I)

Weapons Site	Type of Inspection[a]	OSI Observations/Techniques
Heavy-bomber bases (includes weapon storage areas)	Baseline data, data update, new facility, and close-out	Host exhibits bombers at base by type; team inspects one bomber of each type; team observes distinguishing features of bombers and ALCMs, then compares with reference data;[c] photographs[b] are taken; in weapon storage areas team may use neutron detector if nuclear ALCMs are declared nonnuclear; team counts inventories of each type of nuclear-armed bomber and ALCM
Mobile-missile bases	Post-exercise dispersal	Team posts perimeter monitor around restricted area; team counts missiles and launchers within allowed areas, using procedures similar to data update inspections for mobile missiles, as above
Any of above bases after completion of close-out inspections	Formerly declared facilities	Team conducts OSIs for treaty limited items (TLIs) using procedures for data update OSI for the appropriate categories

[a] The types of inspections, defined in START, are listed in Charts VII-D and G of this report.

[b] May request photographs if there are ambiguities.

[c] Reference data includes MOU and data given in subsequent notifications and declarations.

[d] Must include all deployed road missiles assigned to a specified site. Rail-mobile missiles are restricted to rail garrisons and inspected in a similar way.

CHART VII-F.
Conversion, Elimination, and Verification Procedures (START I)

Weapons System	Conversions/ Elimination Procedures	Verification
ICBM silos	Missiles and other equipment not to be eliminated are removed more than 1000 m from the silo; eliminate the silo by excavation to 8 m or explosion to a depth of 6 m	NTM and cooperative measures only; observe with satellite photos, etc.; other side provides notifications of each step; silo area must be visible for entire process plus 90 days
SLBM launchers	Submarine moved to elimination facility; all SLBMs removed, in the open; remove complete missile sections or all launch tubes and superstructure; all removed launch tubes are cut in half; thereafter, submarine may be used only for uses other than SNDV carriers	NTM and cooperative measures only; observe with satellite photos etc.; other side notifies and keeps process visible for start and for 10 days thereafter
Mobile ICBMs and launch canisters	Remove RVs, guidance and control systems; may remove propellant, penetration aids, etc., before OSI; launchers, canisters, stages, and motors are destroyed by demolition or crushing; RV platform, rocket nozzles, etc., are cut into pieces	OSI team arrives by standard procedures, confirms types of missiles to be eliminated; team observes entire elimination process; team leader and host write report confirming elimination
Mobile launchers and related structures	Road-erector launchers and rail-car launchers cut into two pieces; other hardware and structures similarly eliminated	OSI team arrives as above; team observes entire elimination process; report is written

CHART VII-F. (Cont.)
Conversion, Elimination, and Verification Procedures (START I)

Weapons System	Conversions/ Elimination Procedures	Verification
Heavy bombers, former heavy bombers (elimination)	Before OSI, engines and equipment not part of airframe are removed; for elimination: tail is severed, wings are removed, fuselage is cut in two pieces	NTM, with notification, observes entire process; may make OSI by request; procedures similar to above
Heavy bombers (conversion)	Bombers with long-range nuclear ALCMs may be converted to nuclear non-ALCM bombers. Nuclear-armed bombers may be converted to nonnuclear. Details are specified in the elimination/conversion protocol (see ref. 10).	NTM with notifications; OSI may be requested at a particular site; procedures similar to above

CHART VII-G.
On-Site Inspections under START I and II

Type Inspection[a]	OSIs	Sites	START I	START II
Baseline data (≤165 days after EIF)	≤10 at once	BM, HB	yes	yes
Data update	15/year	BM, HB	yes	yes
New facility	1 each facility	BM, HB	yes	yes
Suspect site	≤2 each	MOU 7/91	yes	yes
RV	10 per year	ICBM, SLBM	yes	4 added RV OSIs per year
Post-exercise dispersal	as notified	mobile ICBM	yes	yes
C/E	as notified	C/E	yes	yes
Close out	1 per site	BM, HB	yes	yes
Formerly declared facility	≤3 year	ICBM, SLBM	yes	yes
Tech characteristic exhibit (BMs)	1 each type	host select	yes	yes
Distinguish exhibit (HB, ALCM)	1 each type	host select	yes	yes
Baseline exhibit HB, nonnuclear	as needed	host select	yes	yes
Continuous monitor (mobiles, production)	PPCM	MOU of 7/31/91	yes	yes
Heavy ICBM elimination	as notified	SS-18	no	yes
Heavy ICBM silo conversion	as notified	SS-18	no	yes
HB attribution exhibit	as needed	HB bases	no	yes
HB reorientation exhibit	as needed	HB bases	no	yes

CHART VII-G. (Cont.)
On-Site Inspections under START I and II

BM = ballistic missile (strategic)
HB = heavy bomber (strategic)
OSI = on-site inspection
EIF = entry into force (START I)
MOU = memorandum of understanding
RV = reentry vehicle
ALCM = air-launched cruise missile
PPCM = portal perimeter continuous monitoring
SLBM = submarine-launched ballistic missile
ICBM = intercontinental ballistic missile
C/E = conversion/elimination inspection (see Chart C).

[a] The types of inspections are defined in the START treaties and are described in Chart VII-D and in our earlier reports.[9, 10, 13]

CHART VII-H.
JCIC Agreements and Joint Statements

Agreement Number	Date	Subject
1.	Oct. 23, 1992	Addition of "Annex 1" to the JCIC Protocol provides for operation of JCIC by the five parties.
2.	Oct. 23, 1992	Corrections to Inspections Protocol and to MOU. Inspections at air bases and test ranges, use of tags, etc.
3.		Corrections to coordinate data (Confidential)
4.	Oct. 23, 1992	Amendment to Inspections Protocol. Assigns maximum weight of 3000 kg for equipment brought by one flight of inspectors for continuous monitoring of a facility.
5.	Oct. 23, 1992	Provision of notification time for inventory, repacking, and examination of equipment transported by inspection airplanes.
6.	Nov. 19, 1992	Amends Telemetry Protocol and adds Annex to provide for equipment for playback of telemetry information, etc. Applies until July 1993 and may be extended. (Initial agreement by US, Russia, and Ukraine.)
7.	April 14, 1993	Amends Inspections Protocol. Procedures for additional confirmation of dimensions of first stages of SLBMs.
8.	Nov. 19, 1992	Amends Inspection Protocol and provides for notification of change of flight routes for inspection airplanes.
9.	Nov. 19, 1992	Corrects MOU and amends data on fixed structures for rail-mobile launchers (Kostroma and Bershet sites)

CHART VII-H. (Cont.)
JCIC Agreements and Joint Statements

Agreement Number	Date	Subject
10.	Jan. 28, 1993	US to provide Russia equipment requested for playback of telemetric information. Amends Telemetry Protocol.
11.	April 14, 1993	Provision of tapes and data associated with the analysis of telemetric information and the use of recording media. Amends telemetry protocol.
12.	Oct. 14, 1993	Specifies use of IL-62, IL-76, and IL-96 airplanes for flights to US Amends Inspection Protocol.
13.	Oct. 14, 1993	Pre-inspection restrictions at SLBM bases. Amends Inspections Protocol and MOU.
14.	Oct. 14, 1993	Establishes the points of entry and associated inspection sites for the five parties. Amends Inspection Protocol and MOU.
15.	Oct. 14, 1993	Provides for exhibition of first stage of silo variant of SS-24.
16.	Nov. 4, 1993	Provisions for exhibition with inspection of the RS-12M (variant 2) for silo launcher as early exhibition.
17.	May 4, 1994	Gives specifics of releasability of START information. Specifies telemetric information release and treaty notifications that may not be released until three months after the notification.
18.	May 4, 1994	Logistical and administrative procedures for training and maintenance and for providing replacement parts for telemetry equipment.
19.	May 4, 1994	Detailed procedures for using satellite system receivers. Amends Inspections Protocol

CHART VII-H. (Cont.)
JCIC Agreements and Joint Statements

Agreement Number	Date	Subject
20.	Oct. 13, 1994	Notifications concerning rescheduling of activities. Amends Notifications Protocol.
21.	Oct. 13, 1994	Amends Inspections Protocol regarding inspections of soft-site launchers at test ranges.
22.	Oct. 13, 1994	Changes size criteria in connection with RS-12M, variant 2, for silo launcher. Amends Inspections Protocol and JCIC Agreement 16.
23.	Nov. 3, 1994	Amends Inspection Protocol regarding diplomatic officials meeting and accompanying inspectors, monitors, and air crew members at points of entry. Includes activities at San Francisco (POE) and access through Travis Air Force Base.
24.	Nov. 3, 1994	Amends Inspections Protocol with detailed procedures (seven pages) for the use of radiation detection equipment at weapons storage areas and the use of these detectors to verify that there is no nuclear weapon in a container.
25.	Nov. 3, 1994	Amends the Inspections Protocol regarding the use of radiation detection equipment during long-range, nonnuclear ALCM distinguishability exhibitions. Specifies US and Russian equipment.
26.	Nov. 3, 1994	Provision of summaries for tapes that contain a recording of telemetric information. Amends Telemetry Protocol.
27.	Nov. 3, 1994	Amends Notifications Protocol regarding notification before the change of function of a facility for ICBMs, SLBMs, or bombers.

CHART VII-H. (Cont.)
JCIC Agreements and Joint Statements

Agreement Number	Date	Subject
28.	Feb. 3, 1995	Amends Inspections Protocol so that baseline data inspections begin 85 days after treaty entry into force (EIF) and end 205 days after EIF. Data update and RV inspections begin 205 days after EIF and continue thereafter.
29.	Feb. 3, 1995	Amends MOU and Notifications Protocol regarding changes to boundaries on site diagrams of facilities.
30.	Feb. 3, 1995	Detailed additions to Annex 14 of Inspections Protocol regarding settlement of accounts for costs of inspections, etc.
31.	Feb. 3, 1995	Amends and adds to the Inspections Protocol to help enable Belarus, Kazakhstan, and Ukraine to participate in the conduct of inspections and continuous monitoring on the territory of the US Also elaborates on Agreement 30.
32.	June 23, 1995	Amends and adds to lists of inspection equipment in Inspections Protocol.
33.	June 23, 1995	Amends Notifications Protocol with regard to changes of facility boundaries and notifications of changes in data.
34.	Sept. 28, 1995	Amends and changes Inspections Protocol in detail (10 pages) with regard to use of radiation detection equipment.
35.	Dec. 12, 1995	Amends Notification Protocol and Telemetry Protocol with regard to telemetric information tapes and requires provision of related missile acceleration profiles and other data.

CHART VII-H. (Cont.)
JCIC Agreements and Joint Statements

Joint Statement Number	Date	Subject
1.	Dec. 19, 1991	On designation of parking sites for rail-mobile ICBMs.
2.	Oct. 23, 1992	Refers to Annex I of JCIC Protocol. On consent to be bound by JCIC agreements, Party which did not sign is not bound.
3.	Oct. 23, 1992	Notes that everything shown within site boundary diagram is inspectable except silo training launchers, as agreed.
4.	Oct. 24, 1992	Notes agreement that normal practice will be to inspect cargoes of inspection equipment at the facility to be inspected (even though treaty allows such inspection at point of entry [POE] or airport).
5.	Nov. 19, 1992	Agreed form for JCIC agreements.
6.	Nov. 19, 1992	Parties agree to specific time (number of days) that rights and obligations under treaty begin (refer to 00:00 hours, Greenwich mean time).
7.	Nov. 19, 1992	Limits need for inspection of ICBM emplacement equipment.
8.	April 14, 1993	Parties understand that training model specs may differ from specs for specific ICBMs or SLBMs.
9.	April 14, 1993	Additional confirmation by US of SLBM dimensions.
10.	April 14, 1993	Parties accept list of equipment US provided 10/92 for Votkinsk continuous monitoring.
11.	Oct. 14, 1993	Parties agree that preinspection restrictions at Yagel'naya and Olen'ya SLBM bases may vary from JCIC Agreement 13.

CHART VII-H. (Cont.)
JCIC Agreements and Joint Statements

Joint Statement Number	Date	Subject
12.	Oct. 14, 1993	Agreement on procedures for refueling IL-76 inspection airplanes at Anchorage, AL. Anchorage not at POE.
13.	Oct. 14, 1993	Agreement on list of equipment and specifications provided by US for continuous monitoring at Pavlograd, Ukraine, machine plant.
14.	May 4, 1994	Agree that inspected party shall ensure that satellite system receivers are capable of providing coordinates of silo launchers when satellite signal available. (Note: Satellite system receivers [SSRs] are provided by host.)
15.	May 4, 1994	Parties agree on use of photographs and length measurements of SS-N-8 by US at SLBM facilities during inspections.
16.	Oct. 13, 1994	Parties agree on interpretation of Inspection Protocol with respect to submarines and other items at sub bases. Items not considered within the inspection site or not subject to inspection or preinspection restrictions are indicated.
17.	Oct. 13, 1994	Parties agree that each party shall have right to change function of facilities listed in 1991 MOU. Such changed functions shall be described in applicable notifications.
18.	Oct. 13, 1994	Parties understand that for facilities not listed in MOU but specified in a notification, site diagrams will be provided within 48 hours.

CHART VII-H. (Cont.)
JCIC Agreements and Joint Statements

Joint Statement Number	Date	Subject
19.	Feb. 3, 1995	Parties understand that the US and Russian NRRCs and equivalent Continuous Communication links of Ukraine, Belarus, and Kazakhstan will be used for all notifications. The US will send all its notifications to all four FSU parties. Each FSU party will send its notifications to the US The FSU parties will agree among themselves as to exchange of copies of notifications each sends to the US The four FSU parties may, by mutual agreement, send one notification to US giving aggregate numbers.
20.	Sept. 28, 1995	The parties understand that, during RV inspections, radiation detection equipment may be used to demonstrate that a declared nonnuclear object is nonnuclear, at the discretion of the inspectee.
21.	Sept. 28, 1995	The parties confirm that the first stage of ICBM or SLBM incorporated into a space launch vehicle is subject to the treaty. Provisions for such application spelled out.

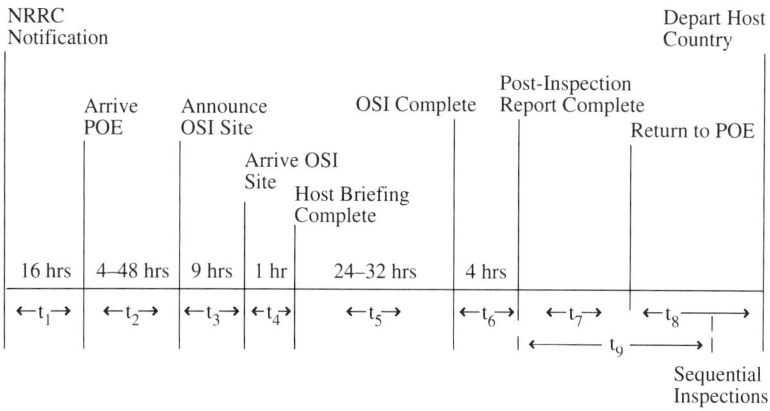

t_1 Inspection team flies (overseas) from home to host POE (includes time from notification).

t_2 Time for team to rest, prepare for inspection; host inspects equipment etc.; team designates site; t_2 = 4–24 hr for data update, suspect site, and RV OSIs.

t_3 Host flies team to specified site (expeditiously).

t_4 Host briefs OSI team upon arrival at inspection site.

t_5 Actual specified OSI takes place (team may request extension).

t_6 Team leader writes, completes report of OSI findings.

t_7 Team returns to POE; announces sequential inspection by this time.

t_8 Team prepares to leave, leaves POE for home, or conducts sequential inspection.

t_9 Team conducts sequential inspection.

Figure VII-1. Durations of time for on-site inspections (does not include PPCM; times shown are for baseline, data update, and other "short-notice" inspections), under START I, as prescribed in the original treaty, reference 6.

Inspection Times (t) in Hours for Fig. VII-1

Type of OSI	t_1	t_2	t_3[a]	t_4	t_5	t_6	t_7	t_8
Baseline Data	≥16	4-48	≤9	1	24[b]	≤4	t_7[c]	24
New Facility	≥16	4-48	≤9	1	24[b]	≤4	t_7[c]	24
Data Update	≥16	4-24	≤9	1	24 + 8[b]	≤4	t_7[c]	24
RV Count	≥16	4-24	≤9	1	t_5 (RV)	≤4	t_7[c]	24
Suspect Site	≥16	4-24	≤9	1	24 + 8[b]	≤4	t_7[c]	24
Conversion or Elimination	≥72	*	*	1	t_5 (C, E)	≤4	*	24
Post-Exercise Dispersal	≥16	48	≤9	1	24 + 8[b]	≤4	t_7[c]	24
Close-Out	≥72	*	≤48	1	24 + 8[b]	≤4	*	24
Formerly Declared Facility	≥16	4-24	≤9	1	24 + 8[b]	≤4	t_7[c]	24
Exhibitions: RV Technical Characteristics	≥72	*	*	1	24[b]	≤4	*	24
Exhibitions: HB, ALCM; distinguishing	≥72	*	*	1	24[b]	≤4	*	24
Exhibitions: nonnuclear HB; baseline	≥72	*	*	1	24[b]	≤4	*	24

[a] See exceptions for mobile-missile sites etc. (ref. 6).

[b] May be extended by mutual agreement as needed to complete inspection.

[c] These times depend on sequential inspections (see inspections protocol ref. 6).

[d] 8-hour extension by agreement.

t_5 (RV) Upon completion of procedures in annex 3 of inspections protocol, ref. 6.

t_5 (C, E) depends on conversion/elimination activities.

* The time durations for these “scheduled” inspections will depend on the host exhibition activities for these cases.

Chapter VIII

The START II Treaty

At the Washington Summit of June 16 and 17, 1992, US President Bush and Russian President Yeltsin signed a "Joint Understanding on Reductions in Strategic Offensive Arms"[1] along with several other agreements.[2] The Joint Understanding called for the United States and Russia to sign a second treaty, based on START I[3] (chapter VII), that would further reduce strategic nuclear deployments. This agreement (to be called START II) called for major reductions in two phases to an aggregate total of no more than 3500 strategic warheads, and for the elimination of all MIRVed ICBMs no later than the year 2003. The new treaty would employ START I procedures for notifications, eliminations, and verification.

START II Negotiations

During the START hearings before the Senate Foreign Relations Committee (SFRC) on June 23, 1992, Secretary of State Baker indicated hope that the Joint Understanding could be converted to treaty language by as early as September 1, 1992. Subsequent negotiations were more difficult. In November 1992, William Clinton won the presidential election from George Bush. Senators Sam Nunn and Richard Lugar,[4] after an urgent fact-finding trip to Russia, held a joint press conference and urged the outgoing Bush administration to do every thing possible to implement START I; to sign a treaty on START II; and to carry out the agreements provided for in the Nunn-Lugar Amendment,[5] which provided American funds ($400 million in 1991 and another $400 million each year thereafter, for several years) to assist with nuclear weapons dismantlement.[4] They also urged the Clinton transition team to support such efforts.

Negotiators for the two parties held several meetings beginning in September. Russian Foreign Minister Kozyrev and US Secretary of State Eagleburger met to discuss treaty language in Stockholm, Sweden, December 13, 1992. Three areas of disagreement[6] were reported:

- Because of costs, Russia did not want to destroy all of its SS-18 heavy missile silos (as first agreed at the June Summit);
- Russia wanted to keep all of its SS-19 MIRVed missiles and download them to one reentry vehicle (RV) each (a regression from the June Summit understanding to fully eliminate all MIRVed ICBMs); and
- The United States wanted to be allowed to convert B-1 bombers to a nonnuclear role and not count as being nuclear-armed.

After intensive negotiations, these and other issues were resolved in START II, which was signed January 1, 1993, in Moscow by Presidents Bush and Yeltsin, very shortly before Bush left office. The treaty as signed relaxes the downloading restrictions of START I to allow additional MIRVed ICBMs to be converted to single-warhead missiles. Russia was allowed to retain 90 modified SS-18 silos and use them for a smaller single-warhead missile (such as the SS-25). START I elimination and verification procedures were enhanced in START II by the requirement of concrete pours and restrictive rings to reduce the size of the new missile that could be placed in the retained SS-18 silos and by the provision of additional on-site inspections (OSIs) of these sites. In addition, all SS-18 heavy ICBMs that are to be removed from the START count will be eliminated (unlike START I, which specifies that missiles be removed from the silos and the silos eliminated). The treaty as signed allows the sides to reorient heavy bombers (particularly the United States B-1) to nonnuclear use (with verification) without having them count against the total 3500 strategic warhead count.

These final negotiations were detailed and difficult, but Ambassador Linton Brooks has reported[7] that they were much more professional and involved less "walking back" by the Russians than the START I negotiations. Completely eliminating MIRVed ICBMs was particularly significant. Such ICBMs are powerful but also vulnerable and, in a time of crisis, the incentive to use them before they can be destroyed is strong.

Description of the START II Treaty

START II, as signed by Presidents Bush and Yeltsin on January 1, 1993, is a bilateral treaty[8,9] between the United States and Russia, but it is based on the five-party treaty, START I (chapter VII). START II reduces deployed strategic nuclear forces to levels much below those in START I. All prohibitions, notifications, and on-site inspection procedures used in START I apply in START II except when specifically changed or modified. We note here START II had not been ratified by the Russian Duma, as of March 1999.

A. START II Warhead and Force Limitations

In addition to reducing total deployed strategic nuclear warheads to 3500, nearly one-half the START I limit, START II will eliminate all MIRVed ICBMs, greatly reducing the hair-trigger (use or lose) nature of cold war deployments. By eliminating all heavy ICBMs (SS-18s, 10 warheads each), START II will achieve a long-time US objective. START II limits are to be achieved by the end of a second phase (no later than January 1, 2003).

A sublimit of 1750 for total warheads has been placed on SLBMs. Rules of counting heavy bombers armed with nuclear weapons are modified so that each bomb, short-range attack missile (SRAM), or ALCM for which each type of bomber is actually equipped, counts as one warhead. These START II force limitations are set on top of the START I limitations and are summarized[9] and compared with START I values in Chart VIII-A.

B. START II Elimination, Conversion, and Verification Procedures

START II uses START I elimination, conversion, and verification procedures (chapter VII) but adds to them in several important ways. START II additions appear in the following categories:

Heavy ICBMs and Silos. All heavy ICBMs (SS-18s) are to be eliminated, either by destruction or by space launch (with notification). For missile eliminations, START I OSI procedures apply. All heavy ICBM silos are to be destroyed according to START I procedures except that up to 90 such silos may instead be converted to silos into which only single-warhead, nonheavy missiles may be inserted. This conversion includes the use of a restrictive ring and concrete in the silos to reduce the diameter and length so that only the allowed missile types may be inserted. OSIs to observe the whole process will be provided. Such inspections do not count against the START I OSI quotas.

Nonheavy ICBMs and SLBMs. These may be downloaded, within strict rules, to bring the warhead counts within the limits and sublimits of the treaty. The 1250 limit is removed on downloaded RVs. START I allows the US Minuteman III, the Russian SS-N-18, and two other missile types for each party to be downloaded by up to four warheads each to single-warhead missiles. START II does not require the elimination and replacement of the RV bus on the downloaded missiles. Also, up to 105 of the Russian SS-19s may be downloaded from six to one warhead each. START II compensates for its relaxation of the START I downloading restrictions by adding 4 RV inspections per year to the START I quota of 10 such inspections per year. These added OSIs are to be used for inspecting former heavy ICBM silos converted for nonheavy missiles with one warhead each. The heavy ICBM (SS-18) elimination and verification procedures and the silo elimination or conversion and verification procedures provided in START II are summarized in Chart VIII-B

Heavy Bombers. Since each deployed bomb and short-range attack missile (SRAM), as well as ALCM, is to count as one warhead in START II, additional exhibitions and inspections are provided to help verify that each deployed bomber is equipped to carry no more than the number of such weapons stated for each type of bomber in the START II data exchange. These inspections include confirmation of stated distinguishing characteristics that may then be observed by NTM. Heavy bombers may be converted to nonnuclear roles and removed from the total warhead counts under specific rules. Such bombers may, one time only, be returned to nuclear roles.[9] The exhibitions and inspections for heavy bombers in START II are summarized in Chart VIII-C.

Chart VII-G summarizes the OSIs provided in START I and lists the additional types of inspections provided in START II.

START II Ratification Process and Difficulties

The first principal delay in START II ratification by both parties was obtaining the entry into force of START I. As previously discussed (chapter VII), this delay resulted from problems in Ukraine, and full implementation of START I did not begin until December 1994.

United States

Another delay came in the US Senate in late 1995. The SFRC held early hearings on the treaty in 1993,[10] following submission of the treaty to the US Senate by President Bush in January 1993.[9] Final action did not occur until the SFRC hearings[11] and actions in 1995.

At the January 31, 1995, session, SFRC chairman Jesse Helms turned the gavel over to Senator Richard Lugar (a former SFRC chairman) to preside at the START II hearings.[11] Lugar presided at all four 1995 hearings, which were held January 31, February 28, March 1, and March 29.

The January 31 witnesses were START Ambassador Linton Brooks, Secretary of State Warren Christopher, and ACDA Director John Holum. All three witnesses strongly supported ratification of the treaty.

Ambassador Brooks[11] noted the following:

- The 3500-warhead limit is important, as is the complete elimination of MIRVed ICBMs in START II.
- The elimination of heavy ICBMs (SS-18s) achieved a decades-old United States objective.
- START II downloading rules prevented converting Russian SS-24s and American MXs into single-warhead missiles.
- The Russians negotiated for converting SS-19s into single-warhead missiles, but the United States objected because of the uploading (break-out) possibility. The compromise arrived at was to allow 105 of the SS-19s to be downloaded because the United States has the ability to take a similar step with its Trident SLBM forces.
- START II allows the United States to reorient the B-1 bomber to conventional roles and not count against START II limits.
- The additional provisions in START II call for eliminating all heavy (SS-18) ICBM missiles, whereas START I only calls for eliminating heavy ICBM silos.

Secretary Christopher noted that the parties had agreed not to ratify START II until START I entered into force, a process that took several years. He emphasized that START II eliminated or reduced the most dangerous types and numbers of ICBMs while allowing the parties (United States and Russia) to retain adequate nuclear deterrent forces. He also noted that START II ratification was an important component of American efforts at the May 1995 NPT review conference to obtain indefinite extension of the NPT.

Director Holum[11] noted that START II ratification was the highest priority for the administration. While de facto arms control was good, formal binding controls (such as START I and II) remain indispensable because they prescribe detailed means of verification, allowing us to "see for ourselves" that pledged reductions are actually made. He noted that ACDA has statutory responsibility to assess for Congress whether arms control agreements are verifiable, adding, "we remain confident that START II is effectively verifiable."

On February 28, CIA Deputy Director Douglas MacEachin testified,[11] indicating strong support for START II. He stated that eliminating all MIRVed systems would aid the monitoring responsibilities of the Central Intelligence Agency (CIA) because discovery of any MIRVed ICBM is a violation and easier to detect than in START I. He also noted that the SS-18 silo conversion requirement (allowed for 90 such silos) would make any attempts to reconvert to SS-18s observable well in advance by NTM.

On March 1, Secretary of Defense William Perry and Joint Chiefs of Staff chairman John Shalikashvilli testified before the SFRC.[11] Perry stated that START II is an integral part of the overall American strategy to reduce the nuclear threat, mainly because it eliminates the most destabilizing strategic weapons. He also noted that the START treaties had withstood the transitions and instabilities within the former Soviet Union. He urged prompt ratification. General Shalikashvilli stated that in the recent review of our nuclear posture, we concluded that START II allows enough of an American nuclear deterrent to be effective under the most difficult scenarios. He expressed strong confidence in the START verification procedures and urged prompt ratification of START II.

On March 29, Jack Mendelsohn (Arms Control Association), Michael Krepon (Stimson Center), and Stephen Hadley (assistant secretary of defense in the Bush administration) all strongly supported START II.

On the other hand, Sven Kraemer[11] (National Security Council staff under four presidents) criticized START I and II for not eliminating warheads removed from strategic nuclear delivery vehicles (SNDVs). He declared that since START II was negotiated, the Russians had adopted a new military doctrine calling for reintegration of the former Soviet states. He noted that the Russians had a program of extensive strategic modernization, including new land-based mobile ICBMs and new SLBM-carrying submarines. He opposed the Russian linkage of START II ratification to the ABM treaty.

Following the hearings, the SFRC was in a position to complete its final report and vote on the treaty for submission to the full Senate. During the summer of 1995, however, committee chairman Jesse Helms held up final committee action, subject to unrelated political goals.[12] The impasse was finally resolved in December 1995. The full committee then voted 18 to 0 to recommend ratification by the full Senate, subject to six conditions and seven declarations.[13] Senator Lugar submitted the recommendation of the SFRC and others to the full Senate on December 22, 1995. Final Senate ratification of START II came on January 26, 1996, three years after its initial submission by President Bush. Excerpts from the final Senate resolution of ratification are given in Appendix C. The final Senate action[14] included 6 conditions and 12 declarations. A significant condition is that before START II enters into force, the president must consult with the Senate before making any reductions below START I levels.

Russia

Proponents had hoped that the Russian Duma might act on START II before the Russian parliamentary election of December 1995. It did not, and subsequently, the strong showing of the Communists and other hard-line parties not allied with President Yeltsin in this election[15] was not conducive to positive action on START II in the Duma. During late 1995, throughout 1996, and well into 1997, political opposition to

START II within Russia became increasingly evident.[16] The Russians have been concerned about American developments in antimissile defense and their relation to the ABM treaty. Some Russian military analysts have voiced concern that eliminating all MIRVed ICBMs in START II places a burden on Russian resources if they are to replace SS-18 and SS-24 missiles with new, single-warhead missiles (such as the SS-25 and SS-27) in sufficient quantity to maintain parity in total strategic force strength. Politically, many Russians expressed concern that the expansion of NATO places them at a strategic disadvantage, and they tie ratification of START II to this NATO issue.[17]

In an effort to encourage Russian ratification of START II, proposals were circulated within the United States arms control community[18] to have Presidents Clinton and Yeltsin agree on a framework for a new treaty (START III) that would reduce deployed strategic warheads to significantly lower levels (such as 2000 to 2500), a level more suitable to present Russian economic considerations. By this scenario, such a framework agreement would be signed by the presidents but not negotiated in treaty form until START II entered into force. The agreement would be a pledge by the United States to negotiate the lower levels desired by the Russians. Proposals were also made to alleviate Russian concerns about NATO expansion with NATO force limits and other assurances.[19]

The March 1997 Summit Agreement

Presidents Clinton and Yeltsin held a summit meeting in Helsinki, Finland, on March 21 to discuss arms control and mutual security interests.[20] Guideline agreements were reached regarding START II and START III, missile defense (and ABM treaty), NATO-Russian cooperation, further Conventional Forces in Europe (CFE) agreement reductions, support for the Chemical Weapons Convention (CWC), and Western-Russian economic cooperation.

The presidents agreed[20] to amend START II as follows:

- The deadline for completing START II reductions will be extended from January 1, 2003, to December 31, 2007.

- All SNDVs that are to be eliminated under START II will be placed in a deactivated status by December 31, 2003. Such deactivation will be accomplished by the removal of their nuclear warheads or by other jointly agreed methods.
- The sides will agree on specific language to accomplish these two amendments and President Yeltsin will submit them to the Duma. Following Duma approval of START II, the amendments will be submitted to the US Senate.

The presidents underscored the importance of prompt ratification of START II by the Duma. The presidents also agreed to the goal of making the current START treaties of unlimited duration.

At the March 1997 Summit, the presidents further agreed that when START II enters into force, the United States and Russia will immediately begin their negotiations on a START III agreement.[20] START III was to include reductions to lower aggregate limits (2000 to 2500) for deployed strategic nuclear warheads. These negotiations were also to include new measures relating to the transparency and destruction of strategic nuclear warheads themselves. (See ref. 21 for a review of START II, its status, and these 1997 summit agreements. START III proposals are discussed in chapter IX.)

Amendments to START II

On September 26, 1997, in New York, the United States and Russia signed amendments[22] to the START II treaty, as agreed at the March Summit. These included a START II protocol to extend the completion date for START II eliminations and reductions and to extend the date by which the interim limitations and reductions (Phase I) of START II must be carried out. The protocol also modified a START II provision that tied early implementation of START II reductions to a program of assistance in facilitating such early reductions (such as with Nunn-Lugar assistance). The new provision states that parties "may conclude an agreement on a program of assistance . . . for accelerating . . . START II reductions." The protocol is subject to ratification by each party and will enter into force on the date when START II itself enters into force.

The Joint Agreed Statement between the United States and Russia records the agreement that Minuteman III ICBM downloading under START II can be carried out at any time before December 31, 2007, the new deadline for completing all START II mandated reductions. This statement ensures that deMIRVing under START II will take place in a stable and equivalent manner, and has no effect on downloading provisions under START I.

The exchange of letters on early deactivation (by Secretary Albright and Foreign Minister Primikov) codifies the 1997 Summit commitment to deactivate by December 31, 2003, all SNDVs that, under START II (with the new protocol), are to be eliminated by December 31, 2007. Such SNDV deactivation is to be achieved by removing the nuclear RVs from the missiles, or by taking other jointly agreed steps. The letters on deactivation will enter into force with START II, when American and Russian experts will immediately begin work on methods of deactivation and on parameters of a US program of assistance to Russia for implementing deactivation. The Russian letter also states that Russia understands that "START III" will be entered into force before this deactivation deadline.

At the time of signing, the administration indicated that it would submit the 1997 START II Protocol to the US Senate for ratification following ratification of START II by the Russian Duma. As this chapter is written, action[23] on START II by the Russian Duma has been very uncertain, as has the future of the Yeltsin government.

See ch. IX for further discussion of START II status and proposed future United States/Russian arms control agreements.

[In April, 2000 after the election of Vladimir Putin as Russia's President, the Russian Duma finally ratified the START II treaty. Duma conditions included the amendments to START II agreed by the parties in September 1997 noted above, and amendments to the ABM treaty agreed in September 1997, and discussed in Chapter IX. These amendments must be acted on by the US Senate if START II is to be entered-into-force.]

References and Notes

1. "Joint Understanding on Reductions in Strategic Offensive Arms," Office of the Press Secretary, The White House, June 17, 1992.
2. Eric K. Graben, "The June 1992 Bush-Yeltsin Summit," CNSS Briefing, Vol. 3, No. 7, (Los Alamos National Laboratory report), July 10, 1992.
3. "START, Treaty Between the U.S. of America and the Union of Soviet Socialists Republics on the Reduction and Limitation of Strategic Offensive Arms," US ACDA, Washington, DC, 1991, 280 pp.; includes the complete text of the treaty, protocols, MOU, and related documents exchanged at signing.
4. Press conference with Senator Sam Nunn and Senator Richard Lugar, "Report from Their Tour of Russian Republics," US Senate Radio and TV Gallery, federal news service, November 25, 1992.
5. "Soviet Nuclear Threat Reduction Act of 1991," US Senate, November 25, 1991, Amendment to H.R. 3807 (known as the Nunn-Lugar Amendment). Testimony of William Burns, SFRC, "Hearings on Weapons Dismantlement in the former Soviet Union," July 27, 1992 (Burns was accompanied by Dr. John Birely, DoD, and Dr. James Turner, DOE). Also see the Statement by Dr. Harold Smith, assistant for atomic energy to the secretary of defense, hearing on cooperative threat reduction, US SASC, July 23, 1993. A description of the Nunn-Lugar program is given in David B. Thomson, "The Nuclear Warhead Dismantling Initiative: The Nunn-Lugar Initiative," CNSS briefing, Vol. 4, No. 4, Nov. 3, 1993 (Los Alamos National Laboratory report); and Katherine E. Johnson, "U.S.-FSU Nuclear Threat Reduction Programs: Effectiveness of Current Efforts and Prospects for Future Cooperation," CISA, Los Alamos National Laboratory report, August 1995.
6. Elaine Sciolino, "U.S. and Russia Fail to Settle Differences on Arms Cut Pact," *New York Times*, December 13, 1992.
7. Linton F. Brooks, "Strategic Nuclear Arms Control: Status and Prospects," CNSS seminar at Los Alamos National Laboratory, February 25, 1994, Los Alamos National Laboratory report LA-UR-94-952 (March 25, 1994).
8. "Treaty between the U.S. of America and the Russian Federation on Further Reduction and Limitation of Strategic Offensive Arms (START II)," signed by the presidents of the US and the Russian Federation, January 3, 1993. This edited version was released by the US ACDA, February 1, 1993.
9. "Message from the President Transmitting the START II Treaty to the U.S. Senate (including its Protocols and Memorandum of Attribution, MOA)," Senate Treaty Doc. 103-1, January 20, 1993. Includes article-by-article analysis.

10. SFRC hearings on the START II treaty, May 11, 18, June 17 and 24, 1993. Doc. 103-325, US GPO, Washington, DC.
11. SFRC hearings on consideration of ratification of the START II treaty held January 31, February 28, March 1, and 29, 1995, Senate Hearing Doc. 104-30, US GPO, Washington, DC, 1995.
12. Spurgeon M. Keeney, Jr., "Holding U.S. Security Hostage," *Arms Control Today*, October, 1995, p. 2.
13. "START II Treaty," SFRC Exec. Report 104-10, 104th Congress, December 15, 1995.
14. Craig Cerniello, "START II Resolution of Ratification," *Arms Control Today*, February 1996, pp. 30–33.
15. Alessandra Stanley, "Unfazed by Election, Yeltsin Vows Not to Change Course," *The New York Times International*, December 21, 1995; and David Hoffman, "Russia Will Not Leave the Road of Reform," *Washington Post*, December 21, 1995. See also Steve Maaranen and Joe Pilat, "The Russian Duma Election," CISA report 96-018(U), February 8, 1996 (Los Alamos National Laboratory internal report).
16. Spurgeon M. Keeney, Jr., "START III Now," and Jack Mendelsohn, "START II and Beyond," *Arms Control Today*, October, 1996, pp. 2–9.
17. Ibid, p. 5.
18. Ibid p. 2, p. 7–8.
19. Michael R. Gordon, "Albright Offers Russia Plan to Erase Fears over NATO," *New York Times International*, February 21, 1997. See also Norman Kemster, "Russia Agrees to European Security Talks with NATO," *Albuquerque Journal*, December 12, 1996, p. A16.
20. "Joint Statement on Parameters of Future Reductions in Nuclear Forces," Presidents Clinton and Yeltsin, Office of the White House Press Secretary, Helsinki, Finland, March 21, 1997. See also White House fact sheet, March 21, 1997. See also ABM Joint Statement and other summit joint statements, White House fact sheets. See also Paul Mann, "Helsinki Summit Spurs Strategic Partnership," *Aviation Week & Space Technology*, March 31, 1997, pp. 24–27; and Jack Mendelsohn and Craig Cerniello, "The Arms Control Agenda at the Helsinki Summit," and "Joint Statements of the Helsinki Summit," *Arms Control Today*, March, 1997, pp. 16–21.
21. David B. Thomson, "The START Treaties: Implementation and Status," CISA, Los Alamos National Laboratory report LA-UR-97-2045 (May 1997).

22. "START II Protocol," Text of Protocol, Joint Agreed Statement, and letters on early deactivation, signed by US Secretary of State Albright and Russian Foreign Affairs Minister Primakov, September 26, 1997, US ACDA (press release and fact sheets), September 26, 1997.
23. During late 1998 and early 1999, successive plans to bring START II to a vote for ratification have continually been delayed because of expressed opposition by many members of the Russian Duma.

CHART VIII-A.
Numerical Force Limitations[a] under START I[b] and II

Weapons System	START I	START II (Phase 1)	START II (Phase 2)
SNDVs (ICBMs, SLBMs, bombers)	1600		
Total throw-weight (metric tons)	3600		
Heavy ICBMs (SS-18s)	154		0
Heavy SLBMs	0		
Total accountable warheads	6000	4250 (3800)	3500 (3000)
Warheads on ICBMs and SLBMs	4900		
Warheads on heavy ICBMs	1540	650	0
Warheads on mobile ICBMs	1100		
Warheads on MIRVed ICBMs		1200	0
Warheads on SLBMs		2160	1750 (1700)
Heavy bombers[c]			

[a] Limits apply to deployed strategic nuclear-armed systems. In columns where value is blank, there is no limit or sublimit for that item in that treaty, but the START I limit applies if the START II value is blank. The lower values in parentheses(), or a still lower value, may be chosen by either party as its limit.

[b] Phases

START I reductions are to be carried out in three phases as follows:

Time from EIF	SNDVs	Warheads
3 years (Dec. 1997)	≤2100	≤9150
5 years (Dec. 1999)	≤1900	≤7950
7 years (Dec. 2001)	≤1600	≤6000

Phase 1 of START II reduction is to occur within the 7-year START I reduction period.

Phase 2 of START II reduction is to occur no later than January 1, 2003. The protocol (signed September 26, 1997, but not ratified) extends this date to December 31, 2007.[22]

START II shall remain in force for the duration of START I.

[c] In START I, each heavy bomber counts as one warhead, regardless of the number of bombs or SRAMs it may carry. Each ALCM counts as one warhead. The rules favor deployment of 150 (for the US) and 180 (for the FSU) heavy bombers equipped for ALCMs. In START II, each bomb, SRAM, or ALCM for which a heavy bomber is equipped counts as one warhead against the total warhead limit.

CHART VIII-B.
Silo and Heavy ICBM Elimination, Conversion, and Verification Procedures[a,b]

Weapons System/Process	Procedures	Verification
ICBM silos/elimination (START I and II)	Missiles and equipment not to be eliminated are removed >1000 m from silo; silo eliminated by excavation to 8 m or by explosion to a 6-m depth	NTM and cooperative measures only; satellite photos, etc.; other side provides notifications at each step; silo area kept visible for entire process plus 90 days
Heavy ICBMs (SS-18s)/elimination (START II)	RVs, electronics, and propellant removed; stages disassembled before OSI team arrival; stages, nozzles, and skirts cut in half and crushed; front section and RV platform cut in two or three pieces (<1.5 m long) Heavy ICBMs may also be eliminated by using them for space launches.	OSI team arrives, confirms types (by START I procedures); team observes entire elimination; team leader and host write report
Heavy ICBM silo conversion (START II)	NRRC notification 30 days before conversion; missile and canister removed; concrete poured (5-m height); restrictive ring installed (<2.9-m inside diameter)	OSI team observes the pouring and measures depth and diameter; team leader and host sign report; inspection does not count against START I quotas

[a] See Charts VII-F and VII-G.

[b] See Refs. 8 and 9 for complete notification and inspection procedures needed (in addition to START I procedures) to carry out START II.

CHART VIII-C.
Exhibitions and Inspections for Heavy Bombers in START II[a]

Type of Inspection	Procedures
(1) Exhibition OSI (one each type, from MOA list) (2) Exhibition inspections of changes in MOA (one each type). Reoriented to nonnuclear or returned to nuclear. (These OSIs are not counted against any START I quota)	Inspection by ≤10 inspectors (START I); 2-hour limit; host provides photographs to demonstrate differences in nuclear-armed/nonnuclear-armed bomber of type that is observable by NTM. Host may shroud parts of bomber except weapons bay, exterior weapons-carrying parts, and exterior parts providing "observable differences."
During START I data update and new facility inspections at airbases, may inspect nuclear-armed bombers to confirm START II MOA data.	START I procedures plus the following: may visually inspect weapons bay and all exterior weapons locations to confirm actual number of nuclear weapons; may inspect for "observable differences" as above
During START I data update and new facility inspections, may inspect heavy bombers reoriented to conventional role	Similar to START I procedures; inspect differences observable by NTM
During START I data update and new facility inspections, may inspect heavy bombers returned to nuclear role	Inspect "observable differences"; visually inspect weapons bay and all exterior weapons locations

[a] See START II treaty article IV, and Exhibitions and Inspections Protocol, ref. 9, for HB conversion options and verification details.

Chapter IX

START III Issues and Related Former Soviet Union Weapons Materials Agreements

Discussions on a new Treaty, START III, began between the United States and Russia at the March 1997 Helsinki Summit.[1] In an effort to achieve Duma ratification of START II, the presidents also agreed to extend the deadline for START II reductions by four years, and agreed to place SNDVs to be eliminated under START II on deactivated status by December 2003. These agreements were codified in a START II Protocol and signed by the two parties in September 1997,[2] as discussed in ch. VIII. At Helsinki, the presidents also agreed to make the current START treaties of unlimited duration, but that proposal has not been submitted for ratification. As noted in ch. VIII, the proposed START III treaty is to reduce the total number of allowed deployed strategic warheads to values below 2500 to alleviate Russian concerns over alleged START II asymmetries. Here in ch. IX, we discuss issues relating to the proposed START III treaty, issues relating to the urgent need for verification and control of numbers of nuclear warheads, and agreements being negotiated between the United States and Russia regarding control of nuclear weapons materials (plutonium and highly enriched uranium, HEU). The status of negotiations pertaining to some of these issues has changed almost daily. Our discussion below pertains primarily to the situation that existed by early 1999.

START III

At Helsinki, the presidents also agreed that when START II enters into force, the United States and Russia will immediately begin their negotiations on a START III agreement[1] that will include the following components:

- Establishment by December 2007 of lower aggregate levels of 2000 to 2500 deployed strategic nuclear warheads for each of the two START II parties;

- Measures relating to the transparency of strategic nuclear warhead inventories and the destruction of strategic nuclear warheads; and
- Other jointly agreed technical and organizational measures to promote the irreversibility of deep reductions, including prevention of a rapid increase in the number of warheads.

At Helsinki, the presidents further agreed[1] that in the context of START III negotiations, their experts would explore, as separate issues, possible measures relating to nuclear-armed, long-range SLCMs, and tactical nuclear weapons systems.

These measures are to include appropriate confidence building and transparency. The presidents also agreed[1] that the sides would consider the issues related to transparency in nuclear materials. We note that the Summit parties agreed that the START III reduction completion date coincides with the amended START II reduction completion date (December 2007).

These Helsinki agreements relating to START II and START III are discussed in ref. 3. An earlier suggestion[4] for the United States to agree to the lower strategic warhead limits (2000 to 2500) was intended to enable a START III agreement to serve to expedite Russian Duma ratification of START II (ch. VIII). This has not yet happened, however, as discussed below.

START III/START II Implementation Issues

During the decades of the nuclear arms buildup of the pre-Gorbachev era, the Soviets had very superior conventional ground forces in Europe (tanks, artillery, manpower), as noted in ch. I. These decades were characterized by dictatorial rule, military buildups at the expense of consumer goods, and decay of the morale and spirit of the Soviet peoples.[5] Gorbachev was able to bring new freedoms to the people, but in his few short years of leadership, he was not able to reverse the economic decay.[5] The breakup of the Soviet Union in 1991 only exacerbated these conditions, particularly in Russia. One result has been a general deterioration of the resources supporting the conventional Russian army with a subsequent lowering of conventional military capability. This has led many in the Russian gevernment to feel a continuing need for nuclear weapons for their security.

With their poor economy and with much uncertainty as to their future defense capabilities, members of the Russian Duma, rightly or wrongly, have expressed a number of concerns relating to START II. The United States has taken initiatives to address these issues, but concerns in the Duma have persisted.

1. Strategic Force Structure Issues

Many of the Russian strategic forces that existed at the time of START I signing (Table 5, 1991) are old[6] and scheduled for elimination by about 2009, during the first fifteen years of START I. These include such systems as the SS-N-19, SS-N-6, and SS-N-18, which are all SLBMs. Old ICBMs include the SS-11, SS-13, and SS-17, all of which had been eliminated as of January 1998 (Table 9).

The START II requirement to eliminate all MIRVed ICBMs, including the downloading to 1 RV each in the case of the 105 allowed SS-19s, will leave the Russians with only about 475 ICBMs (note Table 10). A projected Russian strategic nuclear force structure under START II (say by year 2007) might then look like the following:

Russian Example A

SS-19s	105 warheads
SS-25s, SS-X-27s	370 warheads
SLBMs (SS-N-20, 23)	1448 warheads
Bombers (with ALCMs)	904 warheads
Total	**2827 warheads**

By virtue of eliminating all the heavy SS-18s, the Russians might have little capability[6] left to attack hard targets without building new forces.

Russian defense spokesmen indicate that an economically strapped defense budget will impose a capability under START II considerably less than shown above. Aleksey Podberezkin (deputy chairman, Duma International Affairs Committee) and Anton Surikov[7] (information-analyst, Center of Institute of Defense Research in Moscow) say the naval SLBM forces are degrading swiftly because of underfunding and will "shrink threefold by 2007." They say that, under present plans,

Russia will "evidently have 6-7 missile submarines with 700-1000 warheads by 2010, and ten such subs with 1300 warheads by 2015." They also say the Russian heavy bomber force future is "even more dismal." The 79 heavy bombers available today carry about 800 nuclear bombs and ALCMS, but only 6 of these bombers are "modern," the Tu-160, carrying a total of about 144 ALCMs. They[7] state that unless production is resumed at the Kazan aircraft enterprise (presumably at considerable cost), the bomber component of their triad will consist of only the 144 ALCMs, plus some capability with about 80 other bombers by, say, the year 2005. They admit that present plans and production rates call for the production of up to about 300 SS-X-27 single RV missiles (successfully tested modernized successor to the road mobile SS-25) by year 2005, and about 200 more by the year 2010, again at significant economic cost.[7]

With these assumptions, we could project (by year 2007) a force structure under START II like the following:

Russian Example B

SS-19s	105 warheads
SS-25s, SS-X-27	740 warheads
SLBMs	700 warheads
Bombers	~235 warheads
Total	**~1780 warheads**

We note that Russian Example A may be compared with US plans[6] under START II (as of 1995) to deploy the following:

US Example A

Minuteman III (@ 1 RV)	500 warheads
Trident (D-5, @ 5 RVs)	1680 warheads
Bombers (B-52H and B-2)	1260 warheads
Total	**3440 warheads**

In the case of the Trident II (D-5), the ALCMs, and the B-2 bomber component of the ALCM force, the United States is planning[6] to use its most modern and effective weapons. In the case of the SS-X-27, the Russians are planning to build more of their newest and recently tested single warhead missile, but at the significant cost of new production.

Noting differences in projected force structures such as in Russian Example B and US Example A, Podberezkin and Surikov[7] argue that Russia should not ratify START II. They state that this projected imbalance between US and Russian forces would put Russian security at risk, and that this imbalance would be exacerbated by any US deployment of missile defenses. They also note that with this imbalance with the United States, Russians have greater concerns about how to balance China's increasing nuclear missile capability. As a solution, Podberezkin and Surikov[7] propose that Russia and the United States continue to implement START I, and that Russia plan to modernize or replace about 150 of the SS-18 heavy ICBMs to be eliminated under START II, giving them 1500 warheads not included in the examples above. They say this force would give them a hard target capability; and, also, the SS-18 force, with its heavy payload, has over a ton of countermeasures (per missile), making the force more suitable to guarantee deterrence in the face of a US ABM system.[7] They claim that this SS-18 force enhancement could be accomplished within only 2 to 3% of the present military budget. In a later report, Surikov no longer supports retaining SS-18s.

Aleksay Arbatov (deputy chair, Duma Defense Committee) and Col. Petr Romashkin, in a contrary opinion,[8] agree with the general force structure assumptions of Russian Example B, but point out that the stronger US economic position makes it much easier for the United States to maintain its START I force levels than for the Russians, whose forces are not presently getting sufficient maintenance attention and note that this will get worse so that Russia cannot afford to try to maintain START I levels. They state[8] that "it is enormously better to ratify START II and go on to START III talks." They note that the conditions for shifting to START III talks can be spelled out in the Duma decree of ratification of START II.

As noted above, the Helsinki agreements included a START III treaty with a strategic warhead limit of 2000 to 2500. We show, as only one possible scenario for a US force structure under START III, the following:

US Example B

Minuteman III (@ 1 RV)	300 warheads
Trident II (D-5, @ 5 RVs)	1200 warheads
Bombers	
B-2 (20 @ 16 ALCMs)	320 warheads
B-52H (40 @ 10 ALCMs)	400
Total (approx.)	**2220 warheads**

US Example B provides use of most of the Trident II missiles planned[6] under START I and presently counted as deployed SNDVs, retains some MM III ICBMs to retain the triad, uses all the planned B-2 bombers (our most modern and penetrating bomber), and uses a significant number of old reliable B-52s to provide an option to the expensive B-2s. This example illustrates that it should be economical and efficient for the United States to achieve START III reductions as proposed at Helsinki, and perhaps even to offer to go as low as 1800-2000 warheads, with modest additional decreases in each leg of the triad. Other example force structures may be equally appropriate.

As previously suggested,[4,3] the author has believed a simple US agreement to go to these START III levels might be quickly negotiated with the Russians as a START III treaty (separate from the needed but more complicated negotiations on warhead verification procedures) or as a simple additional amendment to START II. If negotiated as a simple new treaty, it could be timed to go into effect simultaneously with START II to alleviate the Russian concerns and help regain the momentum of US/Russian nuclear arms control accomplishments.

2. ABM Treaty Issues

Despite the alleviation of economic needs of the Russians by going to START II levels and below, several political and/or military issues have also contributed to opposition to START II in the Duma. Among the most contentious has been the ABM treaty.[9] As noted in ch. II, the ABM (antiballistic missile) treaty (signed in 1972, amended in 1974) limited the United States and the USSR to one ABM site each with <100 launchers per site. The United States never deployed missiles at its ABM site.

Since Reykjavik the Russians have been concerned[10] about US strategic missile defense (SDI) and during the START negotiations have insisted on strict adherence to the ABM treaty of 1972. Some Russians state that with its present superior economic and technical base, the United States could break out of the ABM treaty and create a strategic defense force that could greatly reduce the effectiveness of the Russian strategic deterrent force. This issue has been raised strongly in the Duma with respect to START II, and Yeltsin's transmittal letter to the Duma stated "It goes without saying that the START II treaty can be fulfilled only providing the United States preserves and strictly complies with the bilateral ABM treaty of 1972." For some years, the United States has been pursuing theater missile defense (TMD) research partly as a hedge against missile attacks by third parties and/or rogue states, and has been negotiating a "demarcation agreement" with the Russians that clarifies that a US theater missile defense deployment will not abrogate the ABM treaty.

Such an agreement was negotiated and signed[11] in September 1997 as part of the package agreed upon at the Helsinki Summit to alleviate Russian concerns about START II. The entire package of agreements relating to the ABM treaty and the START II (ch. VIII) treaty was signed September 26, 1997,[11,2] in conjunction with the annual session of the United Nations General Assembly. The package included a Memorandum of Understanding (MOU), an amendment to the ABM treaty that extends it to include Russia, Belarus, Ukraine, and Kazakhstan in place of the USSR in the original 1972 treaty between the United States and the USSR. The MOU provides that the four FSU "successor states" would be limited to a single antiballistic missile (ABM) system deployment area at any one time. The Standing Consultative Commission (SCC) of the original treaty is expanded to include all four of the successor states along with the United States. The MOU provides that each party is subject to the First and Second Agreed

Statements (and their respective "Common Understandings") upon entry-into-force of the MOU as an amendment to the ABM treaty. The First and Second Agreed Statements were signed separately by the SCC ambassadors for the respective parties (Stanley Riveles for the United States). The MOU is subject to ratification by each of the parties using their respective constitutional processes.

The First Agreed Statement limits the tested characteristics of interceptor missiles to capabilities less than the agreed ABM capabilities needed to intercept ICBMs. This demarcation is defined as follows:

- the velocity of the interceptor missile does not exceed 3 km/sec over any part of its flight trajectory,
- the velocity of the target-missile does not exceed 5 km/sec over any part of its flight trajectory, and
- the range of the ballistic target-missile does not exceed 3500 kilometers.

The Second Agreed Statement reaffirms the parties' commitment to the ABM treaty as a measure to "strengthen strategic stability" and states that the parties "have the option" to deploy effective systems to counter ballistic missiles "other than strategic ballistic missiles." It further states that "systems to counter ballistic missiles will not be deployed by the parties for use against each other." The Second Agreed Statement reaffirms the specific demarcation characteristics given above for the First Agreed Statement. The use of the SCC to resolve technical questions concerning these agreements is affirmed.

The Agreement[11] on Confidence Building Measures included in this package includes a system of notifications of interceptor missile tests or launches and related assurances.

In signing this package of agreements clarifying the ABM treaty, the United States hopes to encourage positive Duma action on START II, but strong support in the US Congress for ballistic missile defense has made this issue difficult.[12] More recently, the United States has informally proposed amending the ABM treaty to move the location of the allowed site from Grand Forks, SD, to a more generally useful location (such as Alaska). The Russians have not yet agreed.

3. Russian Political and Economic Issues

Russians have expressed much concern for the sheer expense[9] of START II implementation. This includes the cost of physically destroying (or converting) all the SS-18 and SS-24 Silos (and/or rail launchers), and all the MIRVed missiles themselves. The costs of eliminating missile submarines, their nuclear power plants, and their spent nuclear fuel is formidable.[9] Since, under START II plans, the United States must only destroy 50 MX MIRVed Missiles and can more easily download MM IIIs and Tridents, some in the Duma argue that the treaty places an "unfair" heavier financial burden on them.[9] The author notes however, that the older Russian systems have to soon be taken out of service anyway, and the United States is helping with Nunn-Lugar funds.[13]

Equally important have been Russian concerns about NATO expansion.[14] The end of the cold war resulted in the breakup of the Warsaw pact as well as the dissolution of the Soviet Union. The Eastern European nations of Poland, Czechoslovakia, and Hungary applied for admission to NATO, were recently admitted, and the actions were ratified by the US Senate in the spring of 1998.

Those Russians who are inclined to retain their "cold war thinking" (noted in ch. I) see this expansion of NATO as a threat to them, particularly with their weakened conventional military forces.[14] In an effort to alleviate this concern, the NATO-Russian Founding Act was negotiated and signed by NATO and Russia in 1997 to provide for mutual consultations on an institutional basis (such as periodic meetings of the NATO and Russian military and diplomatic staffs) to encourage and promote cooperative activities in the mutual interests of both Russia and NATO.[15]

Some reports[16] from Moscow have indicated that the September 1997 agreements (amending START II and clarifying the ABM treaty) described above (and in ch. VIII) have helped pave the way for positive Duma action on START II, but they also indicate that some Russians are interested in negotiating limits on uploading, as discussed at the Helsinki 1997 Summit, even though these could hold up[3] the reductions proposed at Helsinki for START III.

Perhaps most important to START II ratification has been the status of the Russian government itself and the conflicts between President Yeltsin and the strong Communist and nationalist factions in the Duma.

During 1998, while facing severe economic conditions, Yeltsin used three different prime ministers to run his government: Chernomyrdin, who had held the post for five years; Sergei Kiriyenko; Chernomyrdin (acting); and Foreign Minister Primakov, who was nominated and confirmed in September.[17]

During 1998, Yeltsin made a significant effort to obtain ratification of START II, with then Foreign Minister Primakov and Defense Minister Sergeyov making strong presentations to the Duma in support of the treaty, but as of this writing, Duma action is in doubt.[18]

Nuclear Warhead Verification Issues

As the United States and Russia have drawn down their deployed nuclear weapon delivery systems, verification of nondeployed warheads has become most urgent. The 1997 Helsinki Summit agreement pointed to future negotiations involving a number of nuclear warhead verification or transparency issues.[19–21] Early deactivation is tied to a START II amendment (ch. VIII), and transparency agreements were proposed as components of the START III negotiations, such as transparency of strategic nuclear warhead inventories, destruction of strategic nuclear warheads, measures to prevent rapid increase in deployments, and promotion of irreversibility of deep reductions. Finally, the Summit parties agreed that their experts should explore the transparency of long-range SLCMs, tactical nuclear systems, and nuclear materials. In the following seven subsections, the author briefly discusses potential WH verification regimes from a purely speculative point of view. We note that, for the most part, negotiations for these seven warhead regimes are not formally under way. Our discussion relates to the March 1997 Summit agreements but is meant to apply more generally.

1. Early Deactivation

The protocol amending START II to extend the date of final reductions was accompanied by an exchange of letters calling for early deactivation (by the year 2003, ch. VIII) of those SNDVs to be eliminated by the year 2007. This deactivation may be achieved by removing the reentry vehicles (RVs) from the missiles or "other jointly agreed steps." The verification issue is how to determine, over a period of up to four years, that RVs removed (or otherwise deactivated) from ballistic missiles are not later restored when the SNDVs are still deployed and/or not otherwise eliminated. In the case of fixed-silo-based ICBMs, this might be accomplished by requiring that the RVs be permanently removed and the buses left open, unshrouded, and available to observation at any time by inspection and NTM. Continuous TV monitoring could also be used. Negotiators need to develop a verification regime that ensures that adaptable RVs are not stored in close proximity so that a number of MIRVed ICBMs could be clandestinely and quickly reloaded in sufficient numbers to significantly upset the balance of forces. RVs removed from specific missiles could be physically destroyed (under observation), but their nuclear warheads (physics package) would need to be removed from the RVs before such elimination, and a regime for tracking those warheads might also be needed (regime 2, DSNW, below). In the case of deactivated SLBMs, procedures might be negotiated that allow complete viewing of all the SLBM tubes every time (or at appropriate intervals) the particular submarine makes port at an SLBM base. Tamper-proof seals on deactivated SLBM tubes should be used. If the SNDV whose START II warhead count is to be reduced is a bomber, the nuclear bombs may be removed and the bomber slated for destruction and left under observation (NTM/OSI) at the elimination site, or converted to nonnuclear weapon status by START II/START I conversion and reorientation procedures. The number of yearly short-notice RV inspections and data update inspections should be increased over the START I and II quotas (ch. VIII).

It seems unlikely that MIRVed ICBMs, MIRVed SLBMs, or bombers under continuous observation with all their RVs (or nuclear bombs) deactivated by removal could be reloaded in large numbers without eventual detection, but the verification regime needs to be negotiated to the satisfaction of both parties.

2. Destruction of Strategic Nuclear Warheads (DSNW)

A regime for verifying that particular nuclear warheads removed from SNDVs covered by the START treaties are actually eliminated might be developed and negotiated. The goal could be to verify that the nuclear material from warheads removed from specified SNDVs has been converted to a point where it can no longer be used for nuclear warheads without chemical reprocessing and mechanical fabrication. This regime would require using on-site inspection of the actual removal of the RVs or warheads from the missiles (or bombers). In START I and II, warheads are now removed before the on-site inspection of the elimination of the delivery vehicles.

In this very difficult DSNW regime the inspectors would be present, under complex procedures yet to be negotiated, at the SNDV site during the warhead removal. The inspectors would tag and seal the "box" containing the removed warhead at the time of the removal. In this scenario, the removed warheads would then be shipped to an agreed-on elimination facility (presumably on a different day or week), and inspectors would check the tags and seals (tamper proof) before the transport of these warheads and again at their entry into the elimination facility. We assume that the parties do not want to disclose the details of the warhead designs (such as mass or geometry of pits), so the warhead would be disassembled inside the facility. Inspectors, only allowed outside, would use PPCM to monitor all materials entering and exiting the facility. Unclassified nuclear material (plutonium, uranium) removed from the conversion facility could be monitored by the PPCM using radiation measurements and direct observation and then placed under IAEA-type monitoring procedures for transport and storage. Classified nonnuclear weapons components (such as high explosives, timing and fusing devices, and critical hardware, but containing no plutonium or HEU) would be removed from the facility in special containers and monitored at the PPCM exit using agreed-on radiation measurements such as are now used in START I for nonnuclear ALCMs. Removal of bare pits would require special procedures to confirm agreed-to attributes that the item is a pit without disclosing its mass or geometry. Such pits would be tagged and sealed in their containers, shipped to an agreed-upon storage area, and similarly monitored with PPCM.

The allowed kinds of radiation measurements used for monitoring the initial removal of warheads from the SNDVs, as well as the entry and exit of classified items through the PPCM, will require considerable negotiation by the parties since the host party does not want to disclose classified information.

The complex DSNW regime of verification outlined here is but an example of how one might achieve the goal, and may by itself be too difficult to negotiate when we consider that each party has many other types of unaccounted-for nuclear warheads in its inventories. However, achieving this DSNW regime could provide experience and techniques that would be valuable in future agreements to account for all stored and/or nondeployed warheads.

3. Prevention of Rapid Buildup of Strategic Warheads (PRBSW)

The Helsinki Summit agreement to negotiate measures to "prevent a rapid increase in the number of warheads" was somewhat vague, so here we divide it into two regimes: (a) measures pertaining to rapid increase in any of all types of nuclear warheads, and (b) measures pertaining to the rapid buildup of deployed strategic warheads. Regime (a) pertains to total inventories of all nuclear warheads and is treated in regime 7 below. Regime (b) can be addressed in terms of preventing a START II or START III "breakout," in which a sudden imbalance of deployed strategic forces might be attempted.

Such an occurrence could most likely be instigated by a party rapidly and clandestinely attempting to rearm a significant number of MIRVed ICBMs awaiting elimination, rapidly uploading MIRVed SLBMs, and/or rapidly loading a large number of nonnuclear armed bombers with nuclear weapons. Inhibition of such a breakout in nuclear-armed SNDV capability is first provided in the START I/START II elimination and verification procedures. The stretch-out of required elimination time in the START II protocol[2] may introduce a need to add to the verification that SNDVs, scheduled for elimination and sitting with their nuclear warheads removed, cannot be rapidly and clandestinely rearmed. A system of continuous monitoring with television cameras might also be implemented. Such a breakout threat may not really be a realistic scenario today for either party. But increased verification, such as adding to the quota of START I/START II data-update and RV inspections per year, might add to the confidence of both the US and Russia in ratifying a START III treaty which greatly reduces deployed strategic warheads below present START II levels. These increased verification measures might be accompanied by required elimination of the MIRV platforms and by a ban on testing MIRVs.

4. *Strategic Nuclear Warhead Inventories (SNWI)*

Under START I, deployed nuclear warhead inventories are presently verified only through notifications, data exchanges, and inspections of the SNDV deployments. Once nuclear warheads are removed for elimination, there is presently no regime for tracking their location, and there is no present accounting of nuclear warheads designed as replacements or spares for SNDVs. It should be possible, through the use of tags and direct inspections, to develop a regime of codification of warheads removed from SNDVs, as discussed in case 2 (DSNW) above. However, for reserve, spare, and stored nondeployed warheads, there is no way of knowing whether or not such warheads, even if declared as one type or another, are really designed for use in strategic vehicles (SNDVs). Only a careful and very intrusive inspection by qualified engineers and technicians, with detailed knowledge of both the warheads and the delivery vehicles, could confirm what type of delivery vehicle the warhead might be designed to mate, unless the warhead is stored in its mated RV. We assume at this point that neither side is prepared for this degree of intrusiveness, which would expose so much nuclear weapon design information to the other side.

Specific numbers of nuclear warheads (in marked, sealed boxes) could be declared as strategic or other type of warheads, observed with radiation detectors and counted by inspectors, stored in agreed upon storage facilities, and monitored with PPCM. All other storage areas and possible clandestine areas would be considered nonnuclear and subject to short notice OSIs with sensitive radiation detectors.

Such a comprehensive SNWI regime might be negotiated, but probably not in time for START III.

5. *Nuclear-Armed SLCMs*

During earlier START negotiations, the Russians had wanted to limit nuclear-armed sea-launched cruise missiles (SLCMs) but the United States had resisted because of verification difficulties [22] with such systems (ch. VII, chart VII-A). This was resolved in START I by including separate "declaratory limits" of nuclear-armed long-range

SLCMs for each side (Chart VII-B), where "long-range" was defined as SLCMs having a range >600 km. The agreement stated that neither party was to exceed 880 such deployed SLCMs. The agreement also stated that the parties would each year exchange confidential information as to the number of nuclear-armed SLCMs in the range 300 km to 600 km deployed at sea. The annual data exchanges have taken place since START I entry into force.[22] As of January 1998, each side has reported that long-range nuclear-armed SLCM deployments are zero, with no plans to deploy such SLCMs in the next five years.[22]

At Helsinki, the SLCM issue was brought up again by the Russians for near-term discussions.[20] As a separate arms control regime, verification of inventories of warheads previously removed from SLCMs will be hard to accomplish, since, as with other types of warheads, there is no verified baseline data for nondeployed nuclear-armed SLCMs. Those that are deployed, or stored in declared facilities, might be verified by methods similar to those for nuclear-armed ALCMs. If increased transparency or verification is desired, onboard verification of deployments on naval vessels will be desirable. If it is desirable to achieve an arms control regime of zero or just a few dozen nuclear armed SLCMs, it might be possible to store allowed nuclear-armed SLCMs within specified storage areas monitored with PPCM. Deployments on a limited number of specified naval vessels might be verifiable using NTM, OSIs at port calls, and tamper-proof onboard seals. Distinguishing nuclear-armed SLCMs from nonnuclear SLCMs is important since the US has used many hundreds of nonnuclear armed SLCMs (Gulf War, 1991, Kosovo, 1999). Such inspections could utilize radiation detectors.

6. Tactical Nuclear Systems

In September/October of 1991, Presidents Bush and Gorbachev, in separate unilateral statements, announced[23] that the United States and Russia would withdraw their ground-based and many other tactical nuclear weapons from forward deployment areas in Europe. This has occurred and many nuclear warheads have been removed from these tactical systems and some dismantled. However, there has been no regime of notifications, declarations of deployed and nondeployed tactical warheads, or verification of these warheads.

If the United States and Russia desire to achieve a meaningful verification regime for their tactical nuclear weapons, they will need to agree on the categories of weapons to be limited or eliminated, provide for a complete data exchange of the categories and numbers of weapons, and provide START-like baseline data and inventory inspections. The author suggests, as an example, a regime that would involve putting all allowed and declared tactical nuclear weapons within storage areas monitored by PPCM. The storage areas might be analogous to the restricted areas used for road-mobile ICBMs in START I (ch. VII, Charts VII-B and VII-E). These weapons would be available for deployment in some theater area only under very extreme "threats to extreme national interests." All other tactical nuclear weapons would be declared and transported to agreed upon elimination facilities. The elimination facilities would be monitored with PPCM, and after the allowed period for transport of weapons to the appropriate storage areas, no tactical nuclear weapons would be allowed outside of the agreed areas and facilities. NTM and short-notice OSIs would be provided to monitor tactical weapons within the territories of the parties. A goal could be to reduce the allowed tactical nuclear weapons of both parties to an agreed-upon value (less than 1000, significantly less than the allowed total of strategic warheads.) Detection of any unauthorized nuclear-armed tactical nuclear weapons outside the allowed area would indicate a violation of the agreement.

7. Nuclear Warheads and Verification

The six possible verification regimes discussed above all involve nuclear warheads that were designed for specific types of delivery systems. It should be noted that, in general, nuclear warheads may be used for more than one type of delivery system. Nondeployed and/or stored nuclear warheads may be adapted for a variety of delivery systems. The problem of verifying the presence of nuclear warheads without disclosing design details is, of course, complex. The problem of determining the presence of significant numbers of undisclosed or hidden nuclear warheads in vast geographical areas is even more difficult. As one pursues the goal of transparency, arms limitations, and more comprehensive verification, the problem of verifying the disposition of all types of nuclear warheads becomes more crucial and should be given high priority. It becomes particularly important in two cases: (1) the need to prevent excess nuclear warheads or nuclear materials in the former Soviet Union (FSU) from falling into the hands of third parties (for example, Iraq, North Korea, Iran, or terrorist groups); and (2) in proposed (ch. X) multilateral arms control treaties in which total numbers of nuclear weapons might be reduced to very low levels (hundreds). Efforts to address case 1, such as the Nunn-Lugar program and bilateral nuclear materials disposition agreements, are discussed below. As discussed in ch. X, case 2 regimes would require intrusive verification of all warheads, whether deployed or stored.

The Nunn-Lugar Initiative

In the fall of 1991, President Mikhail Gorbachev (of the former USSR) requested Western help in dismantling nuclear weapons, and President George Bush proposed US cooperation on the storage, transportation, dismantling, and destruction of nuclear weapons. In November 1991, in response to their concern over control of nuclear warheads within the emerging independent republics of the Soviet Union, Senators Sam Nunn (D), Chair of the Senate Armed Services Committee (SASC), and Richard Lugar, a ranking Republican on the Senate Foreign Relations Committee (SFRC), initiated legislative action resulting in an amendment to H.R. 3807 (dealing with European defense issues) which created[13] the "Nuclear Threat Reduction Act of 1991." This action provided $400 M to aid the former Soviets in dismantling their nuclear weapons. These FY92 funds came through presidential transfers from other designated Department of Defense (DoD) accounts. The program under this act provided for US cooperation with the former Soviet Union (FSU) to

- destroy nuclear, chemical, and other weapons;
- transport, store, and safeguard such weapons before their destruction; and
- establish verifiable safeguards against proliferation of such weapons.

The US financial assistance through the 1991 Nunn-Lugar Act, now known as the Cooperative Threat Reduction (CTR) program, was contingent on the recipient's commitment to

- make substantial investment of its own resources for these purposes;
- forgo any modernization or replacement program that exceeds legitimate defense needs;
- forgo any use in new nuclear weapons of fissionable materials from destroyed nuclear weapons;
- facilitate US verification of weapons destroyed under the Act;
- comply with all relevant arms control agreements; and
- observe internationally recognized human rights.

Congressional appropriations for the CTR Program have averaged about $400 M per year since FY92. The technical assistance was distributed by way of specific agreements with each party (Russia, Belarus, Ukraine, and Kazakhstan). During FY92, negotiations on specific projects included armor blankets for nuclear weapons containers, emergency response equipment and training, fissile material storage containers, design of a specific nuclear materials storage facility, and US provision of security upgrade kits to be installed in Russian nuclear weapons rail cars. Examples of the earliest such agreements actually signed (announced at the April 1993 Summit) for implementation included $130 M to assist Russia in eliminating SNDVs, $75 M for procurements for a nuclear materials storage facility, and $10 M for assistance in civil nuclear material control, accountability, and security.[24]

When the program became known as the CTR program in FY93, it expanded[24] to include a range of activities designed to stabilize the FSU nuclear weapons military complexes. These measures included funding for efforts to improve fissile material protection control and accounting (MPC&A).

Despite difficulties[24] in the early implementation of the programs, much progress has been achieved. By November 1997, it could be reported[25] that the CTR program had assisted the four FSU states (Russia, Belarus, Ukraine, and Kazakhstan) with the elimination (or reduction) of their weapons of mass destruction (WMD), proliferation prevention efforts, and the dismantlement or transformation of infrastructure associated with these weapons. CTR projects are helping convert 17 WMD factories to civilian use. Through the Science and Technology Centers, partly supported initially by the CTR program, opportunities have been created for 15,000 FSU weapons scientists and engineers in peaceful civilian research.[25]

In Russia, CTR assistance helped remove about 1500 strategic nuclear warheads from deployment sites. CTR is helping Russia to centralize fissile materials derived from dismantled nuclear weapons into limited numbers of safe and secure storage areas, assisting in the design and construction of a fissile material storage facility at Mayak, Russia, and designing and fabricating storage containers. Discussions are now under way regarding transparency arrangements to be used at MAYAK. CTR has provided a Nuclear Weapons Automated Inventory Control and Management System which will provide for monitoring and tracking nuclear weapons destined for dismantlement. CTR has provided 4000 armored blankets for weapons transit, 115 kits for rail cars (for nuclear weapons transit), supercontainers for transporting nuclear weapons, and emergency response training and equipment. CTR has provided enhancements for up to 50 nuclear weapons storage sites. CTR has also provided substantial support for Russian chemical weapons destruction programs.[25]

In Ukraine, CTR assistance enabled early deactivation (removal of warheads) of all 46 deployed SS-24 ICBMs (10 RVs each), and of all 130 SS-19 ICBMs(780 warheads). CTR assistance also enabled nearly 2000 ICBM and ALCM warheads to be returned to Russia for dismantlement.[25]

In Kazakhstan, CTR is helping eliminate 120 SS-18 launchers and launch control silos, and 28 test launchers. CTR also helped return 104 SS-18 missiles to Russia.[25]

In Belarus, CTR assisted in removing 36 SS-25 ICBM missiles, their launchers, and their nuclear payloads from Belarus to Russia. CTR has contracted for eliminating the 36 SS-25 launch pads. DoD plans to provide Belarus with the support necessary to dispose of its 1000 MT of liquid rocket fuel.[25]

The CTR program continues to help these FSU states in meeting their obligations under the START I treaty and the CWC (Chemical Weapons Convention). We count on CTR to continue this assistance if START II enters into force and many more nuclear weapons are dismantled.

Agreements on US/Russian Nuclear Weapons Materials

Concurrent with the perceived need for and implementation of the Nunn-Lugar program was the realization that political and economic instability in the FSU could drastically weaken the security[26] of hundreds of tons of plutonium and HEU used for building nuclear weapons.[27] These materials are used or stored at several dozen military and civilian sites within Russia and at several sites in other FSU states. The Soviet Union is believed[26] to have produced over 1200 metric tons of HEU, and 150 to 200 tons of plutonium. About half of the material is in nonweapon-usable form or condition. The United States has pursued several kinds of agreements with Russia to help control the disposition of these weapons-grade fissile materials, as discussed below.

MPC&A

Starting in 1992, the United States proposed to Russia and other FSU states the creation of joint programs for improving the effectiveness of nuclear material protection, control, and accounting (MPC&A). The US initiatives were originally part of the DoD's CTR program (Nunn-Lugar) and, since September 1995, have been directed by the DOE's Russia-FSU Nuclear Materials Security Task Force.[26] DOE relies on technical experts from US national laboratories (such as Los Alamos) who work directly with their counterparts in Russia and the FSU to design and install improved MPC&A systems. DOE officials have signed agreements for MPC&A cooperation with more than 50 nuclear sites in the FSU, mostly in Russia, and by early 1998, joint work was under way at all of these sites.[26] New site-wide MPC&A systems have been installed at 17 of these sites, and over 1000 Russian and FSU personnel have received US-supported MPC&A training. Since 1994, MPC&A activities have been conducted on a Laboratory-to-Laboratory basis with scientists and engineers at US laboratories, under guidance of the US government, working directly with their counterparts in the Russian laboratories and institutes on specific projects.[28] Los Alamos is a lead laboratory for this effort and, working with other US laboratories, works with Russian facilities to develop systems for entry control, nondestructive assay measurements, item control functions, and inventory verification. Since 1995, the program has expanded to include 41 Russian institutes and other facilities, and another 13 facilities in other FSU states. The United States provides equipment and technical support, and the Russians provide Russian equipment and methods. An example is the Kurchatov Institute, where a basic MPC&A system (providing effective physical protection and computerized nuclear material accounting) has been installed at an area where HEU experiments are conducted. Two large nuclear material sites, Tomsk-7 and MAYAK, are now also implementing advanced protection technologies.[28]

Despite the many accomplishments of the program, large quantities of weapons-usable nuclear materials in Russia and the FSU remain inadequately secured.[29] The problem of sustaining the effectiveness of the newly installed systems also needs review, and the overall goals will require many years of sustained effort.[26]

Agreements on Highly Enriched Uranium (HEU)

On February 18, 1993, the United States and Russia signed an agreement ". . . Concerning the Disposition of Highly Enriched Uranium Resulting from the Dismantlement of Nuclear Weapons in Russia." By this agreement, the parties are to convert as soon as practical the HEU resulting from dismantlement of Russian nuclear weapons into low enriched uranium (LEU) for fuel in commercial nuclear reactors, and are to establish appropriate measures to fulfill the nonproliferation, physical security, material accounting and control, and environmental requirements with respect to HEU and LEU subject to the agreement.[27] For several years, the United States has been working to enhance transparency measures associated with the agreement for the purchase by the United States from Russia of LEU blended down from 500 tons of HEU removed from former Soviet weapons systems. Since 1996, the United States has had access to documentation associated with dismantled weapons, and to the receipt and storage areas for Russian HEU weapons components arriving from dismantlement facilities. The United States has the right to perform radiation measurements on HEU weapons components and HEU oxide in sealed containers.[27] The United States also has the right to install enrichment and flow-measurement equipment at the blend points in Russian facilities. As noted above, a major CTR project involves assistance in designing and constructing a storage facility for fissile materials from dismantled warheads.

In November 1996, the United States and Russia reached a new agreement[30] accelerating the pace of the 1993 HEU purchase agreement. The new arrangement provides for a 50% increase in the amount of LEU that the United States will receive in the subsequent five years. Hence, by the year 2001, Russia is expected to convert to LEU the HEU equivalent of about 7500 nuclear warheads. The US Enrichment Corporation (USEC) is the US government's agent for the purchase agreement. In January 1994, USEC signed the original 20-year purchase agreement with MINATOM (and with TENEX, the Russian government's executive agent) to implement the 1993 agreement. When completed, the USEC will have purchased approximately 15,000 metric tons of Russian LEU at a cost of about $12 billion. The LEU will eventually be sold as fuel for commercial power reactors worldwide. This would be equivalent to about 22,000 nuclear warheads. By November 1996, the USEC had received 371 metric tons of LEU (diluted from 9.9 tons of HEU).[30] In recent months, world market conditions have impeded these HEU/LEU purchase agreements. An FY99 congressional funding initiative led by Senator Domenici is aimed at keeping the program afloat.[30] In March 1999, the United States and Russia signed a contract implementing the HEU agreements.[30]

Agreements on Plutonium

In 1992, General Brent Scowcroft, national security advisor to President Bush, submitted a request to the National Academy of Sciences' Committee on International Security and Arms Control (CISAC) for a full-scale study of the management and disposition options for plutonium. The Clinton administration confirmed CISAC's mandate in January 1993. After a broad-based study, involving input from many individuals, including those from the US DOE laboratories, other US government agencies, and private organizations in the US arms control community, CISAC published its report[31] in March 1994. The report noted the large amounts of HEU and plutonium that would become excess to the nuclear weapons needs of Russia and the United States, and stated that the existence of this material "constitutes a clear and present danger to national and international security."

The report recommended that the United States negotiate the following actions with Russia.[31]

- Develop a new Weapons and Fissile Material Regime that would include the following:
  - declarations of stockpiles of nuclear weapons and all fissile materials;
  - cooperative measures to confirm these declarations;
  - an agreed halt to production of fissile materials for weapons; and
  - agreed, monitored net reductions from these stockpiles.
- Develop a reciprocal regime of secure, internationally monitored storage of fissile materials and ensure that the inventory could be withdrawn only for nonweapons uses.
- Pursue long-term plutonium disposition options that
  - minimize plutonium storage time in weapons usable form;
  - safeguard such plutonium storage with same security and accounting as with nuclear weapons;
  - convert plutonium to form that is difficult to recover for weapons use; and
  - meet high standards of public protection and worker health.
- Pursue new international arrangements to improve safeguards and physical security over all forms of plutonium and HEU worldwide.

The report[31] noted two principal differences in plutonium and HEU. First, HEU may be diluted with other U isotopes into LEU, which cannot sustain a nuclear explosion, but can be used for reactor fuel. LEU requires an expensive and complex process (more likely observable) to enrich it into weapons-grade HEU. Plutonium cannot be diluted with other plutonium isotopes to make it unusable for weapons, so it must be diluted chemically with other elements, a process more easily reversed by a potential proliferator. Thus, plutonium management requires much more security. Second, the use of plutonium fuels is generally more expensive worldwide (because of the high fabrication and handling costs associated with plutonium toxicity). Few of the world's approximately 400 nuclear power reactors are designed (or licensed) to handle plutonium. These differences play a role in the agreements discussed here on HEU and plutonium disposition.

Following a January 1994 joint statement by Presidents Clinton and Yeltsin, in which the leaders tasked their experts to jointly "study options for long-term disposition of fissile material, particularly plutonium," US and Russian representatives met in May 1994 (Moscow), January 1995 (Los Alamos), January 1996 (Livermore), and three more times to produce a detailed joint report[32] in September 1996. The joint study elucidated the technical issues involved and reported on much of the detailed work that the parties had done to address issues including Russian work to convert weapons "pits" to unclassified forms and methods to resist theft and diversion. The report[32] listed various disposition options and concluded that the United States and Russia need not use the same plutonium disposition technologies. However, such disposition should proceed in parallel with "the goal of reductions to equal levels of military plutonium stockpiles," and stated "it is advisable for both sides to declare how much weapons plutonium, and in what forms, is excess to their military needs."

The GAO produced a detailed report [33] on many technical/political issues related to US-Russia plutonium disposition efforts. It noted the need for future binding agreements with Russia on these issues. The report also indicated that the immobilization of plutonium may be more costly or complicated than was believed earlier.[31]

Recent agreements and issues regarding Pu are discussed below.

Plutonium Production Reactor Agreement

On September 23, 1997, Vice President Gore and Russian Federation Chairman Chernomyrdin signed the US-Russian Plutonium Production Reactor Agreement,[19,34] which entered into force immediately. Under the agreement, Russia's three plutonium production reactors, currently in use, must be converted by the year 2000 to no longer produce weapons-grade plutonium. The United States will provide assistance for this conversion under the CTR program. The total cost of the core-conversion project, estimated at $150 M, will be divided between the two parties. The 10 other Russian plutonium production reactors, and all 14 such US reactors have already been shut down, and under the agreement, must remain permanently out of operation. Russia commits not to use, in nuclear weapons, any of the weapons-grade plutonium it produces in the three operating reactors. The United States is given the right to monitor an estimated 4.5 to 9 tons of such plutonium that will have been produced by these reactors since 1995. The agreements' extensive monitoring regime will provide the US and Russian monitors unprecedented access to each other's nuclear warhead production facilities to ensure that closed facilities remain closed. In addition, the United States will be able to monitor the recently produced plutonium to ensure that it remains out of nuclear warheads. A Joint Implementation and Compliance Commission (JICC) was established to resolve any issues that might arise.[19,34]

Plutonium Management Agreement

In July 1998, the United States and Russia signed an agreement[35] on "... Scientific and Technical Cooperation in the Management of Plutonium that has been Withdrawn from Nuclear Military Programs." This agreement will provide (a) a scientific and technical basis for decisions on how plutonium subject to the agreement shall be managed and (b) establish a framework for continued and expanded cooperation for such plutonium management. The agreement calls for proceeding to a pilot-scale demonstration of plutonium technologies; cooperate in developing techniques for conversion of metallic plutonium into oxide suitable for MOX (mixed oxide) fuel for power reactors; disposal of immobilized forms of materials containing plutonium in deep geological formations; and related activities. The parties are to establish a US-Russian Joint Steering Committee on Plutonium Management, which shall coordinate and agree on work under this agreement. Steering committee decisions will be made by consensus. The agreement outlines its scope and implementation in 14 articles.

On September 2, 1998, Presidents Clinton and Yeltsin signed[36] a "Joint Statement of Principles for Management and Disposition of Plutonium Designated as No Longer Required for Defense Purposes."

In the statement, the United States and Russia agreed to take the following actions:

- Each convert about 50 tons of plutonium withdrawn in stages from nuclear military programs into forms unusable for nuclear weapons;
- Cooperate to pursue this goal through consumption of plutonium fuel in existing nuclear reactors, or in the immobilization of plutonium in glass or ceramic mixed with high-level radioactive waste;
- Expect the comprehensive effort for the management and disposition of this plutonium to be broad-based and multilateral, and welcome close cooperation with other countries;
- In cooperation with others, develop and operate an initial set of industrial-scale facilities for converting plutonium to fuel for the above-mentioned existing reactors;
- Seek to develop acceptable methods for transparency measures, including international verification and stringent standards of MPC&A; and
- Agree upon appropriate financing arrangements.

The statement called for taking into account the July 1998 agreement (above) and called for negotiations to conclude the agreement by the end of 1998.

Trilateral Agreements with IAEA

In December 1997, technical experts from the United States, Russia, and the IAEA met at a technical workshop at the Lawrence Livermore National Laboratory (LLNL) to exchange views and demonstrate verification and monitoring technologies that might be used for IAEA inspections of sensitive components containing plutonium, without revealing classified information.[37] The focus of this "trilateral workshop" was on measurement physics approaches with "information barriers" to protect classified information while permitting the IAEA to draw independent conclusions. In March 1998, a follow-up workshop was held at Obninsk, Russia. The objective of the workshops is to provide the IAEA inspectors with the means of determining that declared nuclear materials actually have been removed irreversibly from nuclear weapons without disclosing sensitive information such as weapons design.

The US "attribute verification team" believes[37] that all standard monitoring methods (such as radiation measurements) for this monitoring task will reveal some classified information, but they also believe[37] that it will be possible to construct instruments that analyze sensitive measurement data that would, using "information barriers," reveal only unclassified results to the inspector. An example of the "information barrier" approach would be an instrument which might reveal only that the value of a measured parameter is above or below an agreed threshold. Personnel of the US DOE national laboratories are conducting experiments and analyses of this approach, and are working with their Russian counterparts and the IAEA to define functional requirements and procedures for using US and/or Russian instruments.

On September 21, 1998, during the General Conference of the IAEA, US Secretary of Energy Bill Richardson issued a statement[38] outlining important areas needed for progress on the control of fissile materials. These included new DOE programs to help execute the plutonium agreements described above, and included support for the United States/Russia/IAEA Trilateral agreement to apply IAEA verification measures to the weapons plutonium to be safeguarded under the Clinton/Yeltsin agreement of September 2.

On September 22, 1998, Secretary Richardson met with Evgueny Adamov (Russian minister of atomic energy) and Mohamed El Baradei (IAEA director general) to review progress made under the trilateral agreements.[38] They agreed that technical work would continue, to enable verification activities to commence at the earliest practical time. The parties are seeking to develop model verification agreement to use as a basis for an IAEA verification regime for weapons-originated fissile materials to be implemented through independent bilateral agreements. Using these, the states may submit to IAEA verification any weapon-originated fissile material or other fissile material released from defense programs. The model agreement anticipates that other states may undertake similar arrangements in conjunction with future arms reductions. It was agreed that the three principals would meet again in September 1999 to review progress and plan the next steps.[38]

The participants were invited to send experts to two workshops at the Los Alamos National Laboratory and at other US DOE facilities.

US/Russian Joint Steering Committee on Plutonium Disposition

The "US/Russian Joint Steering Committee on Plutonium Management and Disposition," as established by the US/Russian Plutonium Management Agreement of July 1998 (discussed above), held its first meeting in Moscow, December 10-12, 1998.[39] The July 1998 agreement had assigned the Steering Committee responsibility for

- development of the overall work program within the scope of the agreement;
- prioritization, coordination, review, and approval of the cooperative projects under the agreement;
- resolution of any disputes that may arise with respect to the scientific and technical work; and
- such other matters as the two governments agree are within the scope of the agreement.

The Steering Committee is also responsible for reviewing and approving implementation for the performance of the joint research projects and experiments that the Joint Steering Committee authorizes. By the July 1998 agreements, its decisions are taken by consensus.

At this inaugural meeting, the Steering Committee agreed to review the progress and the program for US/Russian scientific and technical work in plutonium management and disposition with a view toward developing an agreed-upon coordinated plan and schedule to guide the transition to implementation of a comprehensive plutonium disposition program. It was agreed that DOE and MINATOM enlist other appropriate governmental agencies in the Steering Committee discussions to ensure full expressions of the viewpoints of the two governments. The two co-chairs of the Steering Committee will actively facilitate the involvement of all appropriate entities.

The Steering Committee agreed on the following:

- US-Russian joint scientific work in plutonium disposition will continue under auspices of the US laboratories and Russian institutes under the general direction of DOE and MINATOM;

- In most cases, the laboratory-institute contracts will continue as the vehicles for carrying out the joint studies and programs; and
- The existing framework of Joint Working Groups under the auspices of the Steering Committee will continue as the effective way to proceed, with each working group co-chaired by designated laboratory/institute officials. Additional entities may be used if needed.

Existing working groups reported an assessment of information available from other countries, such as the French/German program to support use of mixed oxide (MOX) fuel. The MOX fuel test at RIAR is considered one of the critical path items for MOX development. Oak Ridge National Laboratory and the Kurchatov Institute have begun work on cost and schedules for the MOX fuel program option. The Fast Reactor Working Group has worked on breeding blanket, MOX core, and other plutonium conversion projects. Reports and plans were reviewed on use of MOX fuel in thermal reactors, and on immobilization of wastes containing plutonium.

The Steering Committee also took up planning and implementation of a joint US/Russian development of High Temperature Gas-Cooled Reactor (HTGR) technology to dispose of military plutonium. The US Congress has appropriated $ 5 M (FY99) to support this effort. A new HTGR joint working group was established to manage the project.

The Steering Committee expects to meet twice each year, with the next meeting set for June 1999 in the United States. The co-chairs will hold an interim executive session in the spring.

Accelerated Plutonium Disposition

US Senator Pete Domenici (R-NM) has urged[40] the establishment of an accelerated program for disposing of about 50 tons of the excess Russian plutonium. This program sets a goal of 10 tons per year to be moved through conversion of classified shapes to unclassified ones and into safeguarded storage. By changing the shapes (chemically or mechanically) of weapons pits, the plutonium can be expeditiously put into a form for storage that may utilize IAEA safeguards. If careful storage and inventory controls are used, this conversion could alleviate the urgent need to dispose of the weapons-grade plutonium directly through a reactor-fuel-burning process that the Russians are not prepared to accomplish at the desired rate of ten tons per year. In a supplemental appropriation initiated by Senator Domenici, Congress has provided about $200 M for FY99 to help facilitate US/Russian plutonium agreements.

Ambassador John Holum (ACDA Director, 1994–99) has been designated undersecretary of state for Arms Control and International Security Affairs and will direct these ongoing negotiations with Russia on disposition of weapons materials.[41]

References and Notes

1. "Joint Statement on Parameters of Future Reductions in Nuclear Forces," President Clinton (United States) and President Yeltsin (Russia), Office of the White House Press Secretary, Helsinki, Finland, March 21, 1997.
2. "START II Protocol," text of protocol, Joint Agreed Statement, and Letters on Early Deactivation, signed by US Secretary of State Albright and Russian Foreign Affairs Minister Primakov, September 26, 1997, US Arms Control and Disarmament Agency (press release and fact sheets), September 26, 1997.
3. David B. Thomson, "The START Treaties: Implementation and Status," Los Alamos National Laboratory report LAUR-97-2045 (May 1997).
4. Spurgeon M. Keeney, Jr., "START III Now," and Jack Mendelsohn, "START II and Beyond," *Arms Control Today*, October 1996, pp. 2–9.
5. Paul Kennedy, "Preparing for the Twenty-First Century," Random House, NY, 1993, ch. 11.
6. Amy F. Woolf, "START II: Central Limits and Force Structure Implications," CRF Report 93-35F updated May 9, 1995, Congressional Research Service (CRS), Library of Congress, Washington, DC, 20540-7460. Also see Paul Podvig, "The Russian Strategic Forces: Uncertain Future," published in *Breakthroughs* (Spring 1998, Vol. VII, No. 1, pp. 11–21), Security Studies Program of MIT, Cambridge, MA.
7. Aleksey Ivanovich Podberezkin and Anton Viktorovich Surikov, "A Treaty Giving the United States Advantages: START II Ratification Should be Revisited After 2000," Moscow Nezavisimoye Voyennoye Obozreniye, February 20–26, 1998, No. 7, p. 6, FBIS translated text, FBIS-SOV-98-089. Podberezkin is deputy chairman of the Duma International Affairs Committee, and Surikov is director of the Information-Analyst Center of Institute of Defense Research (Moscow).
8. Aleksey Arbatov and Petr Romashkin, "There is No Alternative to START II Ratification: Since Russia Extremely Needs the Next Treaty, START III," Moscow Nezavisimoye Voyennoye Obozreniye, Feb. 20–26, 1998. FBIS Translated Text, March 30, 1998, FBIS-SOV-98-089. Arbatov is deputy chairman of the State Duma Defense Committee, and Romashkin (a reserve Col.) is consultant to Yabloko group in the State Duma.
9. Yuri K. Nazarkin and Rodney W. Jones, "Moscow's START II Ratification: Problems and Prospects," *Arms Control Today*, September 1995, pp. 8–14.

10. At the Reykjavik Summit in 1986, Presidents Reagan and Gorbachev agreed on many of the basic parameters of the START treaty (ch. VII), but the Soviets objected strongly to the US Strategic Defense Initiative (SDI) claiming it would lead to violation of the ABM treaty. This disagreement dampened the momentum of the START agreements. During 1987-88, the Soviets continued to oppose the US SDI program, even though they were continuing their own SDI research (See ACDA, "Annual Report to Congress," 1988, pp. 9–24. Issued March 14, 1989). The ABM treaty of 1972, as amended by the 1974 Protocol, limits each side to one ABM site and 100 launchers at that site (see "Arms Control and Disarmament Agreements," US ACDA, 1982 ed., pp. 158–163).
11. "ABM Treaty Agreements" signed September 26, 1997. Includes Joint Communiqué on the Signing of the ABM Treaty Documents," signed by US Secretary of State Albright, Russian Foreign Minister Primakov, Belarussian Foreign Minister Antonovich, Kazakhstan Foreign Minister Tokayev, and Ukrainian Foreign Minister Udovenko. Includes an MOU amending the ABM treaty of 1972 for it to include the four (nuclear weapon) successor states of the USSR, two Agreed Statements each with a separately signed Common Understanding. The Joint Communiqué also includes a Confidence Building Measures Agreement; and the Regulations of the Standing Consultative Commission (SCC) of the ABM treaty. The complete package of agreements, with Fact Sheets, released by the US Arms Control and Disarmament Agency (ACDA), Washington, DC, September 26, 1997.
12. Jack Mendelsohn, "The United States-Russian Strategic Arms Control Agenda," *Arms Control Today*, pp. 12–16, November/December 1997, the Arms Control Association, Washington, DC.
13. The Nunn-Lugar Initiative. See "Soviet Nuclear Threat Reduction Act of 1991," US Senate, November 25, 1991, Amendment to H.R. 3807 (known as the Nunn-Lugar Amendment); Press conference with Senator Sam Nunn and Senator Richard Lugar, "Report from the Tour of Russian Republics," Senate Radio and TV Gallery, Federal News Service, November 25, 1992. Testimony of William Burns, SFRC Hearing on Weapons Dismantlement in the former Soviet Union, July 27, 1992 (Burns was accompanied by Dr. John Birely, DoD, and Dr. James Turner, DOE). Statement by Dr. Harold Smith, assistant to the Secretary of Defense for Atomic Energy. Hearing on Cooperative Threat Reduction (CTR), Armed Services Committee, US Senate, June 23, 1993.
14. Susan Eisenhower, panel member, "Advancing the Arms Control Agenda: Pitfalls and Possibilities," *Arms Control Today*, Vol. 28, No. 1, January/February 1998, pp. 14–16.

15. Jack Mendelsohn, "The NATO-Russian Founding Act," *Arms Control Today*, May 1997, pp. 19–20. Also see pp. 21–24.
16. Rodney W. Jones, "Trip Report for the START II Project," Carnegie Endowment for International Peace, Washington, DC, November 19–22, 1997. The report included a visit by Rodney Jones and Michael Nacht to the Carnegie Moscow Center (CMC) and a Seminar on "START II Ratification: End game in Moscow?" attended by Alexi Arbatov, US Senator Richard Lugar, Anton Vasiliev, Anton Surikov, Gennady Khromov, and other Russian officials.
17. During the last half of 1998, the status of Russian President Boris Yeltsin's government remained in question because of Yeltsin's poor health and the strength of opposition parties in the Duma. During one two-month period, the position of Russian Federation Prime Minister changed places three times. Former Foreign Minister Primakov became prime minister in September 1998 and through April 1999.
18. Radio Free Europe Report, February 9, 1999, report of Interfax Interview. Duma Security Committee chairman Viktor Ilyukhin stated that the Duma will debate START II ratification in March, 1999, but he does not think START II will be ratified then. Aleksandr Pikaev of the Moscow Carnegie Center, reported in "Novae Vremyu" (February 1999), " . . . chances for Duma ratification of START II have never been so small." The Jamestown Foundation Monitor (January 6, 1999) reviewed recent Russian Press reports on START II and noted that prospects in the Duma indicate both favorable and unfavorable outcomes for ratification.
19. Annual Report to Congress for 1997, US ACDA, Washington, DC, July 1998, pp. 14–25. Nuclear warhead dismantlement was discussed by Cote and Kerr, pp. 107–115, in ref. 56, ch. I. Warhead Transparency is discussed by Steve Fetter, "A Comprehensive Transparency Regime for Warheads and Fissile Materials," *Arms Control Today*, January/February 1999, pp. 3–7.
20. Jack Mendelsohn and Craig Cerniello, "The Arms Control Agenda at the Helsinki Summit," and "Joint Statements of the Helsinki Summit," *Arms Control Today*, March 1997, pp. 16–21.
21. Spurgeon Keeny, Jack Mendelsohn, John Rhinelander, and John Steinbruner, " Arms Control and the Helsinki Summit: Issues and Obstacles in the Second Clinton Term," *Arms Control Today,* March 1997, pp. 9–15.
22. SLCM monitoring was studied in detail in the report "Monitoring Limits on Sea Launched Cruise Missiles," Office of Technology Assessment (OTA) report to the US Congress, July 1991, updated

November 1991, published 1992. Pursuant to the Separate Declaratory Limits on SLCMs (ch. VII and Charts VII-A and VII-B) in the original START I treaty package, signed July 31, 1991 (ref. 6 in ch. VII), the sides have exchanged data on SLCMs in December 1994 (concurrent with the START I data exchange at EIF) and each year thereafter. These SLCM declarations by the US and Russia have stated that zero long-range (>600 km) nuclear-armed SLCMs are deployed by each party, and that as of the January 1998 data exchange, neither party has plans to deploy such SLCMs. Pursuant to the START I agreement, declarations of deployments of shorter range nuclear-armed SLCMs (300 km <range<600 km) are exchanged annually but kept confidential. At START EIF, Belarus, Ukraine, and Kazakhstan each reported that they had no nuclear-armed SLCM deployments either, and as NPT states, had no plans for such. Source: Separate Declarations by the US and Russia Regarding Their Sea-Launched Cruise Missiles, December 1997, US ACDA, Washington, DC, pvt. comm. LCDR Darryl Bates and Richard Hertman, ACDA, October, 1998.

23. Annual Report to Congress for 1991, US ACDA, Washington, DC, 1992. Also see Annual Report to Congress for 1993, US ACDA, Washington, DC, March 1994. For specifics of tactical nuclear weapons withdrawn, see pp. 66–67, SFRC Rpt. 102-53 (ref. 14, ch. VII).

24. Early activities relating to the Nunn-Lugar Initiative are reported in "Quarterly Report On Program Activities for Facilitation of Weapons Destruction and Nonproliferation in the Former Soviet Union," April 30, 1993, DoD, Report to US Congress (House and Senate); Also see David B. Thomson, "The Nuclear Warhead Dismantling Assistance Initiative: The Nunn-Lugar Initiative," CNSS Briefing, Vol. 4, No. 4, November 3, 1993 (Los Alamos National Laboratory report LA-UR-93-3805); and Katherine E. Johnson, "US-FSU Nuclear Threat Reduction Programs: Effectiveness of Current Efforts and Prospects for Future Cooperation," CISA report, August 1995 (Los Alamos National Laboratory report LALP 95-223).

25. William S. Cohen, "Proliferation: Threat and Response," DoD report, November 25, 1997, DoD News Release and Press Briefing Transcript (with press briefing slides). See section on "Department of Defense Response: CTR Activities, Objectives, and Accomplishments." (http://www.defense link.mil./pubs/prolif97/secii.html#department)

26. James E. Doyle, "Improving Nuclear Materials Security in the Former Soviet Union: Next Steps for the MPC&A Program," *Arms Control Today*, March 1998, pp. 12–18.

27. Control of weapons grade fissile materials is reported in ref. 19, pp. 26–30, and pp. 123.
28. "Non-proliferation and International Security," NIS Division Brochure, Los Alamos National Laboratory, February, 1998, LALP-97-216. See pp. 6–7 for role of Center for International Security Affairs (LANL) and the Los Alamos role in the MPC&A program. For an overview of the joint efforts of the United States, Russia, and NIS states to improve MPC&A systems, see "Partnership for Nuclear Material Security," Office of Arms Control and Nonproliferation, US DOE, January 1997 (21-page brochure).
29. Prepared testimony of Rose E. Gottemoeller, director of the Office of Nonproliferation and National Security, DOE, before the US Senate Appropriations Committee, March 3, 1998.
30. Craig Cerniello, "United States, Russia Amend HEU Deal, Accelerating Implementation Pace," *Arms Control Today*, November/December 1996, p. 16. In mid-1998, world market conditions deflated the price of LEU and threatened the HEU purchase agreement. Senator Domenici led a congressional rescue with a special FY99 appropriation. See Walter Pincus, *Washington Post*, November 1, 1998, p. A12. In March 1999, the US and Russia signed a $325-M implementation contract; see John Fialka, *The Wall Street Journal*, March 22, 1999.
31. "Management and Disposition of Excess Weapons Plutonium," Committee on International Security and Arms Control, National Academy of Sciences, National Academy Press, Washington, DC, March 1994.
32. Report of the "Joint United States/Russian Plutonium Disposition Study," US DOE, September, 1996. The US delegation included Bruce MacDonald (OSTP), chair; Howard Carter (DOE), deputy chair; Steve Cochran (LLNL); Paul Cunningham (LANL); James Stiegler (ORNL); and Stephen Passman (SNL). The Russian delegation included Nikolai Yegorov (Minatom), chair; Valery Bogdan (Minatom), deputy chair; and V. I. Solonin (IIM); Anatoli Zrodnikov (IPPE); and Vladimir Kagramanian (IPPE).
33. "Nuclear Nonproliferation and Safety-Uncertainties About the Implementation of United States-Russian Plutonium Disposition Efforts," report to the Committee on Foreign Relations, US Senate, GAO/RCED-98-46, January 1998.
34. "Agreement Concerning Cooperation Regarding Plutonium Production Reactors," signed by US Vice President Al Gore and Russian Federation Chairman Chernomyrdin, in Moscow, September 23, 1997, US ACDA, 1997.

35. "Agreement between the . . . United States and the . . . Russian Federation on Scientific and Technical Cooperation in the Management of Plutonium that has been withdrawn from Nuclear Military Programs," signed by US Vice President Al Gore and Russian Federation chairman, July 24, 1998, in Moscow, International Programs, US DOE, Washington, DC, July 30, 1998.
36. "Joint Statement of Principles for Management and Disposition of Plutonium Designated as No Longer Required for Defense Purposes," signed in Moscow by US President William Clinton and Russian President Boris Yeltsin, September 2, 1998.
37. N. J. Nicholas, M. W. Johnson, D. G. Langner, B. L. Fearey, and J. W. Tape, LANL; T. B. Gosnell and S. J. Luke, LLNL; H. R. Martin, B. W. Smith, PNNL; and D. J. Mitchell and K. W. Marlow, SNL; "Instrument Recommendations for Trilateral Initiative Attribute Verification Measurement Technologies," 1998, LA-UR-98-2084. The Trilateral Initiative for IAEA verification of fissile material excess to defense needs was announced on September 17, 1996, at the IAEA General Conference by DOE Secretary O'Leary, Russian Minatom Minister Mikhailov, and IAEA Director General Blix.
38. Statement by US Secretary of Energy Richardson, at the IAEA General Conference, Vienna, Austria, September 21, 1998. USIA Washington file. For results of the trilateral meeting, see "Statement on Behalf of the Russian Federation, the United States, and the IAEA," press release, IAEA, September 1998.
39. Protocol of the meeting of the US/Russian Joint Steering Committee on Plutonium Management and Disposition in Moscow, Russia, December 10–12, 1998. Signed by Ernest J. Moniz, undersecretary of energy at US DOE, and Valentin Borisovich Ivanov, first deputy minister, Ministry of the Russian Federation for Atomic Energy.
40. Statement of Senator Pete V. Domenici, US Senate, September 18, 1998. Also see John Fleck, "Plutonium Plucked Out of Nukes," *Albuquerque Journal*, December 8, 1998. Report on visit to Los Alamos by Senator Domenici (head of Senate Special Task Force on Plutonium Disposition) with group of Congressional staff members to be briefed on a new DOE/LANL program to chemically convert weapons plutonium pits to unclassified plutonium oxide for eventual use as reactor fuel. Also see Deon Daugherty, "Domenici Urges Faster Action on Plutonium" *Los Alamos Monitor*, December 8, 1998.
41. John D. Holum, "The Arms Control Agenda After ACDA," *Arms Control Today*, March 1999, pp. 3–8.

Chapter X

Multilateral Nuclear Arms Control and Future Needs

The Nuclear Nonproliferation Treaty (NPT) has played a major role in restricting[1] the development and possession of nuclear weapons by many nation-states, as discussed in ch. IV. The indefinite extension[2] of the NPT at the 1995 review conference by 175 nations attests to its importance as a cornerstone in the regime of limiting nuclear weapons. Many nonnuclear weapon states (NNWS) who are party to the NPT have long urged[2] the major nuclear weapons states (NWS) to (1) make more rapid progress in ending the arms race and moving to much lower levels of nuclear deployments than currently agreed in START II and (2) move toward "nuclear disarmament" as called for in Article VI of the NPT itself. A number of experienced former US arms control policy makers have also recently urged[3] moving toward a "long-term objective of eliminating all weapons of mass destruction." Certainly the nuclear superpowers have long been criticized by many NNWS for the asymmetry of the NPT, which allows only five nations to possess nuclear weapons. If the superpowers really succeed in bringing their inventories of nuclear weapons down to much lower values (below those of START III proposals, ch. IX), and if the CTBT enters into force, it will remain to be seen how much pressure will still be applied by the NNWS for the NWS to go to zero.

The vital role that nuclear deterrence played during the cold war and may continue to play in the immediate future has recently been addressed by the National Academy of Sciences[4] and the National Research Council.[5] In this chapter, we note the role of nuclear deterrence, review some of the proposals for very major reductions in numbers of nuclear weapons, emphasize the role and needs for effective verification, and indicate some possible future paths for multilateral nuclear arms control.

The Role of Nuclear Deterrence

The role of nuclear weapons in US security policy has gone through a series of phases during the past 50-some years since they were developed in the Manhattan project. First they were used at Hiroshima and Nagasaki to end World War II and prevent the heavy American and Japanese casualties anticipated in an invasion of Japan. Next they were deployed during the early decades of the cold war to counterbalance the vastly superior Soviet conventional forces in Europe and deter Soviet attack, as discussed in ch. I and II. During the later stages of the cold war, when the two sides maintained a rough parity of nuclear forces, the policy of "mutual assured destruction" prevailed, and each side was presumably deterred by the fear that neither could "win" a nuclear war and that both sides would suffer massive casualties and destruction if a superpower war broke out. It is widely accepted or believed that the mere existence of large numbers of survivable nuclear weapons by the United States and the Soviets deterred their use.[4,5]

Now we are in a period of more friendly relations between the United States and Russia, with major nuclear force reductions and comprehensive verification well under way. Today, however, Russian defense analysts speak in terms of their nuclear weapons as a deterrent against external threats, given their weakened conventional forces (ch. IX). US defense planners prudently suggest that US nuclear force inventories should remain comparable to those of the Russians, as a hedge against some future more aggressive Russian government.[6]

Another major concern now is that one or more third parties or rogue states will threaten to use, or acquire and threaten to use, nuclear weapons. US nuclear weapons, albeit at much lower levels than now available, could remain as a deterrent to such use against the United States or its allies. However, nuclear deterrence is most effective when the potential aggressor being deterred is a rational nation state responsible for the lives of a major population. Terrorists, and/or suicide terrorists, such as the frequent bombers in the middle east who readily kill dozens or hundreds of innocent persons, represent a different kind of threat against which nuclear deterrence may have minimal effect.

The NRC panel[5] notes that the role of nuclear weapons in the post-cold war environment is a matter of some controversy. They state "Most agree that the threat of nuclear weapons use is appropriate to deter the threat or use of nuclear weapons against us and also against allies protected by the US shield." They note there is disagreement on whether it would be appropriate to invoke a nuclear response to chemical or biological attacks on the United States or its allies, and disagreement as to when to use nuclear weapons in response to attacks, with only conventional weapons, on the United States or its allies. This Goodpaster panel[5] concluded, however, that "Nuclear weapons, at whatever numbers our treaty commitments allow, will remain a cornerstone of US national security." Hopkins[5] and Maaranen add that ". . . in the present state of (international) turmoil and uncertainty, complete elimination (by the US) of nuclear weapons, or their entire removal, is very unwise."

The National Academy of Sciences (NAS) panel[4] on "The Future of US Nuclear Weapons Policy," concluded that "the dilemmas and dangers of nuclear deterrence as practiced by the United States in the past can and should be alleviated in the post-Cold War security environment by confining such deterrence to the core function of deterring nuclear attack, or coercion by threat of nuclear attack, against the United States or its allies." They state further, however, "Given adequate conventional forces, the active and conspicuous role given nuclear weapons during the cold war can be greatly reduced without significant adverse effect." They add "The committee believes that Russia and the other NWS can be persuaded to reach a comparable conclusion." Finally they add "As long as nuclear weapons exist, this very existence will exert a deterrent effect–existential deterrence-against unrestricted conventional war among the major powers."

Here we note the role certain states place on nuclear deterrence. For example, Israel, India, and Pakistan each have nuclear weapons programs (see Table 11) and each to some degree perceive nuclear deterrence as necessary to their security, given animosities of their neighbors.

The NAS panel strongly recommends,[4] however, a continued program of progressive verified mutual reductions in nuclear weapons by the major NWS, as does the Stimson Group,[3] Goodby-Feiveson,[7] and others.[8] In view of the US pledge in NPT Article VI (above), we now consider various nuclear arms reduction proposals by others, and then suggest some goals and milestones.

Proposals for Very Deep Reductions in Nuclear Weapons

The Four-Phase Stimson Center Proposal

In December 1995, the Henry L. Stimson Center released results[3] of an in-depth report on its project on eliminating weapons of mass destruction. They proposed to "devalue" weapons of mass destruction and seek an "evolutionary" nuclear posture of careful phased reductions combined with an up-front, long-term commitment to eliminate all such weapons. Alterations in the US nuclear posture would be gradual, with the condition that other states would cooperate.

Phase I is the current phase, with the US and Russia working to implement START II and move to reduced levels in the range of 2000 deployed warheads. During this phase, new measures to increase the transparency of each party's nuclear forces would be introduced.

In Phase II, based on stable and cordial relations among the five declared NWS, all five states would reduce their inventories to hundreds of warheads each. The only military role of nuclear weapons would be to deter nuclear attack. Cuts in force levels would include steps to remove many (or all) such weapons from active alert status. Transparency and safety measures would be extended to the smaller nuclear powers. They state that resolving long-standing conflicts will require a new commitment to strengthen regional institutions and organizations (to achieve conditions for Phase II).

In Phase III, all nuclear weapons states would reduce their arsenals to tens of nuclear weapons each. This would require widespread embracing of new principles and mechanisms for national security. National sovereignty would be preserved but states would rely on regional and global collective security systems for their security. Intrusive verification would be essential.

During the final phase, Phase IV, an international community of sovereign states would have (or require) effective and reliable security alternatives to the threat of mass violence and sufficiently stringent verification and safeguard regimes to allow for the complete elimination of nuclear weapons from all countries. In this "zero" nuclear weapons phase, however, the safeguards regime would have to provide the international community with the appropriate tools to respond rapidly to any aggressor attempting to extract short-term gain from a position of nuclear monopoly.

For Phase IV, the Stimson panel states "it is presumed that the United States and other currently nuclear armed states would preserve components of their nuclear arsenals under international safeguards. If these safeguarded facilities were sufficiently dispersed and protected, it would take a major preemptive strike by tens of nuclear weapons for a violator of the total ban to minimize chances for a retaliatory nuclear response." Thus even this phase may retain an element of nuclear deterrence.

Goodby-Feiveson Proposals

Goodby and Feiveson[7] warn that the next few years may be critical in the efforts to continue the arms control progress initiated by START and other recent arms control measures. They note that Russia has delayed ratification of START II for reasons we have discussed in chs. VIII and IX. They note that the future arms control agenda of China is presently uncertain and that the NPT will be reviewed again in year 2000. They warn that Russia and the United States still maintain ICBMs on hair trigger, controlled by cold-war command structure and doctrine with early warning and nuclear release procedures regularly exercised. Given the conditions in Russia, they regard the security of Russia's nuclear weapons as uncertain.[7]

To alleviate these dangers and regain the momentum in the arms control agenda, Goodby and Feiveson suggest[7] a three-stage program:

Firstly, carry out in detail the general outline of the Helsinki Summit (chs. VIII and IX), including the START III agreement to (1) reduce to 2000–2500 deployed warheads for each party and (2) shift most strategic nuclear weapons away from rapid-launch procedures, partly by removing warheads from missiles and storing them in separately monitored sites. Demated missiles and warheads (or nose cones) may be monitored by bilateral agreement. They note that dealerting missile submarines may be more difficult, so portions of the SLBM fleets may need to be kept at sea, but not all of them. They also suggest that for the START III reductions to be most meaningful, the nonstrategic nuclear warheads (tactical and SLCMs, for example) must be more fully eliminated and a comprehensive warhead verification regime established.

Secondly, by five years after completion of the first stage, establish a limit of 1000 nuclear warheads of all types, complete with comprehensive warhead verification. During this stage, efforts should be made to bring China, the United Kingdom, and France into the regime by freezing their nuclear weapons at their current values.

Thirdly, by the year 2015 to 2020, the United States, Russia, China, and United Kingdom/France in combination would each reduce their nuclear stockpiles to 200 warheads, most of them deactivated. Deactivation would be accomplished mostly by separating nuclear warheads from their launchers (or delivery systems) and placing both warheads and launchers in storage on the territory of the owner-state under multilateral monitoring. A few tens of weapons for each party would be survivably deployed as a nuclear deterrent. Some specific deployment options are suggested, and comprehensive verification is assumed.

Goodby and Feiveson[7] conclude that initiation and achievement of this program will lead to the creation of arrangements that will forestall nuclear weapons proliferation worldwide.

Strategic Escrow

Stansfield Turner[8] presents an eloquent discussion on the need to reduce the role and numbers of nuclear weapons and then suggests a plan to bypass some of the slow process of arms control negotiations. Turner suggests that the United States unilaterally remove perhaps 1000 strategic warheads from operational strategic launchers and place them in "strategic escrow," that is, in designated storage areas some distance from their launchers. Russia would be invited to place observers at each of the storage sites, with duties limited to counting the number of nuclear warheads going into storage, keeping track of whether any were moved, and conducting surprise inventories to ensure none were clandestinely removed. They would also be allowed to check that other warheads had not been placed on the strategic vehicles from which the escrowed warheads had been removed. These observers would have no authority to prevent the United States from moving any warheads from one point to another, but they could report to Moscow if we did.

The hope would be that the Russians would follow the US example and remove up to 1000 warheads from their strategic vehicles with reciprocal inspections by the United States These reciprocal unilateral actions would allow the two parties to develop a bilateral verification regime on a working basis, without having to agree to a detailed intrusive verification regime in advance. Turner suggests[8] that the advantage of these incremental unilateral steps is that if they were violated early on, before the verification was fully established, the asymmetry in the removal of the first 1000 warheads would not upset too much the START I 6000 warhead limit, or even the START II 3500 warhead limit. Serious violations resulting in deployment asymmetries could be corrected by simply restoring the warheads to their original delivery systems. Turner argues[8] that precedence for an initial removal of, say, 1000 warheads from deployment was set when President Bush in 1991 simply ordered all US ground-based and sea-based tactical nuclear weapons unilaterally withdrawn from forward land bases and from naval ships, a step which President Gorbachev followed within weeks, and which President Yeltsin subsequently maintained. Turner noted that the first unilateral steps taken by the presidents (withdrawing 1000 warheads) would not require difficult parliamentary approvals. We note, however, that these promised Russian withdrawals have never been formally fully verified.

If the first "WH removal" increment is successful, the parties could proceed to a second increment of warheads, perhaps 2000 to 3000, and the process could gain real momentum. Turner suggests[8] that the United States and Russia could use this process of initiatives and reciprocation (over several years) to get down to a number like 2000 (START III level) or even as low as 1000 deployed strategic warheads with the other 6000 or so (former strategic warheads) in strategic escrow. He believes this could be accomplished well before START II's target of 3500 warheads by year 2003 (now 2007).

Once this process was well established, the United States and Russia could move[8] in a number of directions:

- Observers from the other side could be positioned at all storage sites for reserve warheads, with arrangements made to store reserve warheads at some distance from the weapons systems to which they could be mated (that is, ICBM warheads moved and stored at bomber bases rather than at an ICBM complex). This would increase the time for reconstitution and more likely signal its occurrence.
- Observers could also be placed at storage sites for all tactical warheads on each side. It would be important to locate the storage separate from the delivery systems (for example, siting warheads for cruise missiles on nuclear bases other than airfields)
- Components such as guidance sets from weapons and plutonium pits from warheads could be removed and placed at separate storage sites to further complicate and delay reassembly and reconstitution. This process could be reversed if one side did not follow. [Author's note: Temporary pit removal may not be technically practical and we suggest that pit removal most likely must occur at special disassembly facilities such as Pantex (for the US), so should occur at a later stage of a verified arms reduction process when reconstitution is not anticipated for those particular warheads. Guidance sets, though expensive, could be replaced by spares.]
- The casings of some warheads in storage could be deliberately damaged to the point that they could be reconstituted (remounted on delivery vehicles) only with a complete reworking. These warheads would not be denied their owners, just made less accessible. [Author's note: This may be considered a bit wasteful by both Russia and the United States, for what it accomplishes.]
- Warheads could be dismantled. Turner suggests delaying this, preferring to store entire warheads rather than the dismantled plutonium and highly enriched uranium for which there is as yet no firm control in Russia's nuclear program. [Author's note: Given the priority that the United States is now giving to plutonium and highly enriched uranium control in Russia (ch. IX), we may prefer to dismantle many of the warheads, under verification.]

- Some new international agency could be invited to install observers at all storage sites to give the rest of the world more confidence that the superpowers were making the reductions called for in the NPT. A new organization would need to be created, or new ground rules added to the IAEA.

Turner states[8] that the above "strategic escrow" process should pause when the United States and Russia had each reduced to about 1000 deployed strategic warheads. He calls this whole first step "Phase 1."

Turner's Phase 2 would be to negotiate how to organize to continue downward in numbers of deployed warheads; how to include the other nuclear powers (China, United Kingdom, and France, and perhaps bring in Pakistan and India); and how to arrange for the intrusive multinational verification procedures that would be necessary to give each party the assurances that the reductions were taking place.[8]

Turner's Phase 2 endpoint[8] of this program of strategic escrow would be as follows:

- All nuclear warheads, worldwide, would be in internationally supervised storage at some distance from their launchers.
- A limit of not more than 200 warheads and accompanying launchers would be set for each nuclear power.
- Observers would be in place to provide warning of any effort to mate warheads to delivery vehicles.

A serious constraint to this program, appropriate storage space in Russia for nuclear warheads (or pits), is currently being alleviated by the Nunn-Lugar program (ch. IX). Turner suggests his "strategic escrow" plan could jump-start the international nuclear arms control process.

Progressive Constraints—NAS Study

The Committee on International Security and Arms Control of the National Academy of Sciences (NAS) recently sponsored a comprehensive study[4] on "The Future of US Nuclear Weapons Policy," chaired by Major General William F. Burns. This report recognizes the value of nuclear deterrence (noted above) but recommends shifting the focus of US nuclear policy to a program of progressive constraints. The proposed constraints include the following:

- Move as quickly as possible to the START III level of 2000-2500 deployed strategic warheads, as proposed at the Helsinki Summit (ch. IX), deferring for a brief time the more difficult issues of overall verification of warheads. This START III can be accomplished within the technical framework of START I and II. Agreeing to the 2000 warhead total should encourage Duma ratification of START II (as we suggest in ch. IX and in ref. 3, ch. IX). The NAS study also states that the 2000 level would more than adequately fulfill the core deterrent function for both sides.
- Further reductions, say to 1000 total warheads, will be needed to bolster the NPT regime and to help persuade the other NWS (declared and undeclared) to join this arms control process. This regime should include limitations and verification on all nuclear warheads-regardless of type, function, stage of assembly, associated delivery vehicle, or basing mode. Such limits and verification of total warhead inventories would minimize reversibility of reductions and diminish possibility of rapid breakout. Such limits would force the eventual dismantling of thousands of additional warheads, improve stability of the nuclear balance, and demonstrate the commitment of the United States and Russia to very deep reductions.

  Verifying these limits will require transparency measures well beyond those negotiated in START.

  The necessary verification regime will require a data exchange which includes the following:
  - current location, type, and status of all nuclear weapon devices;
  - description of facilities at which nuclear explosive devices have been designed, assembled, tested, stored, deployed, maintained, and dismantled; and
  - relevant operating records of these facilities.

  The report states that perhaps the simplest way to verify the data exchange would be to conduct both scheduled and unannounced inspections of nuclear weapons storage sites. Inspectors could verify the number of warheads at a declared site using simple radiation detection equipment. They acknowledge that verification technologies would have to protect the secrecy of nuclear weapon design information. They suggest that as part of the verification regime, warheads would be counted as they entered a dismantling facility, and the "pits" counted as they exited.

The committee chose 1000 warheads each, for the US and Russia, as the goal of this reduction regime to address three issues: (1) survivability, (2) performance of the core-deterrent function, and (3) the need to bring the other nuclear powers into an overall regime before the United States and Russia go much lower.

- Eliminate the hair trigger. The report[4] states that the United States and Russia may take steps, separately but in parallel with the inventory reductions, to eliminate the continuous-alert practice and reduce the launch-readiness status of deployed forces in ways that could be transparent to the other side. Reducing the likelihood of surprise attack in a stabilizing fashion is a challenging but achievable goal.
- Over the longer term, the United States and Russia, together with the other nuclear powers, should search for ways to assure each other that all nuclear weapons, including SLBMs and mobiles, are incapable of being used quickly and without warning.
- Reducing to a level of, say, 300 nuclear warheads. In this regime, the United States and Russia would each reduce to a few hundred total nuclear warheads and the other nuclear powers would reduce to even lower values or zero. This regime will require even more verification accuracy than that stated above. The committee uses an example model of 300 warheads, of which >100 are secure, survivable, and deliverable. They discuss the issues related to force structures, stability, and needed infrastructure for such a regime.
- The NAS study[4] considered the goal of the "complete prohibition of all nuclear weapons," as stated in the preamble to the NPT, and concluded, "Complete nuclear disarmament will require continued evolution of the international system toward collective action, transparency, and the rule of law; a comprehensive system of verification; and a new or expanded international agency with vigorous powers of inspection." They added, " . . . the committee believes that the potential benefits of comprehensive nuclear disarmament are so attractive . . . that increased attention is now

warranted to studying and fostering the conditions that would have to be met to make prohibition desirable and feasible."

Other Calls for Nuclear Weapons Reductions/Abolition

Over the years, of course, other individuals or private groups have called for major reductions and/or abolition of nuclear weapons. A recent such call[9] was issued by 117 civilian leaders from 46 nations, including former presidents Jimmy Carter and Mikhail Gorbachev. The statement recommended six measures:

1. Remove nuclear weapons from alert status;
2. Separate warheads from delivery vehicles and place in secure storage;
3. Halt production of weapons-grade fissile materials;
4. End nuclear testing pending entry-into-force of CTBT;
5. Negotiate further US/Russian nuclear arms reductions (bypass START II status);
6. Obtain an unequivocal commitment by the other declared and nondeclared NWS to join the reduction process on a proportional basis as the United States and Russia approach their arsenal levels, within an "international system of inspection, verification and safeguards."

The statement also called for the "development of a plan for the eventual implementation, achievement and enforcement of the distant but final goal of elimination."

International Regime of Plutonium and Highly Enriched Uranium (HEU) Control

The plans presented above all call for the control of weapons-grade nuclear materials. In ch. IX we discussed the present approaches to bilateral control of such Pu and HEU by Russia and the United States. In its 1994 study[10] the National Academy of Sciences stated that the safeguards for fissile materials by the United States and Russia should "set a standard for a regime of improved management of such materials in civilian use throughout the world." They said negotiations should be pursued to

1. create a global cutoff of all unsafeguarded production of fissile materials;

2. use the US-Russian safeguarded storage regime recommended by the NAS (ch. IX) as a basis for a broad international storage regime for fissile materials, including registration and safeguards for all civilian separated plutonium and uranium;
3. extend the US-Russian declaratory regime to a global regime of public declarations of stocks of fissile materials;
4. agree on higher standards of physical security for these materials, with an international organization given authority to inspect sites to monitor whether the standards are met; and
5. agree on international approaches to manage reprocessing and use of plutonium to avoid building up excess stocks.

The achievement and implementation of such an international fissile-material-control regime most likely will depend on the success of the US-Russian bilateral negotiations discussed in ch. IX.

Perceived Obstacles to Nuclear Disarmament or Deep Reductions

A number of experienced nuclear policy professionals are skeptical of negotiations to achieve deep reductions of the magnitudes discussed above. For example, in 1998 Senate testimony on the CTBT, Kathleen Bailey stated that potential nuclear proliferants could defeat the goals of the CTBT (and the NPT) by building nuclear weapons without testing and threatening cities, and/or testing nuclear devices at yields below, say, 500 tons and evading the CTBT's verification system (see ref. 47 in ch. III). During testimony in 1995 on START II, Sven Kraemer pointed to a 1995 unclassified CIA report that stated ". . . at least twenty countries, at least half of them in the Middle East or South Asia already have or may be developing weapons of mass destruction and ballistic missile delivery systems." In opposing START II, Kraemer (see ref. 11, ch. VIII) noted increasing international threats, declining US defense budgets, and recalled the statement "weakness provokes aggression." Kraemer noted that such friendly nations as Germany, Japan, South Korea, and Taiwan have forgone nuclear weapons because they could depend on the US nuclear umbrella. If the United States were to agree to go to "zero," or very low levels, some of these nations might be tempted to get their own nuclear weapons.

These kinds of issues must be addressed if the goals for deep reductions proposed in the previous sections are to be achieved. It may be well understood by many[3,4,7] who propose deep reductions that the international negotiations and agreements necessary to achieve their goals, with the necessary step-by-step verification, will not be easy. In the following sections the author discusses verification issues and suggests some future directions for arms control. The author notes, however, that perhaps the most important obstacle to deep nuclear reductions is a lack of greatly improved international mutual security mechanisms well beyond those currently provided by the UN Security Council (note discussion with respect to the NPT, ch. IV). Discussion of the needs and possible goals needed to achieve such improved international security is well beyond the scope of this book, but the author poses it as a challenge to the US policy community.

Needed Multilateral Verification and Nuclear Arms Limitation Regimes

At present there is no multilateral international regime of verification for nuclear weapons, nuclear warheads, and/or delivery systems for nuclear weapons. If the proposals outlined above calling for major reductions (by the United States, Russia, and others) of nuclear weapon inventories down to values of several hundreds of warheads are to be realistic, multilateral verification regimes will be necessary. The NAS study,[4] for example, details a number of verification tasks needed for achieving such warhead reductions. Much work must to be done, however, by the US arms control community and the appropriate US government agencies to prepare the United States to take initiatives in international negotiations to achieve the techniques and international institutions needed for the required comprehensive verification. The US OSIA (ch. VI) has developed into a very effective organization for helping carry out a wide variety of US verification tasks, not only for the INF and START treaties, but also in support of the UNSCOM/IAEA inspections in Iraq, in support of the Conventional Forces In Europe (CFE) treaty, in support of the Chemical Weapons Convention (CWC), and in preparations for the Open Skies treaty. To achieve the new multilateral regimes needed for warhead verification and suggested future reductions, the author believes that a new international institution will be needed to provide efficient and effective verification, to take advantage of logistics and techniques developed by the OSIA, and to apply new verification mechanisms needed for nuclear warheads and delivery systems.

International Verification Agency (IVA)

Here the author suggests the creation of a new international agency, perhaps called the International Verification Agency (IVA), to centralize and carry out the multilateral data exchanges, on-site inspections, and other activities needed to provide for the comprehensive nuclear arms verification suggested in this chapter. This agency would be responsible for codifying and verifying the inventories of all nuclear weapons (such as nuclear armed missiles) and nuclear warheads (deployed, nondeployed, and stored) worldwide.

The agency would be responsible for creating and utilizing a world wide system of data exchanges to codify the declarations of parties to specific treaties regarding their nuclear warhead inventories. In the case of nonnuclear weapon parties to the NPT, it would codify the absence of such inventories. The new agency would utilize experience, technical expertise, and available data from the United States and FSU NRRCs (ch. VI). The new agency might establish principal NRRC-like data centers in several appropriate international centers such as Vienna, Moscow, and Washington. Each such center would have appropriate communications with capitals of all participating nations.

The agency would be responsible for establishing a system of international on-site inspections, and cooperative measures, capable of verifying the data exchanges described above. The types, locations, conditions, and rights to conduct the inspections would of course need to be negotiated with the necessary parties in multilateral treaties in a series of international arms control initiatives designed to achieve the major nuclear arms reductions such as proposed by the NAS[4] and others discussed above.

In proposing such a new international verification agency, we do not suggest that it be meant to replace the IAEA, UNSCOM, or any of the US/FSU verification agreements now in place for the INF and START treaties. Rather it would be developed carefully with a strong institutional base, involving as many nuclear and nonnuclear weapons parties as possible with the goal of adding membership and evolving into a really strong and effective mechanism worldwide. The IAEA inspection regimes would continue in their present role, concentrating on the monitoring and control of nuclear materials (uranium and plutonium, etc.). The new agency would concentrate on the verification of the presence or absence of nuclear weapons themselves. There would be much room for collaboration between the two agencies, just as there has been with the IAEA, UNSCOM, and the US OSIA.

The new agency would not need to be responsible for monitoring the CTBT, since that treaty establishes a comprehensive and specialized verification regime designed to detect nuclear explosions. The new agency would obviously have areas of collaboration with the CTBTO (CTBT organization, ch. III) since suspect tests might lead to suspect weapons, etc.

The US OSIA (DTRA) could be utilized to provide extensive technical and logistical support to the new agency, just as it has for UNSCOM activities. The Russian inspection agencies could be invited to contribute along with the US OSIA (DTRA). To strengthen the international agency, the United States might agree to make available certain kinds of NTM information to facilitate inspections.

The form and structure of the new international verification agency, proposed here, would of course depend much on the results of comprehensive multilateral negotiations. The agency should be efficient in structure, capable of acting directly and swiftly when needed, and not subject to a unilateral veto. We suggest that the need is great and the time is long overdue to begin discussions needed to achieve such an organization.

Now we suggest several needed specific multilateral limitation and verification regimes.

Ballistic Missile Verification and Limitations

In the INF and START treaties, the United States and Russians have agreed to comprehensive data exchanges and OSIs (on-site inspections) for monitoring reductions and/or eliminations of ballistic missile deployments. The United States is currently involved in attempting to expand[11] the Missile Technology Control Regime (MTCR) to include China and other nations. This regime is designed to reduce spread of missile technology among the nations that possess such technology and to other parties. We suggest that much more is needed. Ballistic missiles equipped to carry nuclear, chemical, and/or biological warheads represent a growing threat worldwide, as emphasized by the Rumsfield Report.[12] Ballistic missiles must be strictly limited in number, and nuclear-armed missiles must be limited worldwide, with certain categories prohibited. All MIRVed ICBMs (fixed site) worldwide should be prohibited as in START II. We suggest the ballistic missile verification regimes of the START and INF treaties be expanded to include all nations. All nations who agree to the regime would declare annually the numbers, types, and locations of their ballistic missiles, submitting this data to an international verification agency (IVA, as suggested above). A regime of inspections, similar to the OSIs in the INF and START treaties, would be included in the agreement and would be conducted by the international verification agency (perhaps at first assisted by the US OSIA and/or experienced Russian inspectors). A series of treaties or agreements may be needed to bring all the NW states into the verification regime with appropriate sublimits for the numbers of ballistic missiles allowed each NW state party. For example, the United States and Russia could initially be limited to START III values, and China, United Kingdom and France frozen at their present (1999) values. Future reductions would be negotiated. In this suggestion, all other states should be prohibited from having nuclear armed ballistic missiles. Other nations would of course be allowed peaceful space launchers which would be brought under the verification regime. To facilitate negotiations, the United States and Russia could agree not to deploy short-range, ground-based, offensive ballistic missiles (shorter range than already prohibited by the INF treaty).

Bombers and Cruise Missiles

In START I and II, the United States and Russia have placed restrictions on the numbers of nuclear armed bombers (with and without ALCMs) and placed declaratory limits on nuclear armed SLCMs (chs. VII and VIII). In the INF treaty, intermediate-range GLCMs are prohibited (ch. V). These limitations may readily be proposed for the other NWS parties to the NPT (China, France, United Kingdom). Many NNWS parties may understandably desire to have defense forces that include non-nuclear-armed bombers and perhaps cruise missiles.

In future arms control treaties, these should be allowed within negotiated numerical limits, but placed under strict verification regimes. In START, the Russians agreed to the use of radiation detectors to nonintrusively confirm that declared non-nuclear-armed ALCMs were indeed nonnuclear. It should be possible to negotiate a world-wide multilateral regime of on-site inspections of declared nonnuclear armed bombers (with or without ALCMs) to confirm that declared bomber/ ALCM deployments are indeed nonnuclear. This may require additional short notice inspections, PPCM around critical air bases, and other features.

To achieve effective multilateral regimes will require both innovation and strength of purpose on the part of arms control negotiators.

A similar challenge may await multilateral negotiations involving SLCMs.

Stored Nondeployed Warheads

The proposals by others[3,4,7,8,9] for drastic reductions in nuclear deployments worldwide all generally include a goal of several hundred warheads as a desired upper limit to be allowed. If we use the NAS study[4] as an example, the United States and Russia could each be limited to <300 nuclear warheads with, say, about 100 deployed and the remainder stored or nondeployed. For the United States, Russia, and many other nations to achieve enough confidence in such a regime to agree to it, it will be necessary to achieve high confidence in the verification of stored nondeployed warheads, a verification regime untested at this time. Limited numbers of warheads, each in separate storage containers, may be placed in agreed storage facilities and individually counted as they are inserted. The agreed-on storage sites could include highly secured underground facilities protected against surprise attack. International PPCM may be set up around each storage facility and declared warhead containers counted (and tagged) if they are removed for a stated purpose. All other objects removed from the facility would be verified for their nonnuclear character with radiation detectors. Removed warheads would be monitored as to their ultimate use, especially if moved to a deployment site.

If carefully designed, such a verification system, also utilizing START and INFT type procedures to keep track of the deployed nuclear-armed delivery systems, could give confidence as to the declared total inventories of nuclear weapons.

Nondeployed or stored warheads can be small and easy to hide, however, so a strict regime of challenge inspections, including "anywhere anytime" provisions, would be needed for the international verification agency (IVA), backed up by US OSIA (now DTRA) and other appropriate organizations. Though many inspections of many types of facilities could be provided,[13] backed up by the NTM of several nations, it may be impossible to fully confirm that clandestine nuclear warheads are not hidden anywhere in any particular nation (or group of allied nations). The final effectiveness of this regime may require the ability of the international community to impose severe penalties on any nation caught violating the agreements with clandestine storage or deployments of nuclear weapons. The UNSCOM experience in Iraq demonstrates that this problem remains to be solved. Thus the author believes that it would not be prudent for the United States to agree to ultimately reduce its deterrent nuclear weapons inventory below the approximately 300-WH value suggested by the NAS.

The Open Skies Treaty

As noted in ch. II, in 1955 President Eisenhower first proposed[14] Open Skies to the Soviets as a bilateral proposal to allow for wide ranging aerial inspections between the super powers to warn against surprise attack. His proposal, made before space-based reconnaissance satellites were available, could have served as a confidence-building measure to reduce tensions, but the Soviets rejected it. For the United States and Russia, space-based satellite photography[15] became available in the 1960s and satisfied most United States needs for the clandestine aerial photography the United States had practiced over the Soviet Union in the late 1950s with U-2 flights.[14,15] During the 1970s and

1980s the United States continued to use fixed-wing aircraft (U-2R and SR-71) flights to conduct surveillance over areas they could fly safely, such missions being less expensive for some short flight missions.[15]

Many European nations are concerned about military facilities or activities of their neighbors, but do not by themselves have the resources to make detailed satellite observations. Some of these states are in regions where long-standing political or ethnic disputes, held back by the cold war, could resurface. Because of these and related concerns, President Bush proposed a multilateral Open Skies initiative in May 1989, as a means to help ease tensions.[16] Canada and Hungary joined the US initiative. After the breakup of the Soviet Union and many negotiations[17] involving NATO and former Warsaw Pact nations, the Treaty on Open Skies was signed (Table 12) by the United States and 24 other nations at Helsinki on March 24, 1992.[18,19,16,20] After favorable actions[16,19,20] by the Senate Foreign Relations Committee during which spokesmen from both the Bush and Clinton Administrations supported the agreement, the Open Skies Treaty was ratified by the US Senate on August 6, 1993.[21]

We note that the Open Skies Treaty is not of itself an arms reduction or limitation treaty. The Preamble to the Open Skies Treaty notes that its primary objectives include openness, transparency, and confidence building. It recognizes the potential of the treaty to cover areas and states parties beyond those of the original signatories. It notes the possibility of using the open-skies regime to facilitate arms control agreements and to aid in crisis management. It sets forth that all territories of all the parties are open for aerial observation. The treaty provides for the status and types of aircraft that may be used for overflights, the types and specifications of sensors used during overflights, specific maximum annual quotas of overflights that each party accepts over its territories, and annual quotas of overflights that each party or group of observer parties may conduct over the territory of specified observed parties. The treaty provides in detail [16–18,20] for the conduct of overflights including mission plans, notifications, certification. Specified sensors include optical cameras, video cameras with real time display, infrared scanning devices, and synthetic aperture radar.

Sensors must be commercially available to all parties. Resolution is limited so that large objects such as tanks and trucks may be distinguished, but small details such as difference in Russian tank types (with similar appearance) can not be determined.

The treaty provides[17,20] for an Open Skies Consultative Commission (OSCC), with one representative from each party, to facilitate implementation. The OSCC meets regularly to consider questions of compliance, resolve ambiguities, and provide for accession of new members. The OSCC may consider improvements in the verification instrumentation, but OSCC decisions (or recommendations) are made by consensus. Total overflight annual quotas for treaty members range from 4 each for small nations (such as Hungary and Greece), to 12 each for larger nations (such as United Kingdom, France, and Ukraine), and up to 42 each for the United States and Russia. Active quotas varied from party to party depending on the number of overflight requests anticipated.

The treaty is of unlimited duration and any party may withdraw with six months notice. Any party may submit amendments, and if three parties so request, a review conference will be convened to consider amendments. Any amendment shall be subject to approval of all state parties. The treaty will go into effect when at least 20 parties have ratified it, including all parties with quotas greater than 8 (these are the United States, Russia, United Kingdom, Germany, Canada, France, Italy, Turkey, and Ukraine). By late 1998, ratifications were still needed from Ukraine and Russia/Belarus for treaty entry-into-force.[22]

Through the accession of new members, the treaty may be expanded to include new areas of possible concern and bring new nations into a regime of openness and possible cooperation (such as India/Pakistan and in the Middle East).

Though not a nuclear arms reduction treaty, the Open Skies Treaty may serve as a confidence building measure, encourage other multilateral mutual security negotiations, encourage the NPT regime by reducing the fear of surprise attack, and help encourage the international community to negotiate the much needed multilateral verification mechanisms such as the IVA suggested above.

A Strategy for the Future

Unilateral initiatives (not requiring treaties) by the United States and its close allies are vital to reducing the threat of weapons of mass destruction (nuclear, chemical, biological) from terrorist, rogue nations, and traditional adversaries. These initiatives have been emphasized by many, including the DoD.[23] The scope of this book, however, is limited primarily to describing the history, content, and the effectiveness of the existing formal nuclear arms control treaties and some of those treaty proposals that might be initiated in the near future. The author believes that bringing all nuclear weapons under an umbrella of the formal treaty process, combined with robust verification regimes, and coupled with success in the nuclear materials control regimes discussed or proposed in ch. IX and this chapter, will optimize the chance for success in the overall efforts to reduce the threats from terrorists, rogue states, and/or any potential new militancy by former adversaries or others.

To achieve their stated goals for nuclear arms control and nonproliferation, the author believes that the United States and the international community must make a renewed effort to establish the goals and negotiate the treaties and agreements necessary to strengthen international security and greatly reduce the dangers of unlimited nuclear weapons.

Here we suggest a Sixfold approach. Each of these initiatives should be undertaken on its own merits and not be held back dependent on success of one or more of the others.

First, very high priority must be given to achieving entry-into-force of START II, either as presently signed and modified (ch. VIII) or by further reducing the deployed warhead limits to alleviate the stated Russian concerns as discussed in chs. VIII and IX. The large numbers of warheads still deployed on ICBMs and other strategic delivery vehicles (>7000 WHs shown in Table 10) still represent a hair trigger threat of great magnitude (particularly if there is a political breakdown in Russia).

Second, the efforts to bring HEU and plutonium in the FSU under international safeguards should be continued with the utmost urgency. As discussed in ch. IX, Senator Domenici and others consider this a very serious proliferation threat because of the large amount of FSU plutonium for which the accounting and control are questioned. Pu and HEU Controls are urgent because, as discussed in ch. IV and listed in Table 11, there are at least seven countries, not recognized as nuclear weapon states by the NPT, that have, or are considered desirous of obtaining, nuclear weapons. Some clandestine leakage of unaccounted or unsafeguarded plutonium and HEU from the FSU could eventually end up in one or more of these nations, as well as in the hands of terrorists.

Third, the United States and Russia must continue and accelerate discussions to achieve a comprehensive nuclear warhead verification regime such as suggested at the 1997 Helsinki Summit and discussed in ch. IX. A comprehensive warhead verification regime would make feasible additional United States/Russian agreements to limit all nondeployed warheads to values comparable to START III deployed warhead limits. As shown in Table 11, Russia is believed to still possess over 22,000 nuclear warheads, more than 60% of which are nondeployed and undeclared, as discussed in ch. IX. The need to work toward regimes to bring these warheads under control and accountability is urgent both to alleviate concerns for possible clandestine transfer of some of them to outside powers, and to the promotion of the overall arms reduction agenda suggested by this chapter. These negotiations will require resolution of continued US/Russian differences over theater missile defense and the ABM treaty.

Fourth, the United States with like minded partners should promote negotiations to establish an international regime of HEU and plutonium controls such as outlined and recommended by the NAS[10] and discussed in this chapter. As noted above (second initiative) seven or more nations are considered desirous of becoming (or recognized as) nuclear weapon states. Others might join them unless the nonproliferation regime is strengthened.

Fifth, the author strongly recommends the initiation of multilateral negotiations to achieve creation of a strong and durable international verification agency (IVA) as discussed above. Developing the mechanisms to work toward the goal of effective verification of numbers and locations of all nuclear warheads must proceed hand in hand with, or precede, future negotiations on reductions to hundreds of warheads urged by others.[4,7–9] As we have noted, the suggested IVA should also include the capability to verify the locations and inventories of all ballistic missiles. We again note that the IVA should strive for the capability to help determine if nonnuclear weapon members of the NPT indeed have "zero" nuclear-armed weapons.

Sixth, we urge the initiation of parallel multilateral treaty negotiations to achieve staged reductions by the nuclear-weapon NPT parties to nuclear warhead totals in the range of ~300 (lower for all but the United States and Russia) as proposed by the NAS[4] and others discussed above. An important early stage of this initiative could be a multiparty treaty reducing United States and Russian inventories to 1000 warheads each with lower sublimits for deployed ICBMs, SLBMs and bombers (as in START). This stage could limit China and United Kingdom/France (in combination) to no more than about 300 total warheads each, values a little under what they have now (see Table 11). All MIRVed ICBMs would be banned. All other parties would be limited to zero nuclear weapons. The rationale for this stage was discussed by the NAS study[4] outlined in this chapter. Verified limitations to apply to all nations on armed offensive ballistic missiles should be negotiated as part of this initiative.

We must particularly note that special considerations would be needed to bring India, Pakistan, and Israel into these new arms control regimes, as well as into the NPT as NNWS and/or even into the CTBT.[24] India and Pakistan have long-standing animosities, India feels threatened by China's nuclear weapons, and Israel has long been surrounded by adversaries. All have nuclear capabilities as shown in Table 11. Under present conditions, neither Israel nor India is likely to formally agree to "zero" nuclear weapons. Pakistan is unlikely to agree to "zero" unless India does. When the NPT was signed, needed "security assurances" for the NNWS were recognized by a UN Security Council Resolution and separate statements by the United States, United Kingdom, and the USSR to "seek immediate Security Council action" to provide assistance to any NNWS that was subjected to nuclear aggression or threats (ch. IV). Given the inconsistent history of the Security Council and its veto, such assurances have not been sufficient to satisfy India, Pakistan, or Israel. Even Ukraine was concerned about its future security at the time of its accession to the NPT (ch. VII). Other NNWS may desire stronger security assurances if they are to remain in the NPT. The author believes that the resolution of this problem will require new initiatives by the United States and/or other nations, and ideally could result in the creation of new regional collective security agreements and/or institutions. This need has been recognized by others[3,4] and noted earlier in this chapter. Some first-stage transparency and confidence-building measures might be negotiated among India, Pakistan, China, and their neighbors, and by Israel and her neighbors as a means of gaining confidence. Even the Open Skies Treaty could play a role. Further discussion of these needs is beyond the scope of this book, but the author urges new attention to this subject by the US policy community.

The six specific initiatives proposed here are each important of themselves and can lead to valuable agreements and actions, but they are obviously synergistic. Implementation of START II and/or START III may be necessary to move the international community to the fifth and sixth initiatives, but progress on the sixth might encourage the Russians to proceed with the first. Much progress and experience has been gained from the arms control treaties presently in force. To move forward and proceed vigorously toward goals as suggested here indeed represents a challenge to the US arms control community, to congressional leaders, and particularly to the responsible executive branch officials.

References and Notes

1. "Treaty on the Nonproliferation of Nuclear Weapons, Arms Control and Disarmament Agreements," 1990 Edition, US Arms Control and Disarmament Agency, Washington, DC (ACDA, 1990 Ed.). Background, pp. 89–97; treaty text, pp. 98–102.
2. Lewis A. Dunn, "High Noon for the NPT," *Arms Control Today* (ACT), pp. 3–9, July/August 1995. Also see Mitchell Reiss, "Nuclear Rollback Decisions: Future Lessons," pp. 10–15, ACT, same issue.
3. General Andrew J. Goodpaster, chair "An Evolving US Nuclear Posture," Second Report of the Steering Committee, Project on Eliminating Weapons of Mass Destruction, Report No. 19, December 1995, the Henry L. Stimson Center (Washington, DC). Goodpaster was assistant to President Eisenhower during the 1950s.
4. Major General William F. Burns, (retired, study chair), "The Future of US Nuclear Weapons Policy," Committee on International Security and Arms Control, National Academy of Sciences, National Academy Press, Washington, DC, 1997. Burns was director of ACDA during the latter years of the Reagan administration.
5. John C. Hopkins and Steven A. Maaranen (LANL), "Nuclear Weapons in Post-Cold-War Deterrence," Appendix E in "Post-Cold-War Conflict Deterrence," National Research Council (NRC) Study on the Future of Deterrence, National Academy Press, Washington, DC, 1997. Also see the Executive Summary of this NRC report, chaired by General Andrew Goodpaster (retired).
6. Edward L. Warner, III, Assistant Secretary of Defense (Strategy and Threat Reduction), Statement at Hearings on Nuclear Deterrence, Strategic Forces Subcommittee, Senate Armed Services Committee (SASC), March 31, 1998.
7. James E. Goodby and Harold Feiveson, "Ending the Threat of Nuclear Attack," Center for International Security and Arms Control, Institute for International Studies, Stanford University, Stanford University Press, May 1997. Goodby was principal US negotiator for nuclear security and dismantlement during the early 1990s.
8. Stansfield Turner, "Caging the Nuclear Genie," Westview Press, Boulder, CO, 1997. Admiral Stansfield Turner was director of the CIA under President Carter.
9. Butler and Cranston, "Statement on Nuclear Abolition," issued February 2, 1998, on behalf of 117 civilian leaders from 46 nations (including former presidents Jimmy Carter and Mikhail Gorbachev), reported in *Arms Control Today*, January/February 1998, p. 34, by Craig Cerniello.

10. "Management and Disposition of Excess Weapons Plutonium," Committee on International Security and Arms Control, National Academy of Sciences, National Academy Press, Washington, DC, 1994.
11. Howard Diamond, "U.S. Renews Effort to Bring China into Missile Control Regime," *Arms Control Today*, March 1998, p. 22.
12. Donald H. Rumsfield, chair, "Report of the Commission to Assess the Ballistic Missile Threat to the United States Pursuant to Public Law 104–201, 104th Congress," Unclassified Exec. Summary, July 15, 1998.
13. Allan S. Krass," The United States and Arms Control: The Challenge of Leadership," Praeger Publishers, Westport, CT, 1997. For portal monitors, see "MPC&A Technical Note #1," DOE, June 1998.
14. Dwight D. Eisenhower, "Waging Peace," Doubleday & Co, Garden City, NY, 1965; Chapter XX.
15. William C. Potter, editor, "Verification and Arms Control," Lexington, MA, Lexington Books, 1985.
16. "Treaty on Open Skies," US Senate Foreign Relations Committee Report, Executive Report 103-5, August 2, 1993.
17. Peter Jones, "Open Skies: A New Era of Transparency," *Arms Control Today*, May 1992, pp. 10–15.
18. "Message from the President, August 12, 1992, transmitting the Treaty on Open Skies, with Twelve Annexes, signed at Helsinki on March 24, 1992," US Senate Treaty Doc. 102-37, 1992 (includes article-by-article analysis).
19. "Treaty On Open Skies," Hearing of the Committee on Foreign Relations, US Senate, September 22, 1992, Sen. Hrg. 102-910.
20. David B. Thomson, "The Treaty on Open Skies," CNSS Briefing, Vol. 5, No. 2, July 25, 1994 (Los Alamos National Laboratory report).
21. "Treaty on Open Skies," Resolution of Ratification, US Senate in Executive Session, Congressional Record, S10800-10804, August 6, 1993.
22. Open Skies Status, US ACDA, January 13, 1999. (Pvt. Comm.)
23. William S. Cohen, " Proliferation: Threat and Response," DoD report, November 25, 1997, ref. 25, ch. IX.
24. Strobe Talbott, "Dealing with the Bomb in South Asia," Foreign Affairs, March/April 1999. An excellent review of the India/ Pakistan problem and US efforts to alleviate it.

Table 1. Parties to the Limited Test Ban Treaty

Country	Signature	Deposit of Ratification	Deposit of Accession
Afghanistan	08/08/63	03/12/64	
Algeria	08/14/63		
Argentina	08/08/63		11/21/86
Australia	08/08/63	11/12/63	
Austria	09/11/63	07/17/64	
Bahamas			08/13/76
Bangladesh			03/11/85
Belgium	08/08/63	03/01/66	
Benin	08/27/63	12/15/64	
Bhutan			06/08/78
Bolivia	08/08/63	08/04/65	
Botswana			01/05/68
Brazil	08/08/63	12/15/64	
Bulgaria	08/08/63	11/13/63	
Bunkina Faso	08/30/63		
Burma	08/14/63	11/15/63	
Burundi	10/04/63		
Byelorussian S.S.R.	10/08/63	12/16/63	
Cameroon	08/27/63		
Canada	08/08/63	01/28/64	
Cape Verde			10/24/79
Central African Republic			12/22/64
Chad	08/26/63	03/01/65	
Chile	08/08/63	10/06/65	
China (Taiwan)	08/23/63	05/18/64	
Colombia	08/16/63		
Costa Rica	08/09/63	07/10/67	
Cyprus	08/08/63	04/15/65	
Czechoslovakia	08/08/63	10/14/63	
Denmark	08/09/63	01/15/64	
Dominican Republic	09/16/63	06/03/64	
Ecuador	09/27/63	05/06/64	
Egypt	08/08/63	01/10/64	
El Salvador	08/21/63	12/03/64	
Ethiopia	08/09/63		
Fiji			07/18/72
Finland	08/08/63	01/09/64	

Table 1. Parties to the Limited Test Ban Treaty (Cont.)

Country	Signature	Deposit of Ratification	Deposit of Accession
Gabon	09/10/63	02/20/64	
Gambia			04/27/65
German Democratic Republic	08/08/63	12/30/63	
Germany, Federal Republic of	08/19/63	12/01/64	
Ghana	08/08/63	11/27/63	
Greece	08/08/63	12/18/63	
Guatemala	09/23/63	01/06/64	
Haiti	10/09/63		
Honduras	08/08/63	10/02/64	
Hungary	08/08/63	10/21/63	
Iceland	08/12/63	04/29/64	
India	08/08/63	10/10/63	
Indonesia	08/23/63	01/20/64	
Iran	08/08/63	05/05/64	
Iraq	08/13/63	11/30/64	
Ireland	08/08/63	12/18/63	
Israel	08/08/63	01/15/64	
Italy	08/08/63	12/10/64	
Ivory Coast	09/05/63	02/05/65	
Jamaica	08/13/63		
Japan	08/14/63	06/15/64	
Jordan	08/12/63	05/29/64	
Kenya			06/10/65
Korea, Republic of	08/30/63	07/24/64	
Kuwait	08/20/63	05/20/65	
Laos	08/12/63	02/10/65	
Lebanon	08/12/63	05/14/65	
Liberia	08/08/63	05/19/64	
Libya	08/09/63	07/15/68	
Luxembourg	08/13/63	02/10/65	
Madagascar	09/23/63	03/15/65	
Malawi			11/26/64
Malaysia	08/08/63	07/15/64	
Mali	08/23/63		
Malta			11/25/64
Mauritania	09/13/63	04/06/64	
Mauritius			04/30/69

Table 1. Parties to the Limited Test Ban Treaty (Cont.)

Country	Signature	Deposit of Ratification	Deposit of Accession
Mexico	08/08/63	12/27/63	
Mongolia	08/08/63	11/01/63	
Morocco	08/27/63	02/01/66	
Nepal	08/26/63	10/07/64	
Netherlands	08/09/63	09/14/64	
New Zealand	08/08/63	10/10/63	
Nicaragua	08/13/63	01/26/65	
Niger	09/24/63	07/03/64	
Nigeria	08/30/63	02/17/67	
Norway	08/09/63	11/21/63	
Pakistan	08/14/63		03/03/88
Panama	09/20/63	02/24/66	
Papua New Guinea			11/13/80
Paraguay	08/15/63		
Peru	08/23/63	07/20/64	
Philippines	08/08/63	11/10/65	
Poland	08/08/63	10/14/63	
Portugal	10/09/63		
Romania	08/08/63	12/12/63	
Rwanda	09/19/63	12/27/63	
San Marino	09/17/63	07/03/64	
Senegal	09/20/63	05/06/64	
Seychelles			03/12/85
Sierra Leone	09/04/63	02/21/64	
Singapore			07/12/68
Somalia	08/19/63		
South Africa			10/10/63
Spain	08/13/63	12/17/64	
Sri Lanka	08/22/63	02/05/64	
Sudan	08/09/63	03/04/66	
Swaziland			05/29/69
Sweden	08/12/63	12/09/63	
Switzerland	08/26/63	01/16/64	
Syrian Arab Republic	08/13/63	06/01/64	
Tanzania	09/16/63	02/06/64	
Thailand	08/08/63	11/15/63	
Togo	09/18/63	12/07/64	
Tonga			07/07/71

Table 1. Parties to the Limited Test Ban Treaty (Cont.)

Country	Signature	Deposit of Ratification	Deposit of Accession
Trinidad and Tobago	08/12/63	07/14/64	
Tunisia	08/08/63	05/26/65	
Turkey	08/09/63	07/08/65	
Uganda	08/29/63	03/24/64	
Ukrainian S.S.R.	10/08/63	12/30/63	
Union of Soviet Socialist Republics	08/05/63	10/10/63	
United Kingdom	08/05/63	10/10/63	
United States	08/05/63	10/10/63	
Upper Volta	08/30/63		
Uruguay	08/12/63	02/25/63	
Venezuela	08/16/63	02/22/65	
Western Samoa	09/05/63	01/15/65	
Yemen Arab Republic (Sana)	08/13/63		
Yemen, People's Democratic Republic of (Aden)			06/01/79
Yugoslavia	08/08/63	01/15/64	
Zaire (New Dem Rep of Congo)	08/08/63	10/28/63	
Zambia			01/11/65
Total	**108**	**94**	**23**

Source: US Arms Control and Disarmament Agency, ACDA, "Arms Control and Disarmament Agreements," 1982 Edition and 1996 Edition.

Table 2. Comprehensive Test Ban Treaty

Country	Voted in favor	Signed	Ratified[a]
Afghanistan	Yes	---	---
Albania	Yes	09/27/96	---
Algeria	Yes	10/15/96	---
Andorra	Yes	09/24/96	---
Angola	Yes	09/27/96	---
Antigua and Barbuda	Yes	04/16/97	---
Argentina	Yes	09/24/96	12/04/98
Armenia	Yes	10/01/96	---
Australia	Yes	09/24/96	07/09/98
Austria	Yes	09/24/96	03/13/98
Azerbaijan	Yes	---	---
Bahamas	Yes	---	---
Bahrain	Yes	09/24/96	---
Bangladesh	Yes	10/24/96	---
Barbados	Yes	---	---
Belarus	Yes	09/24/96	---
Belgium	Yes	09/24/96	---
Belize	Yes	---	---
Benin	Yes	09/27/96	---
Bhutan	No	---	---
Bolivia	Yes	09/24/96	---
Bosnia and Herzegovina	Yes	09/24/96	---
Botswana	Yes	---	---
Brazil	Yes	09/24/96	07/24/98
Brunei	Yes	---	---
Bulgaria	Yes	09/24/96	---
Burkina Faso	Yes	09/27/96	---
Burma	Yes	---	---
Burundi	Did not vote	09/24/96	---
Cambodia	Yes	09/26/96	---
Cameroon	Yes	---	---
Canada	Yes	09/24/96	12/18/98
Cape Verde	Yes	10/01/96	---
Central African Republic	Did not vote	---	---
Chad	Did not vote	10/08/96	---
Chile	Yes	09/24/96	---
China	Yes	09/24/96	---
Colombia	Yes	09/24/96	---

Table 2. Comprehensive Test Ban Treaty (Cont.)

Country	Voted in favor	Signed	Ratified[a]
Comoros	Did not vote	---	---
Congo, Peoples Republic of	Yes	10/04/96	---
Costa Rica	Yes	09/24/96	---
Cole d'Ivoire	Yes	09/25/96	---
Cook Islands		12/05/97	---
Croatia	Yes	09/24/96	---
Cuba	Abstain	---	---
Cyprus	Yes	09/24/96	---
Czech Republic	Yes	11/12/96	09/08/97
Denmark	Yes	09/24/96	12/21/98
Djibouti	Yes	---	---
Dominica	Yes	---	---
Dominican Republic	Did not vote	10/03/96	---
Ecuador	Yes	09/24/96	---
Egypt	Yes	10/14/96	---
EI Salvador	Yes	09/24/96	09/14/98
Equatorial Guinea	Did not vote	10/09/96	---
Eritrea	Did not vote	---	---
Estonia	Yes	11/20/96	---
Ethiopia	Yes	09/25/96	---
Fiji	Yes	09/24/96	10/10/96
Finland	Yes	09/24/96	01/15/99
France	Yes	09/24/96	04/06/98
Gabon	Yes	10/07/96	---
Gambia	DNV	---	---
Georgia	Yes	09/24/96	---
Germany	Yes	09/24/96	08/20/98
Ghana	Yes	10/03/96	---
Greece	Yes	09/24/96	---
Grenada	Yes	10/10/96	08/19/98
Guatemala	Yes	---	---
Guinea	Yes	10/03/96	---
Guinea-Bissau	Yes	04/11/97	---
Guyana	Yes	---	---
Haiti	Yes	09/24/96	---
Holy See	---	09/24/96	---
Honduras	Yes	09/25/96	---
Hungary	Yes	09/25/96	---

Table 2. Comprehensive Test Ban Treaty (Cont.)

Country	Voted in favor	Signed	Ratified[a]
Iceland	Yes	09/24/96	---
India	No	---	---
Indonesia	Yes	09/24/96	---
Iran	Yes	09/24/96	---
Iraq	Did not vote	---	---
Ireland	Yes	09/24/96	---
Israel	Yes	09/25/96	---
Italy	Yes	09/24/96	02/01/99
Jamaica	Yes	11/11/96	---
Japan	Yes	09/24/96	07/08/97
Jordan	Yes	09/26/96	08/25/98
Kazakhstan	Yes	09/30/96	---
Kenya	Yes	11/14/96	---
Kuwait	Yes	09/24/96	---
Kyrgyzstan	Yes	10/08/96	---
Laos	Yes	07/30/97	---
Latvia	Did not vote	09/24/96	---
Lebanon	Abstain	---	---
Lesotho	Did not vote	09/30/96	---
Liberia	Yes	10/01/96	---
Libya	No	---	---
Liechtenstein	Yes	09/27/96	---
Lithuania	Yes	10/07/96	---
Luxembourg	Yes	09/24/96	---
Macedonia	Yes	10/29/98	---
Madagascar	Yes	10/09/96	---
Malawi	Yes	10/09/96	---
Malaysia	Yes	07/23/98	---
Maldives	Yes	10/01/97	---
Malawi	Yes	10/09/96	---
Mali	Did not vote	02/18/97	---
Malta	Yes	09/24/96	---
Marshall Islands	Yes	09/24/96	---
Mauritania	Yes	09/24/96	---
Mauritius	Abstain	---	---
Mexico	Yes	09/24/96	---
Micronesia (Federated States of)	Yes	09/24/96	07/25/97
Moldova	Yes	09/24/97	---

Table 2. Comprehensive Test Ban Treaty (Cont.)

Country	Voted in favor	Signed	Ratified[a]
Monaco	Yes	10/01/96	12/18/98
Mongolia	Yes	10/01/96	08/08/97
Morocco	Yes	09/24/96	---
Mozambique	Yes	09/26/96	---
Myenmar		11/25/96	---
Namibia	Yes	09/24/96	---
Nepal	Yes	10/08/96	---
Netherlands	Yes	09/24/96	---
New Zealand	Yes	09/27/96	---
Nicaragua,	Yes	09/24/96	---
Niger	Did not vote	10/03/96	---
Nigeria	Yes	---	---
North Korea	Did not vote	---	---
Norway	Yes	09/24/96	---
Oman	Yes	---	---
Pakistan	Yes	---	---
Palau	Yes	---	---
Panama	Yes	09/24/96	---
Papua New Guinea	Yes	09/25/96	---
Paraguay	Yes	09/25/96	---
Peru	Yes	09/25/96	11/12/97
Philippines	Yes	09/24/96	---
Poland	Yes	09/24/96	---
Portugal	Yes	09/24/96	---
Qatar	Yes	09/24/96	03/03/97
Republic of Korea	Yes	09/24/96	
Romania	Yes	09/24/96	---
Russia	Yes	09/24/96	---
Rwanda	Did not vote	---	---
Saint Kitts and Nevis	Yes	---	---
Saint Lucia	Yes	10/04/96	---
Saint Vincent and the Grenadines	Yes	---	---
San Marino	Yes	10/07/96	---
Sao Tome and Principe	Did not vote	09/26/96	---
Saudi Arabia	Yes	---	---
Senegal	Yes	09/26/96	---
Seychelles	Did not vote	09/24/96	---
Sierra Leone	Yes	---	---

Table 2. Comprehensive Test Ban Treaty (Cont.)

Country	Voted in favor	Signed	Ratified[a]
Singapore	Yes	01/14/99	---
Slovakia	Yes	09/30/96	03/03/98
Slovenia	Yes	09/24/96	---
Somalia	Did not vote	---	---
Solomon Islands	Yes	10/03/96	---
South Africa	Yes	09/24/96	---
Spain	Yes	09/24/96	07/31/98
Sri Lanka	Yes	10/24/96	---
Sudan	Yes	---	---
Suriname	Yes	01/14/97	---
Swaziland	Yes	09/24/96	---
Sweden	Yes	09/24/96	12/02/98
Switzerland	---	09/24/96	---
Syria	Abstain	---	---
Tajikistan	Yes	10/07/96	06/10/98
Tanzania	Did not vote	---	---
Thailand	Yes	11/12/96	---
Trinidad and Tobago	Yes	---	---
Togo	Yes	10/02/96	---
Tunisia	Yes	10/16/96	---
Turkey	Yes	09/24/96	---
Turkmenistan	Yes	09/24/96	02/20/98
Uganda	Yes	11/07/96	---
Ukraine	Yes	09/27/96	---
United Arab Emirates	Yes	09/25/96	---
United Kingdom	Yes	09/24/96	04/06/98
United States	Yes	09/24/96	---
Uruguay	Yes	09/24/96	---
Uzbekistan	Yes	10/03/96	05/29/97
Vanuatu	Yes	09/24/96	---
Venezuela	Yes	10/03/96	---
Vietnam	Yes	09/24/96	---
Yugoslavia	Did not vote	---	---
Western Samoa	Yes	10/09/96	---
Yemen	Yes	09/30/96	---
Zaire (Democratic Republic of Congo)	Yes	10/04/96	---
Zambia	Did not vote	12/03/96	---

Table 2. Comprehensive Test Ban Treaty (Cont.)

Country	Voted in favor	Signed	Ratified[a]
Zimbabwe	Yes	---	---
187 Countries	**158-3-5**	**152**	**28**

Bold face text: One of 44 countries whose ratification is required for entry into force.

[a] Date state deposited instruments of ratification.

Source: US Arms Control and Disarmament Agency Fact Sheets, October 17, 1996, and February 4, 1999.

Table 3. Nuclear Nonproliferation Treaty (NPT) Parties

Country	Signature	Deposit of Ratification	Deposit of Accession
Afghanistan	07/01/68	02/04/70	
Albania			09/12/90
Algeria			01/12/95
Antigua and Barbuda			06/17/85
Andorra			06/07/96
Angola			10/14/96
Argentina			02/10/95
Armenia			07/15/93
Australia	02/27/70	01/23/73	
Austria	07/01/68	06/27/69	
Azerbaijan			09/22/92
Bahamas			08/11/76
Bahrain			11/03/88
Bangladesh			08/31/79
Barbados	07/01/68	02/21/80	
Belarus			07/22/93
Belgium	08/20/68	05/02/75	
Belize			08/09/85
Benin	07/01/68	10/31/72	
Bhutan			05/23/85
Bolivia	07/01/68	05/26/70	
Bosnia and Herzegovina			08/15/94
Botswana	07/01/68	04/28/69	
Brazil			09/18/98
Brunei			03/26/85
Bulgaria	07/01/68	09/05/69	
Burkino Faso	11/25/68	03/03/70	
Burundi			03/19/71
Cambodia			06/02/72
Cameroon	07/17/68	01/08/69	
Canada	07/23/68	01/08/69	
Cape Verde			10/24/79
Central African Republic			10/25/70
Chad	07/01/68	03/10/71	
Chile			05/25/95
China, People's Republic[a]			03/09/92
Colombia	07/01/68	04/08/86	
Comoros			10/04/95

Table 3. Nuclear Nonproliferation Treaty (NPT) Parties (Cont.)

Country	Signature	Deposit of Ratification	Deposit of Accession
Congo, Democratic Republic (formerly Zaire)	07/22/68	08/04/70	
Congo, People's Republic			10/23/78
Costa Rica	07/01/68	03/03/70	
Cote d'lvoire	07/01/68	03/06/73	
Croatia			06/29/92
Cyprus	07/01/68	02/10/70	
Czech Republic			01/01/93
Denmark	07/01/68	01/03/69	
Djibouti			10/16/96
Dominica			08/10/84
Dominican Republic	07/01/68	07/24/71	
Ecuador	07/09/68	03/07/69	
Egypt	07/01/68	02/26/81	
El Salvador	07/01/68	07/11/72	
Equatorial Guinea			11/01/84
Eritrea			03/03/95
Estonia			01/07/92
Ethiopia	09/05/68	02/05/70	
Fiji			07/14/72
Finland	07/01/68	02/05/69	
France[a]			08/03/92
Gabon			02/19/74
Gambia	09/04/68	05/12/75	
Georgia			03/07/94
Germany, Federal Republic	11/28/69	05/02/75	
Ghana	07/01/68	05/04/70	
Greece	07/01/68	03/11/70	
Grenada			09/02/75
Guatemala	07/26/68	09/22/70	
Guinea			04/29/85
Guinea/Bissau			08/20/76
Guyana	07/01/68		10/19/93
Haiti	07/01/68	06/02/70	
Holy See			02/25/71
Honduras	07/01/68	05/16/73	
Hungary	07/01/68	05/27/69	
Iceland	07/01/68	07/18/69	

Table 3. Nuclear Nonproliferation Treaty (NPT) Parties (Cont.)

Country	Signature	Deposit of Ratification	Deposit of Accession
Indonesia	03/02/70	07/12/79	
Iran	07/01/68	02/02/70	
Iraq	07/01/68	10/29/69	
Ireland	07/01/68	07/01/68	
Italy	01/28/69	05/02/75	
Jamaica	04/14/69	03/05/70	
Japan	02/03/70	06/08/76	
Jordan	07/10/68	02/11/70	
Kazakhstan			02/14/94
Kenya	07/01/68	06/11/70	
Kiribati			04/18/85
Korea, North			12/12/85
Korea, South	07/01/68	04/23/75	
Kuwait	08/15/68	11/17/89	
Kyrgyzstan			07/05/94
Laos	07/01/68	02/20/70	
Latvia			01/31/92
Lebanon	07/01/68	07/15/70	
Lesotho	07/09/68	05/20/70	
Liberia	07/01/68	03/05/70	
Libya	07/18/68	05/26/75	
Liechtenstein			04/20/78
Lithuania			09/23/91
Luxembourg	08/14/68	05/02/75	
Madagascar	08/22/68	10/08/70	
Malawi			02/18/86
Malaysia	07/01/68	03/05/70	
Maldive Islands	09/11/68	04/07/70	
Mali	07/14/69	02/10/70	
Malta	04/17/69	02/06/70	
Marshall Islands			01/30/95
Mauritania			10/23/93
Mauritius	07/01/68	04/08/69	
Mexico	07/26/68	01/21/69	
Micronesia			04/14/95
Moldova			10/11/94
Monaco			03/13/95
Mongolia	07/01/68	05/14/69	

Table 3. Nuclear Nonproliferation Treaty (NPT) Parties (Cont.)

Country	Signature	Deposit of Ratification	Deposit of Accession
Morocco	07/01/68	11/27/70	
Mozambique			09/04/90
Myanmar (Burma)			12/02/92
Namibia			10/02/92
Nauru			06/07/82
Nepal	07/01/68	01/05/70	
Netherlands	08/20/68	05/02/75	
New Zealand	07/01/68	09/10/69	
Nicaragua	07/01/68	03/06/73	
Niger			10/09/92
Nigeria	07/01/68	09/27/68	
Norway	07/01/68	02/05/69	
Oman			01/23/97
Palau			04/12/95
Panama	07/01/68	01/13/77	
Papua New Guinea			01/13/82
Paraguay	07/01/68	02/04/70	
Peru	07/01/68	03/03/70	
Philippines	07/01/68	10/05/72	
Poland	07/01/68	06/12/69	
Portugal			12/15/77
Qatar			04/03/89
Romania	07/01/68	02/04/70	
Russia[a,b]	07/01/68	03/05/70	
Rwanda			05/20/75
Saint Kitts and Nevis			03/22/93
Saint Lucia			12/28/79
Saint Vincent and Grenadines			11/06/84
San Marino	07/01/68	08/10/70	
Sao Tome and Principe			07/20/83
Saudi Arabia			10/03/88
Senegal	07/01/68	12/17/70	
Seychelles			03/12/85
Sierra Leone			02/26/75
Singapore	02/05/70	03/10/76	
Slovakia			01/01/93
Slovenia			04/07/92
Solomon Islands			06/17/81

Table 3. Nuclear Nonproliferation Treaty (NPT) Parties (Cont.)

Country	Signature	Deposit of Ratification	Deposit of Accession
Somalia	07/01/68	03/05/70	
South Africa			07/10/91
Spain			11/05/87
Sri Lanka	07/01/68	03/05/79	
Sudan	12/24/68	10/31/73	
Suriname			06/30/76
Swaziland	06/24/69	12/11/69	
Sweden	08/19/68	01/09/70	
Switzerland	11/27/69	03/09/77	
Syria	07/01/68	09/24/69	
Taiwan[c]	07/01/68	01/27/70	
Tajikistan			01/17/95
Tanzania			05/31/91
Thailand			12/02/72
Togo	07/01/68	02/26/70	
Tonga			07/07/71
Trinidad and Tobago	08/20/68	10/30/86	
Tunisia	07/01/68	02/26/70	
Turkey	01/28/69	04/17/80	
Turkmenistan			09/29/94
Tuvalu			01/19/79
Uganda			10/20/82
Ukraine			12/05/94
United Arab Emirates			09/26/95
United Kingdom[a,b]	07/01/68	11/27/68	
United States[a,b]	07/01/68	03/05/70	
Uruguay	07/01/68	08/31/70	
Uzbekistan			05/02/92
Vanuatu			08/26/95
Venezuela	07/01/68	09/25/75	
Vietnam			06/14/82
Western Samoa			03/17/75
Yemen	11/14/68	06/01/79	
Yugoslav Republic of Macedonia (former)			04/12/95
Zambia			05/15/91
Zimbabwe			09/26/91

Table 3. Nuclear Nonproliferation Treaty (NPT) Parties (Cont.)

[a] Nuclear-weapon state.

[b] Depositary state.

[c] The United States recognizes the People's Republic of China as the sole legal government of China but regards Taiwan as bound by the terms of the NPT.

Notes: Nonsignatory states include Cuba, India, Israel, and Pakistan.
Brazil acceded September 18, 1998.
Serbia and Montenegro both claim NPT membership as the sole successor state to Yugoslavia. Their NPT status remains in dispute.

Sources: US Arms Control and Disarmament Agency, "Signatories and Parties to the Treaty on the Nonproliferation of Nuclear Weapons," Fact Sheet, January 23, 1997.

Rodney Jones and Mark McDonough with Toby Dalton and Gregory Koblentz, "Tracking Nuclear Proliferation," Carnegie Endowment for International Peace," Washington, D.C., 1998.

See also http://www.acda.gov/treaties/npt3.txt); November 7, 1997; The Arms Control Association, Washington, DC.

See also http://www.acda.gov/treaties/npt3.htm; June 9, 1999, ACDA.

Table 4. Intermediate[a] and Shorter-Range Missiles[b] to be Eliminated Under the INF Treaty (Data reported in MOU, signed December 8, 1987)[c]

Type	Deployed	Nondeployed	Total	(Warheads)
Soviet Union				
SS-20	405	245	650	(1,215)
SS-4	65	105	170	(65)
SS-5		6	6	
Subtotal[a]	470	356	826	
SS-12/22	220	506	726	(220)
SS-23	167	33	200	(167)
Subtotal[b]	387	539	926	
Total (USSR)	857	895	1,752	(1,667)
United States				
Pershing II	120	127	247	(120)
GLCMs[d]	309	133	442	(309)
Subtotal[a]	429	260	689	(429)
Pershing IA[b]	0	170	170	
Total (US)	429	430	859	(429)

[a] Intermediate-range missiles, defined as having a range of 1,000 to 5,500 kilometers.

[b] Shorter-range missiles, defined as having a range of 500 to 1,000 kilometers.

[c] Data taken from "The INF Treaty, Report of the Committee on Foreign Relations," US Senate Exec. Report 100-15, April 14, 1988, Washington, D.C. (SFRC report).

[d] GLCMs = ground-launched cruise missiles.

Note: Information in parentheses—The SFRC report assumes the nondeployed missiles are not stored with their warheads.

Table 5. USSR and US Strategic Nuclear Deployments (START I Counting Rules Used for Warheads per SNDV), July 31, 1991

Type	Launchers[a]	Warheads/ Launcher[a]	Total Warheads[a]
	USSR		
ICBM			
SS-11	326	1	326
SS-13	40	1	40
SS-17	47	4	188
SS-18	308	10	3,080
SS-19	300	6	1,800
SS-24	89	10	890
SS-25	288	1	288
Subtotal (ICBM)	1,398		6,612
SLBM			
SS-N-6	192	1	192
SS-N-8	280	1	280
SS-N-17	12	1	12
SS-N-18	224	3	672
SS-N-20	120	10	1,200
SS-N-23	112	4	448
Subtotal (SLBM)	940		2,804
Bombers			
Blackjack (ALCM)	15	8[b]	120
Bear (ALCM)	84	8[b]	672
Bear (non-ALCM)	63	1[b]	63
Blackjack (non-ALCM)	0	1[b]	0
Subtotal (Bombers)	162		855
Total (SNDV)	2,500	**Total (Warheads)**	10,271

[a] Values given in MOU, signed July 31, 1991, Chapter VII (Ref. 6).
[b] Attributed by START I bomber/ALCM counting rules.

Table 5. USSR and US Strategic Nuclear Deployments (START I Counting Rules Used for Warheads per SNDV), July 31, 1991 (Cont.)

Type	Launchers[a]	Warheads/ Launcher[a]	Total Warheads[a]
	United States		
ICBM			
Minuteman II	450	1	450
Minuteman III	500	3	1,500
MX	50	10	500
Subtotal (ICBM)	1,000		2,450
SLBM			
Poseidon	192	10	1,920
Trident I	384	8	3,072
Trident II	96	8	768
Subtotal (SLBM)	672		5,760
Bombers			
B-1B	95	1[b]	95
B-52 (non-ALCM)	290	1[b]	290
B-52 (ALCM)	189	10(39@12)[b]	1,968[b]
Subtotal (bombers)	574		2,353
Total (SNDVs)	2,246	**Total (Warheads)**	10,563

[a] Values given in MOU, signed July 31, 1991, Chapter VII (Ref. 6).
[b] Attributed by START I bomber/ALCM counting rules.

Table 6. FSU and US Strategic Nuclear Deployments as of January 1, 1995

Type	SNDVs				Total SNDVs	Total Warheads[a]
FSU	Russia	Kazakhstan	Ukraine	Belarus		
ICBM						
SS-11@1	20				20	20
SS-13@1	20				20	20
SS-17@4	11				11	44
SS-18@10	188	104	0	0	292	2,920
SS-19@6	170	0	130	0	300	1,800
SS-24@10	46	0	46	0	92	920
SS-25@1	318	0	0	36	354	354
Total ICBM	773	104	176	36	1,089	6,078
SLBM						
SS-N-6@1	32				32	32
SS-N-8@1	256				256	256
SS-N-17@1	0				0	0
SS-N-18@3	208				208	624
SS-N-20@10	120				120	1,200
SS-N-23@4	112				112	448
Total SLBM	728				728	2,560
Bombers						
Blackjack/ALCM	6		19		25	200
Bear/ALCM	65		25		90	720
Bear	24		2		26	26
Blackjack	0		0		0	0
Total Bombers	95		46		141	946
Total FSU	1,596	104	222	36	1,958	9,584

[a] Listed warheads are only those as counted on deployed delivery vehicles.

Source: US Arms Control and Disarmament Agency (ACDA), April, 1995.

Table 6. FSU and US Strategic Nuclear Deployments as of January 1, 1995 (Cont.)

Type	SNDVs	Total SNDVs	Total Warheads[a]
	United States		
ICBM			
Minuteman II@1		377	377
Minuteman III@3		532	1,596
MX@10		50	500
Total ICBM		959	2,473
SLBM			
Poseidon@10		48	480
Trident I@8		288	2,304
Trident II@8		192	1,536
Total SLBM		528	4,320
Bombers			
B-1B+B2@1		94+8	102
B-52@1		69	69
B-52 ALCM@10[b]		180	1,860
Total Bombers		351	2,031
Total US		1,838	8,824

[a] Listed warheads are only those as counted on deployed delivery vehicles.
[b] 30@12 by START I bomber/ALCM counting rules.

Source: US Arms Control and Disarmament Agency (ACDA), April, 1995.

Table 7. FSU and US Strategic Nuclear Deployments as of January 1, 1996

Type	SNDVs				Total SNDVs	Total Warheads[a]
FSU	Russia	Kazakhstan	Ukraine	Belarus		
ICBM						
SS-11@1	0				0	0
SS-13@1	0				0	0
SS-17@4	1				1	4
SS-18@10	186	24	0	0	210	2,100
SS-19@6	170	0	128	0	298	1,788
SS-24@10	46	0	46	0	92	920
SS-25@1	351	0	0	18	369	369
Total ICBM	754	24	174	18	970	5,181
SLBM						
SS-N-6@1	16				16	16
SS-N-8@1	232				232	232
SS-N-17@1	0				0	0
SS-N-18@3	208				208	624
SS-N-20@10	120				120	1,200
SS-N-23@4	112				112	448
Total SLBM	688				688	2,520
Bombers						
Blackjack/ALCM	6		19		25	200
Bear/ALCM	63		25		88	704
Bear	20		0		20	20
Blackjack	0		0		0	0
Total Bombers	89		44		133	924
Total FSU	1,531	24	218	18	1,791	8,625

[a] Listed warheads are only those as counted on deployed delivery vehicles.

Source: US Arms Control and Disarmament Agency (ACDA), April, 1996.

Table 7. FSU and US Strategic Nuclear Deployments as of January 1, 1996 (Cont.)

Type	SNDVs	Total SNDVs	Total Warheads[a]
	United States		
ICBM			
MM II@1		281	281
MM III@3		542	1,626
MX@10		50	500
Total ICBM		873	2,407
SLBM			
Poseidon@10		48	480
Trident I@8		208	1,664
Trident II@8		216	1,728
Total SLBM		472	3,872
Bombers			
B-1B+B2@1		93+13	106
B-52@1		56	56
B-52 ALCM@10[b]		172	1,764
Total Bombers		334	1,926
Total US		1,679	8,205

[a] Listed warheads are only those as counted on deployed delivery vehicles.
[b] 22@12 by START I bomber/ALCM counting rules.

Source: US Arms Control and Disarmament Agency (ACDA), April, 1996.

Table 8. FSU and US Strategic Nuclear Deployments as of January 1, 1997

Type	SNDVs				Total SNDVs	Total Warheads[a]
FSU	Russia	Kazakhstan	Ukraine	Belarus		
ICBM						
SS-11@1	0				0	0
SS-13@1	0				0	0
SS-17@4	0				0	0
SS-18@10	186	0	0	0	186	1,860
SS-19@6	170	0	69	0	239	1,434
SS-24@10	46	0	46	0	92	920
SS-25@1	360	0	0	0	360	360
Total ICBM	762	0	115	0	877	4,574
SLBM						
SS-N-6@1	16				16	16
SS-N-8@1	208				208	208
SS-N-17@1	0				0	0
SS-N-18@3	208				208	624
SS-N-20@10	120				120	1,200
SS-N-23@4	112				112	448
Total SLBM	664				664	2,496
Bombers						
Blackjack/ALCM	6		19		25	200
Bear/ALCM	63		25		88	704
Bear	10		0		10	10
Blackjack	0		0		0	0
Total Bombers	79		44		123	914
Total FSU	1,505	0	159	0	1,664	7,984

[a] Listed warheads are only those as counted on deployed delivery vehicles.

Source: US Arms Control and Disarmament Agency (ACDA), April, 1997.

Table 8. FSU and US Strategic Nuclear Deployments as of January 1, 1997 (Cont.)

Type	SNDVs	Total SNDVs	Total Warheads[a]
	United States		
ICBM			
Minuteman II@1		115	115
Minuteman III@3		590	1,770
MX@10		50	500
Total ICBM		755	2,385
SLBM			
Poseidon@10		32	320
Trident I@8		208	1,664
Trident II@8		240	1,920
Total SLBM		480	3,904
Bombers			
B-1B+B2@1		93+17	110
B-52@1		56	56
B-52 ALCM@10[b]		163	1,656
Total Bombers		329	1,822
Total US		1,564	8,111

[a] Listed warheads are only those as counted on deployed delivery vehicles.
[b] 13@12 by START I bomber/ALCM counting rules.

Source: US Arms Control and Disarmament Agency (ACDA), April, 1997.

Table 9. FSU and US Strategic Nuclear Deployments as of January 1, 1998

Type	SNDVs				Total SNDVs	Total Warheads[a]
FSU	Russia	Kazakhstan	Ukraine	Belarus		
ICBM						
SS-11@1	0				0	0
SS-13@1	0				0	0
SS-17@4	0				0	0
SS-18@10	180	0	0	0	180	1,800
SS-19@6	168	0	20	0	188	1,128
SS-24@10	46	0	46	0	92	920
SS-25@1	362[b]	0	0	0	362	362
Total ICBM	756	0	66	0	822	4,210
SLBM						
SS-N-6@1	16				16	16
SS-N-8@1	192				192	192
SS-N-17@1	0				0	0
SS-N-18@3	208				208	624
SS-N-20@10	120				120	1,200
SS-N-23@4	112				112	448
Total SLBM	648				648	2,480
Bombers						
Blackjack/ALCM	6		19		25	200
Bear/ALCM	64		25		89	712
Bear	10		0		10	10
Blackjack	0		0		0	0
Total Bombers	80		44		124	922
Total FSU	1,484	0	110	0	1,594	7,612

[a] Listed warheads are only those as counted on deployed delivery vehicles.
[b] Including two RS-12M (silo version).

Source: US Arms Control and Disarmament Agency (ACDA), April, 1998.

Table 9. FSU and US Strategic Nuclear Deployments as of January 1, 1998 (Cont.)

Type	SNDVs	Total SNDVs	Total Warheads[a]
	United States		
ICBM			
Minuteman II@1		12	12
Minuteman III@3		639	1,917
MX@10		50	500
Total ICBM		701	2,429
SLBM			
Poseidon@10		32	320
Trident I@8		192	1,536
Trident II@8		240	1,920
Total SLBM		464	3,776
Bombers			
B-1B+B2@1		92+20	112
B-52@1		49	49
B-52 ALCM@10[c]		160	1,620
Total Bombers		321	1,781
Total US		1,486	7,986

[a] Listed warheads are only those as counted on deployed delivery vehicles.
[b] Including two RS-12M (silo version).
[c] 10@12 by START I bomber/ALCM counting rules.

Source: US Arms Control and Disarmament Agency (ACDA), April, 1998.

Table 10. FSU and US Strategic Nuclear Deployments as of January 1, 1999

Type	SNDVs				Total SNDVs	Total Warheads[a]
FSU	Russia	Kazakhstan	Ukraine	Belarus		
ICBM						
SS-11@1	0				0	0
SS-13@1	0				0	0
SS-17@4	0				0	0
SS-18@10	180	0	0	0	180	1,800
SS-19@6	160	0	0	0	160	960
SS-24@10	46	0	44	0	90	900
SS-25@1	370[b]	0	0	0	370	370
Total ICBM	756	0	44	0	800	4,030
SLBM						
SS-N-6@1	0				0	0
SS-N-8@1	152				152	152
SS-N-17@1	0				0	0
SS-N-18@3	208				208	624
SS-N-20@10	120				120	1,200
SS-N-23@4	112				112	448
Total SLBM	592	0	0	0	592	2,424
Bombers						
Blackjack/ALCM	6		18		24	192
Bear/ALCM	64		25		89	712
Bear	4		0		4	4
Blackjack	0		0		0	0
Total Bombers	74	0	43	0	117	908
Total FSU	1,422	0	87	0	1,509	7,362

[a] Listed warheads are only those as counted on deployed delivery vehicles.
[b] Including ten RS-12M (silo version).

Source: US Arms Control and Disarmament Agency (ACDA), April 1, 1999.

Table 10. FSU and US Strategic Nuclear Deployments as of January 1, 1999 (Cont.)

Type	SNDVs	Total SNDVs	Total Warheads[a]
	United States		
ICBM			
Minuteman II@1		1	1
Minuteman III@3		650	1,950
MX@10		50	500
Total ICBM		701	2,451
SLBM			
Poseidon@10		32	320
Trident I@8		192	1,536
Trident II@8		240	1,920
Total SLBM		464	3,776
Bombers			
B-1B+B2@1		91+20	111
B-52@1		48	48
B-52 ALCM@10[c]		156	1,572
Total Bombers		315	1,731
Total US		1,480	7,958

[a] Listed warheads are only those as counted on deployed delivery vehicles.
[c] 6@12 by START I bomber/ALCM counting rules.

Source: US Arms Control and Disarmament Agency (ACDA), April 1, 1999.

Table 11. Worldwide Nuclear Warhead Inventories and Nuclear Weapons Status[a]

Country	Delivery Systems	Warheads	Total Warheads[b]
Nuclear Weapons States (as recognized by NPT)			
United States			
Deployed ICBMs & SLBMs[c]	1,165	6,227	
Bombers (START I counting)[c]	315	1,731	
Estimated other warheads		4,112	
Total Warheads			12,070
Russia			
Deployed ICBMs and SLBMs[c]	1,392[d]	6,454[d]	
Bombers (START I counting)[c]	117	908	
Estimated other warheads		15,138	
Total Warheads			22,500
China[f]			
ICBMs and SLBMs[a]	~30	~30	
Other Missiles[a]	~80	~80	
Estimated other warheads			
Total Warheads			>400
France			
SLBMs			
Bombers/other missiles			
Estimated other warheads			
Total Warheads			450
United Kingdom			
SLBMs			
Bombers/other missiles			
Estimated other warheads			
Total Warheads			260
Non-NPT Nuclear Weapons States			
India[e]			~70
Pakistan[e]			~15
Israel[e]			>100

Table 11. Worldwide Nuclear Warhead Inventories and Nuclear Weapons Status[a] (Cont.)

NPT parties as nonnuclear weapon states believed to be high risk

Iraq[e]	Nuclear weapon program dismantled by UNSCOM (Chapter IV).
Iran[e]	Believed to be actively seeking nuclear weapons.[a]
North Korea[e]	Close to having enough plutonium for a nuclear weapon. Agreed to dismantle nuclear weapons program in 1994.[a]
Libya[e]	Extremely limited nuclear infrastructure.[a]

Other States

Belarus,[e] Kazakhstan,[e] and Ukraine[e] have removed all nuclear warheads and have nearly removed all strategic delivery vehicles in conformance with the START I treaty and the Lisbon Protocol (see Chapter VII and Table 10). Have joined NPT and by 1996, agreed to IAEA Safeguards inspections.[a]

South Africa dismantled six nuclear weapons in 1991 and signed NPT and IAEA agreements.[a]

Brazil and Argentine implemented the treaty of Tlatelolco as NNW states (Chapter 4) and have agreed to implement IAEA and bilateral inspections.[a]

Algeria[e] aceded to the NPT in 1995.[a]

Romania[e] terminated a plutonium separation program not subject to IAEA inspections in 1989.[a]

Germany, Japan, Canada, Italy, Hungary, Sweden, Mexico, South Korea,[e] Spain, and many other key nations have signed the NPT as NNW states, accepted IAEA inspections, and are believed in compliance with the NPT.[a] Egypt,[e] Syria,[e] and Poland[e] are NNW state parties to the NPT. See Table 3 for NPT stutus of the other nations.

Table 11. Worldwide Nuclear Warhead Inventories and Nuclear Weapons Status[a] (Cont.)

[a] Rodney W. Jones and Mark G. McDonough, with Toby F. Dalton and Gregory D. Koblentz, "Tracking Nuclear Proliferation, A Guide in Maps and Charts, 1998," Carnegie Endowment for International Peace, 1799 Mass. Ave., NW, Washington, DC 20036, 1998.

[b] Best estimates for total nuclear warheads by Carnegie Endowment.

[c] See Table 10.

[d] Includes 44 MIRVed ICBMs awaiting elimination in Ukraine with warheads removed.

[e] Possesses ballistic missiles (SCUD B or other). See Jones, et al.,[a] pp. 263–264.

[f] See Jones, et al.,[a] for many categories under development.

Table 12. Status of Ratification of the Open Skies Treaty[a]

Party[b]	Treaty Ratified	Date Instrument of Ratification Deposited
Belarus		
Belgium	Yes	06/28/94
Bulgaria	Yes	04/15/94
Canada	Yes	07/21/92
Czech Republic	Yes	12/21/92
Denmark	Yes	11/21/92
France	Yes	07/30/93
Georgia		
Germany	Yes	01/27/94
Greece	Yes	09/09/93
Hungary	Yes	08/11/93
Iceland	Yes	08/25/94
Italy	Yes	10/31/94
Kyrgyzstan		
Luxembourg	Yes	06/28/95
Netherlands	Yes	06/28/95
Norway	Yes	07/14/93
Poland	Yes	05/29/95
Portugal	Yes	11/22/94
Romania	Yes	06/27/94
Russian Federation		
Slovak Republic	Yes	12/21/92
Spain	Yes	11/18/93
Turkey	Yes	11/30/94
Ukraine		
United Kingdom	Yes	12/08/93
United States	Yes	12/03/93

[a] Other states may become members of the treaty, subject to agreement by the current states parties. Other states of the FSU are considered to be initial participants, should they desire.

[b] The parties listed each signed the treaty on March 24, 1992, at Helsinki, except Kyrgyzstan, who signed on February 16, 1993. Ratification by Russia, Ukraine, and Belarus is still required for entry into force. Russia and Belarus shared their overflight quotes at signing.

Source: United States Arms Control and Disarmament Agency (ACDA), May 20, 1994, July 11, 1994, and January 13, 1999.

Appendix A-1

Principal Nuclear Arms Control Treaties[a]

The Antarctic Treaty
Signed December 1, 1959, entered into force on June 23, 1961.
Parties: US, USSR, UK, and ten others.

Limited Test Ban Treaty (LTBT)
Signed August 5, 1963, entered into force on October 10, 1963.
Parties: US, USSR, UK, and 106 others.

Outer Space Treaty
Signed on January 27, 1967, entered into force on October 10, 1967.
Parties: US, USSR, UK, and 89 others.

Latin American Nuclear-Free Zone Treaty (Treaty of Tlatelolco)
Signed on February 14, 1967, entered into force on April 22, 1968.
Parties: 26, with exceptions.

Nonproliferation Treaty (NPT)
Signed on July 1, 1968, entered into force on March 5, 1970.
Parties: US, USSR, UK, and 98 others.

Seabed Arms Control Treaty
Signed February 11, 1971, entered into force on May 18, 1972.
Parties: US, USSR, UK, and 86 others.

Anti-ballistic Missile (ABM) Treaty
Signed on May 26, 1972, entered into force on October 3, 1972.
Parties: US, USSR.

ABM Protocol (Amends ABM Treaty)
Signed July 3, 1974, entered into force on May 24, 1976.
Parties: US, USSR.

Threshold Test Ban Treaty (TTBT)
Signed on July 3, 1974, entered into force on Dec. 1990.
TTBT Verification Protocol Signed June 1990,
and entered into force Dec. 1990.
Parties: US, USSR.

Strategic Arms Limitation Talks (SALT II) Treaty
Signed on June 18, 1979. Expired.
Parties: US, USSR.

Intermediate-Range Nuclear Forces (INF) Treaty
Signed on December 8, 1987, entered into force on June 1, 1988.
Parties: US, USSR.

START I Treaty
Signed July, 1991; Lisbon protocol signed May 23, 1992,
entered into force December, 1994
Parties: US, Russian Federation, Belarus, Ukraine, Kazkhstan.

START II Treaty
Signed on January 3, 1993
Parties: US and Russian Federation.

The Comprehensive Test Ban Treaty (CBTB)
Signed on September 24, 1996
Parties US, Russia, China, U.K., France, and more than 140 states.

---

[a] Source: "Arms Control and Disarmament Agreements," US ACDA, 1996 edition, and related ACDA Documents.

Appendix A-2

Some Related Arms Control Agreements and Treaties[a]

"Hot Line" Agreement
Signed and entered into force on June 20, 1963.
Parties: US, USSR.

"Accidents Measures" Agreement
Signed and entered into force on September 30, 1971
Parties: US, USSR.

"Hot Line" Modernization Agreement
Signed and entered into force on September 30, 1971
Parties: US, USSR.

Interim Agreement (Strategic Arms Limitation, SALT I)
Signed on May 26, 1972, entered into force on October 3, 1972.
Parties: US, USSR.

Prevention of Nuclear War Agreement
Signed on June 22, 1973, entered into force on June 22, 1973.
Parties: US, USSR.

PNE Treaty (Peaceful Nuclear Explosions Treaty)
Signed May 28, 1976
Parties: US, USSR.

US-IAEA Safeguards Agreement
Signed on November 18, 1977, entered into force on December 9, 1980.
Parties: Signed separately between IAEA and each party.

Nuclear Material Convention (Physical Protection)
Signed on March 3, 1980, entered into force on February 8, 1987.
Parties: US, USSR, UK, China, France, and 42 others.

"Hot Line" Expansion Agreement
Signed on July 17, 1984
Parties: US, USSR.

Nuclear Risk Reduction Centers (NRRCs)
Signed and entered into force on September 15, 1987
Parties: US, USSR.

Ballistic Missile Launch Notification Agreement
Signed and entered into force on May 31, 1988.
Parties: US, USSR.

Nuclear Free Zones are also being implemented or developed in the South Pacific, Africa, and Southeast Asia.[b]

---

[a] Source: "Arms Control and Disarmament Agreements" US ACDA, 1996 edition and related ACDA Documents.

[b] See R. Jones, M. McDonough, T. Dalton, and G. Koblentz, "Tracking Nuclear Proliferation," Carnegie Endowment for International Peace, Washington, D.C. (1998), Appendix E.

Appendix B

Selected Highlights from US and Russian Resolutions of Ratification of START I

The US Senate voted 93 to 6 to ratify START I on October 1, 1992. Excerpts[a] from the US conditions and declarations of ratification include the following:

- Russia, Ukraine, Kazakhstan, and Belarus shall be bound by international law to all the obligations of the former USSR under the treaty documents.
- The legal and political obligations of the former USSR reflected in Sen. Doc. 102-20 are included in the obligations assumed by the four former Soviet states in Article I of the May 23, 1992 (Lisbon) Protocol.
- The letters to President Bush from the presidents of Ukraine, Belarus, and Kazakhstan (pledges to become nonnuclear weapons states) are of the same force and effect as the START I treaty.
- The obligations (NPT status) set forth in Article V of the Lisbon Protocol shall have the same force and effect as the START I treaty.
- Condition: If Ukraine, Belarus, and Kazakhstan have not eliminated all their nuclear weapons and strategic offensive arms within seven years of START I entry into force, then the US president shall determine if there is a "changed circumstance" and seek appropriate JCIC and/or US Senate action.
- Declaration: The Senate urges the president to expeditiously seek the destruction of all nuclear warheads from eliminated systems and to facilitate secure safeguarded storage of the nuclear materials withdrawn therefrom.

On November 4, 1992, the Supreme Soviet of the Russian Federation decreed to ratify START I complete with its related protocols, MOU, and related documents, including the Lisbon Protocol of May 23, 1992.[b] Excerpts of conditions and declarations include the following:

- Condition: Entry into force is subject to (prior) accession to the NPT by the Republics of Belarus, Kazakhstan, and Ukraine.

- The Russian government is instructed to elaborate a state program for implementation of the treaty.
- The Russian Defense and Security Committee is to carry out continuous verification of the treaty.

We note here that the Russian requirement that Ukraine, Kazakhstan, and Belarus were to fully accede to the NPT before START I entry into force delayed full START I implementation for many months.

---

[a] Congressional Record (Vol. 138, No. 138, S15955) US Senate, October 1, 1992.

[b] "Supreme Soviet Ratifies START," from Rossiyskaya Gazeta, Moscow, 1st ed., November 21, 1992, BBC Summary of World Broadcasts, November 25, 1992, (LEXISNEXIS Electronic Mail).

Appendix C

Selected Highlights from the US Senate Resolution of Ratification of START II

On January 26, 1996, the US Senate approved a resolution of ratification[a] of START II by a vote of 87 to 4. The resolution included a number of conditions and declarations. Excerpts from the Senate's conditions include the following:

- A condition stipulates that ratification will not require the US to accept any changes to the ABM treaty.
- A condition stipulates that ratification does not obligate the US to provide funding to assist Russian implementation of the treaty.
- A condition on NTM states that the US may pursue its request that Russia abandon its electronic listening post in Cuba.
- In the event that START II does not enter into force, a condition requires the president to consult with the Senate before making any strategic force reductions below START I levels.

Excerpts from the Senate's declarations include the following:

- The US and Russia are encouraged to exchange information on warhead and fissile material stockpiles.
- The US president is asked to regulate the pace of US reductions so as not to allow a strategic imbalance to occur.
- If a non-START party expands its strategic arsenal in a way that threatens the US, the president must consult with the Senate regarding continued compliance with START II.
- A commitment is reinforced that the US maintain a robust stockpile stewardship program, competency in its nuclear weapons laboratories, sufficient nuclear weapons production capabilities, and the right to resume its nuclear weapons testing program if necessary for national security purposes.

---

[a] Craig Cerniello, "START II Resolution of Ratification," *Arms Control Today*, February 1996, pp. 30–33.

Appendix D

Selected Highlights from Testimony of ACDA Director Ron Lehman and START Ambassador Linton Brooks before the Senate Foreign Relations Committee, June 25, 1992[a]

Ron Lehman listed five reasons for ratification of START I.

1. The Soviet strategic arsenal is essentially intact. We can't take for granted that it will be reduced. We must codify the START reductions.
2. The START verification regime will provide explicit rights to access and information independent of internal political shifts (in the independent Republics).
3. The bold agreement to further reduce nuclear strategic arms reached at the June 1992 Summit meeting uses START as a foundation and will depend on START verification provisions.
4. Ratification of START helps advance our nonproliferation goals, particularly in the altered post-Soviet situation.
5. US insistence on verification and strict compliance reinforces political glasnost and the concept of the rule of law. Our emphasis on reduction and stability undermines hawkish opponents of democracy.

Lehman noted that Foreign Minister Eduard Shevardnadze, even after he resigned, emphasized that START I was important in keeping the democratic process on track. Lehman concluded by saying that START has already helped shape events and played an important role in providing for our security.

Linton Brooks gave some background on the process of the Lisbon Protocol, and noted that the treaty is designed to endure. He reviewed the verification regime, including the data exchange in the MOU, the eighty types of notification covering movements and change of status, the twelve types of on-site inspections including up to about twenty-five short-notice inspections per year, and the continuous monitoring.

He noted that the early exhibition inspections of technical characteristics of treaty-limited items have been carried out as agreed. He pointed out the provision (through the JCIC) of special access visits as a formal way to request (with right of refusal) observation of locations not otherwise subject to inspection. Brooks concluded that START was a major step toward a future world of reduced threat and increased openness.

---

[a] Hearings on the START Treaty, SFRC, US Senate, June 23, 25, 26, and 30, 1992, Senate Hearing 102-607, Part 2, US GPO, Washington, D.C., 1992.